The HOUSE PLANT EXPERT

Dr. D.G. Hessayon

1st Impression	300,000
2nd Impression	200,000
3rd Impression	200,000
4th Impression	200,000
5th Impression	200,000

Previous Edition:
BE YOUR OWN HOUSE PLANT EXPERT
18 Impressions   *5,160,000*

Other Books in the EXPERT Series:

THE ROSE EXPERT

THE LAWN EXPERT

THE TREE AND SHRUB EXPERT

BE YOUR OWN GARDENING EXPERT

BE YOUR OWN HOUSE PLANT SPOTTER

BE YOUR OWN GARDEN DOCTOR

BE YOUR OWN VEGETABLE DOCTOR

VEGETABLE PLOTTER

Acknowledgements
The author wishes to acknowledge the painstaking work of Jane Jenks and Peggy Easterling. Grateful acknowledgement is also made for the help received from Joan Hessayon and Angelina Hessayon. John Woodbridge provided both artistry and design work, and Henry Barnett prepared the paintings for this book. Other artists who contributed were June Baker, John Rignall, Jennifer Sumray and Yvon Still.

pbi PUBLICATIONS · BRITANNICA HOUSE · WALTHAM CROSS · HERTS · ENGLAND

Contents

			page
CHAPTER 1	**PLANTS IN THE HOME**		3–19
	Choosing Indoor Plants		4–9
	Buying Indoor Plants		10
	Taking Plants Home		10
	Displaying Indoor Plants		11–19
	The Specimen Plant		12–13
	The Pot Group		14–15
	The Indoor Garden		16–18
	The Terrarium		19
CHAPTER 2	**FOLIAGE HOUSE PLANTS** (Abutilon — Yucca)		20–58
CHAPTER 3	**FLOWERING HOUSE PLANTS** (Acacia — Vallota)		59–78
CHAPTER 4	**FLOWERING POT PLANTS** (Achimenes — Zantedeschia)		79–95
CHAPTER 5	**CACTI**		96–100
CHAPTER 6	**PLANT CARE**		101–110
	Fresh Air		101
	Light		102–103
	Water		104–105
	Warmth		106
	Humidity		107
	Food		108
	Rest		109
	Holiday Care		109
	Cleaning and Polishing		110
	Pruning and Training		110
CHAPTER 7	**POTS AND POTTING**		111–113
	Growing Media		111
	Repotting		112
	Top Dressing		112
	Containers		113
CHAPTER 8	**INCREASING YOUR STOCK**		114–116
CHAPTER 9	**PLANT TROUBLES**		117–122
	Plant Collapse		117
	Cultural Faults		118–119
	Pests		120
	Diseases		121
	First Aid for House Plants		122
CHAPTER 10	**HOUSE PLANT GROWER'S DICTIONARY**		123–125
CHAPTER 11	**PLANT INDEX**		126–128

Printed and bound by Hazell Watson and Viney Limited Aylesbury Bucks. England

ISBN 0 903505 13 4

CHAPTER 1

PLANTS IN THE HOME

You don't need to read a book to learn about the beauty, variety and popularity of house plants — just look around you. Everywhere you will find them, the impressive indoor gardens in public buildings . . . tiny pots on windowsills . . . scores of colourful varieties offered for sale in garden shops.

The charm of house plants may be universal, but many millions of them die needlessly each year. You have to face the fact that your house is not a particularly good home for them – most plants would be much happier in the moist, bright air of a well-lit laundry! So you just can't leave them to look after themselves; each plant needs care and each variety has its own particular requirements. It is the purpose of this book to tell you the secrets of success and the special problems of all the types you are likely to find.

Forget about green fingers. Anyone can grow house plants and make them look attractive. If everything dies as soon as you take it home, then you are making a serious basic mistake and the answer is in these pages. If your plants look sickly and unattractive then it's a matter of poor choice, incorrect upkeep or lack of knowledge about house plant display. Once again the answers are here. True exotics, such as some Orchids and many Bromeliads are quite easy to grow . . . exciting displays are not difficult to make . . . increasing your stock is surprisingly simple . . . here you will find the key.

BASIC RULES

● DON'T DROWN THEM
Roots need air as well as water — keeping the compost soaked at all times means certain death for most plants. Learn how to water properly – see pages 104–5.

● GIVE THEM A REST
Beginners are usually surprised to learn that nearly all plants need a rest in winter, which means less water, less feeding and less heat than in the active growing period.

● ACCEPT THE LOSS OF 'TEMPORARY' PLANTS
Some popular gift plants, such as Cyclamen, Chrysanthemum and Gloxinia will die down in a matter of weeks. You've done nothing wrong — these types are flowering pot plants which are only temporary residents.

● GIVE THEM EXTRA HUMIDITY
The atmosphere of a centrally-heated room in winter is as dry as desert air. Learn how to increase the air humidity – see page 107.

● TREAT TROUBLE PROMPTLY
Expert or beginner, trouble will strike sometime. One or two scale insects or mealy bugs are easily picked off; an infestation may be incurable. Overwatering is not fatal at first, but kills when prolonged. Learn to recognise the early signs of trouble.

● GROUP THEM TOGETHER
Nearly all plants look better and grow better when grouped together. Learn the how and why of plant grouping on pages 14–19.

● LEARN TO REPOT
After a year or two most plants begin to look sickly; in many cases the plant simply needs repotting into a larger container. Learn how on page 112.

● CHOOSE WISELY
The plant must be able to flourish in the home you provide for it. Even the expert can't make a shade-lover survive in a sunny window. Read the rules on pages 4–9.

BASIC TOOLS

COMPOSTS
Needed for repotting and taking cuttings.

POTS
Clay or plastic. 2½, 3½, 5 and 7 inch sizes are the most useful.

FERTILIZER
Feeding is vital during active growth. Use a liquid.

OLD KITCHEN SPOON & FORK
Necessary for top dressing and removing surface crusts.

SOFT SPONGE
Useful for washing leaves.

PEST KILLER
Necessary for greenfly, whitefly and red spider mite control.

MISTER
Vital for increasing humidity, reducing dust and controlling pests.

DRIP SAUCERS
Necessary for catching drainage water, *not* as a means of watering.

STRING
String, wire or plant-ties necessary for climbing varieties.

STAKES
Stakes, trellis or wire hoops necessary for climbing varieties.

SECATEURS
Necessary for pruning. Choose narrow, double-blade sort, not blade-and-anvil.

WATERING CAN
Choose 2–6 pint size. Long, narrow spout essential. Detachable fine rose useful.

There are many additional aids which can be bought by the keen house plant grower. A maximum-minimum thermometer and a hygrometer are extremely useful for checking the temperature and humidity around plants. A propagating frame is a help for difficult cuttings, but rooting bags can be used for propagating most popular plants. A wide range of self-watering pots is now available.

Choosing indoor plants

A bewildering range of plants is now available, and it's all too easy to make a mistake. Look around the homes of your friends to see which plants appear to flourish, but don't be guided by the large specimens in public buildings. These plants are often rented and returned to the nursery when the poor conditions start to have an effect.

You want to buy a plant . . . ask yourself the following six questions and the answers will give you a short list of types which will suit your purpose. Then choose the one which really appeals to you, for that is the most important requirement of all.

QUESTION 1: DO I WANT A PLANT THAT WILL BE PERMANENT?

If you buy a Gloxinia and it starts to die down after a couple of months, you have done nothing wrong – it is a temporary plant. If the same thing happens to an Ivy then you *are* responsible, because it is a permanent plant. Never choose a flowering pot plant if you want to have foliage all year round.

PERMANENT

FOLIAGE HOUSE PLANTS are varieties which will live permanently under room conditions, provided that their needs are met. The foliage remains alive and attractive all year round, although some types need to overwinter in an unheated room.
See A-Z guide, pages 21-58

PERMANENT

FLOWERING HOUSE PLANTS are varieties which will live permanently under room conditions, provided that their needs are met. After flowering, the foliage remains alive but may not be particularly attractive. Some types need to overwinter in an unheated room.
See A-Z guide, pages 60-78

PERMANENT

CACTI are a family of succulents with thickened stems which bear small patches or woolly tufts known as areoles. They are practically always leafless and often spiny. They will live permanently under room conditions and many can be made to flower.
See A-Z guide, pages 98-100

TEMPORARY

FLOWERING POT PLANTS are varieties which are moved away after flowering. Most of them are discarded at this stage, but some can be stored indoors as leafless plants or bulbs whilst others are transferred to greenhouse or garden.
See A-Z guide, pages 80-95

QUESTION 2: HOW MUCH DO I WANT TO SPEND?

The price of a plant in your local shop depends on:

Type: Slow-growing plants, such as Palms, are particularly expensive.

Size: Tall plants may take several years to grow — a 4 ft Rubber Plant will cost you three to four times the price of a 1 ft specimen.

The usual choice is a popular foliage variety in a 3 or 5 in. pot. If you can afford to buy mature specimen plants in a 7 or 10 in. pot then they should be a sound investment, provided you have the space and skill required. If you want lots of foliage and money is strictly limited then buy rooted cuttings or young plants of quick-growing varieties. Feed them and pot on regularly. Even cheaper are easy-rooting cuttings raised at home, potted-up bedding plants and quick-growing climbers grown from seed.

50p

£50

QUESTION 3: DO I WANT A POPULAR PLANT OR A RARITY?

Even if you have been studying and growing indoor plants for many years there will still be some plants illustrated in this book which you will have never seen. These are the rarities, and they are well worth trying if you like to be different and if you respond to a challenge. The High Street stockist is not the place to go — you will need to seek out a specialist supplier — the classified advertisement section of the garden magazines should help. Not all rarities are difficult —Abutilon, Beaucarnea, Carex, Callistemon and Pentas are easier to grow than many popular varieties.

Most people, however, choose the old favourites. These are the ones which are available everywhere and which have shown over the years that they succeed under ordinary room conditions. Even if you choose from the popular group, it is still sometimes possible to obtain an exciting new cultivar — the New Guinea hybrids of Busy Lizzie and the Ellen Danica cultivar of Grape Ivy are good examples.

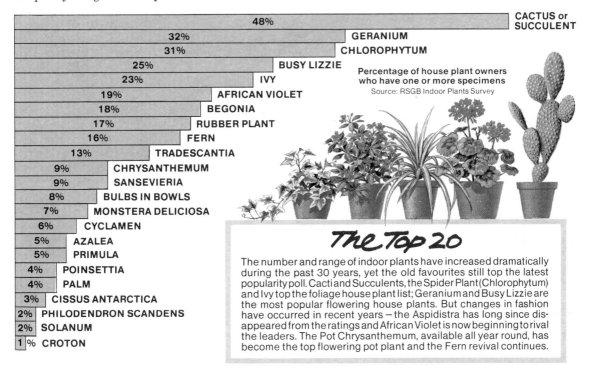

Percentage	Plant
48%	CACTUS or SUCCULENT
32%	GERANIUM
31%	CHLOROPHYTUM
25%	BUSY LIZZIE
23%	IVY
19%	AFRICAN VIOLET
18%	BEGONIA
17%	RUBBER PLANT
16%	FERN
13%	TRADESCANTIA
9%	CHRYSANTHEMUM
9%	SANSEVIERIA
8%	BULBS IN BOWLS
7%	MONSTERA DELICIOSA
6%	CYCLAMEN
5%	AZALEA
5%	PRIMULA
4%	POINSETTIA
4%	PALM
3%	CISSUS ANTARCTICA
2%	PHILODENDRON SCANDENS
2%	SOLANUM
1%	CROTON

Percentage of house plant owners who have one or more specimens
Source: RSGB Indoor Plants Survey

The Top 20

The number and range of indoor plants have increased dramatically during the past 30 years, yet the old favourites still top the latest popularity poll. Cacti and Succulents, the Spider Plant (Chlorophytum) and Ivy top the foliage house plant list; Geranium and Busy Lizzie are the most popular flowering house plants. But changes in fashion have occurred in recent years — the Aspidistra has long since disappeared from the ratings and African Violet is now beginning to rival the leaders. The Pot Chrysanthemum, available all year round, has become the top flowering pot plant and the Fern revival continues.

QUESTION 4: HOW MUCH TIME AND SKILL DO I HAVE?

EASY FOLIAGE HOUSE PLANTS
Aspidistra, Asparagus, Bromeliads, Cissus antarctica, Chlorophytum, Coleus, Cyperus, Dracaena marginata, Fatshedera, Fatsia, Ficus elastica decora, Grevillea, Hedera (mist leaves in winter), Helxine, Howea, Monstera, Neanthe, Philodendron scandens, Rhoicissus rhomboidea, Sansevieria, Saxifraga sarmentosa, Succulents, Tolmiea, Tradescantia, Zebrina.

Some plants have the reputation of being almost as indestructible as plastic. These 'cast-iron' plants include Sansevieria, Cissus antarctica, Fatsia, Fatshedera, Aspidistra, Cacti and other Succulents (if kept dry) and Cyperus (if kept wet). A much larger group are classed as 'easy' — they can tolerate a wide range of conditions and will stand a considerable amount of neglect and poor management. Choose here if you are a beginner or if you have little time to spare for house plant care.

At the other end of the scale is the 'delicate' group. These plants require carefully controlled conditions, which may mean constant temperature, very careful watering or high humidity at all times. Examples are Acalypha, Caladium, Calathea, Codiaeum, Dizygotheca, Ixora and Gardenia. Leave these plants to the experienced house plant grower.

QUESTION 5: WHAT SIZE AND SHAPE DO I WANT ?

Both size and shape are extremely important considerations when choosing a plant. A small, low-growing variety can look completely out-of-place against a large, bare wall . . . a tall, tree-like plant can look distinctly unsafe on a narrow windowsill. Remember that you may be buying a young specimen – in your home a small neat Dracaena or Ficus can become a man-sized tree in a few seasons. There are six basic plant shapes and nearly all indoor plants fit into one or other of these groups. But there are borderline cases, and a few plants will change with age from one shape type to another.

GRASSY PLANTS

GRASSY PLANTS have long, narrow leaves and a grass-like growth habit. Very few true grasses are offered as house plants because their leaf form has never been generally accepted for indoor decoration. Several grass-like plants with long and extremely narrow leaves are listed as indoor plants, but they are not often seen.

Examples: Acorus
Carex
Ophiopogon
Scirpus

Broad-leaved Grassy Plants are much more popular; Chlorophytum comosum is one of the most widely grown of all foliage house plants. Several flowering plants have grassy leaves of this type — good examples are Billbergia nutans, Vallota, Tillandsia lindenii and Narcissus.

BUSHY PLANTS

BUSHY PLANTS are a vast collection of varieties which do not fit into the other groups. The standard pattern is an arrangement of several stems arising out of the compost, with a growth habit which is neither markedly vertical nor horizontal. They may be small and compact like Peperomia or tall and shrubby like Aucuba. Some plants are naturally bushy, regularly producing side shoots; others must be pinched out regularly to induce bushiness. The Secrets of Success listed for each bushy plant will tell you if pinching out is necessary.

Examples: Achimenes
Begonia rex
Coleus
Hypocyrta
Maranta
Pilea

UPRIGHT PLANTS

UPRIGHT PLANTS bear stems with a distinctly vertical growth habit. They vary in height from an inch to the tallest house plants available. Medium-sized upright plants are an essential component of the mixed group, providing a feeling of height to offset the horizontal effect created by rosette plants, trailing plants and low bushes. Tall, upright plants are often displayed as solitary specimens, serving as effective focal points.

Column Plants have thick vertical stems which are either leafless or bear leaves which do not detract from the column effect. Many Cacti and some Succulents have this growth habit.

Examples: Cereus peruvianus
Cleistocactus straussii
Haworthia reinwardtii
Kleinia articulata
Notocactus leninghausii
Trichocereus candicans

Trees are an extremely important group, providing spectacular specimen plants for large displays and the basic centrepiece in collections. All trees have the same basic form — a central branched or unbranched stem bearing leaves with relatively small leaf bases. Some are quite small, such as miniature Succulent 'trees' or a young Croton; others are capable of growing many feet tall.

Examples: Aphelandra
Citrus
Codiaeum
Ficus benjamina
Ficus elastica decora
Laurus
Schefflera

False Palms have stems which are completely clothed by the elongated stem bases when the plant is young. In a mature plant usually only the upper part of the stem is covered by leaves and the characteristically palm-like effect is created. Large false palms are often used as specimen plants in public buildings.

Examples: Beaucarnea
Dieffenbachia
Dracaena
Pandanus
Yucca

CLIMBING & TRAILING PLANTS

CLIMBING & TRAILING PLANTS bear stems which, when mature, are either provided with support to grow upwards or are left to hang downwards on the outside of the container. Many (but not all) varieties can be used in both ways. As climbers they are trained on canes, strings, trellis-work, wire hoops or vertical poles; they can be grown in wall-mounted pots to frame windows or they can be trained up stout supports to serve as room dividers. As trailers they can be used to spread horizontally as ground cover in indoor gardens or left to trail over the sides of pots or hanging baskets.

Climbers are always grown as upright plants. Twining varieties are allowed to twist around the supports provided. Clinging varieties bearing tendrils must be attached to the supports at frequent intervals; if left to grow unattended the stems will soon become tangled together. Varieties bearing aerial roots are best grown on a moss stick (see page 43).

    Examples: Dipladenia
             Passiflora
             Philodendron hastatum
             Stephanotis

Climber/Trailers are extremely useful house plants and many popular varieties belong to this group. When growing them as climbers it is usually advisable not to tie all the stems to a single cane — it is more attractive to spread out the stems on a trellis or on several canes inserted in the pot. When growing them as trailers it is sometimes necessary to pinch out the growing tips occasionally to prevent straggly growth.

    Examples: Ficus pumila
             Hedera
             Philodendron scandens
             Scindapsus

Trailers are always grown as pendent plants, with stems hanging downwards, or as creeping plants, with stems growing along the soil surface. Many trailers have striking foliage or attractive flowers and are best grown in hanging baskets or stood on high pedestals.

    Examples: Begonia pendula
             Campanula isophylla
             Columnea
             Fittonia
             Helxine
             Nertera
             Sedum morganianum
             Senecio rowleyanus
             Zygocactus

ROSETTE PLANTS

ROSETTE PLANTS bear leaves which form a circular cluster around the central growing point. Most rosette plants are low-growing and combine well with bushy and upright plants in Pot Groups and Indoor Gardens.

Flat Rosette Plants have large leaves which lie almost horizontally, forming a loose rosette. African Violet is the best known example; Gloxinia and some Primulas have a similar growth habit.

Succulent Rosette Plants have fleshy leaves borne in several layers and often tightly packed together. The leaves may be horizontal or nearly upright. This arrangement helps to conserve moisture in the natural desert habitat.

    Examples: Aloe humilis
             Aeonium tabulaeforme
             Echeveria setosa
             Haworthia fasciata
             Sempervivum tectorum

Funnel Rosette Plants are common among the Bromeliads. The basal area of the strap-like leaves forms a 'vase' which holds rainwater in the natural tropical habitat. Plants are usually large and spreading.

    Examples: Aechmea
             Guzmania
             Nidularium
             Vriesia

BALL PLANTS

BALL PLANTS are leafless and have a distinctly globular shape. They are all Cacti, and the stem surface may be smooth or covered with hair and spines.

    Examples: Astrophytum
             Echinocactus grusonii
             Ferocactus
             Mammillaria
             Parodia
             Rebutia miniscula

QUESTION 6: WHAT WILL THE GROWING CONDITIONS BE LIKE?

Most people choose a house plant which has the right shape, appearance and price. It is essential, however, that it should also be right for the light and warmth it will receive in its new home. There are three important points to remember:

- **Each plant has its own likes and dislikes.** Some plants need an unheated room in winter, and a few will grow quite happily in full sun, but many would die under such conditions. Don't guess—look up your plants' special needs in the A-Z guides on pages 21-100.

- **A new plant gets homesick even in good conditions.** Many varieties suffer a distinct shock when they are moved from their well-lit and humid glasshouse home to your walled-in and dry living room. Don't assume that the conditions must be wrong if the plant looks jaded for the first few weeks—read page 10.

- **An established plant may adapt to poor conditions.** The Secrets of Success given for each plant in the following pages describe the *ideal* growing conditions; here the plant will flourish. But many plants are capable of slowly adapting to a poorer environment.

TYPE OF SITUATION	N ←	SUITABLE PLANTS
SHADE Well away from a window, but enough light to allow you to read a newspaper		Aglaonema, Aspidistra, Asplenium, Fittonia, Helxine, Philodendron scandens, Sansevieria, Scindapsus (variegation will fade). Any of the Semi-Shade group can be grown here for a month or two; some will survive permanently
SEMI-SHADE Near a sunless window or some distance away from a bright window		Aglaonema, Aspidistra, Dracaena fragrans, Dracaena marginata, Fatshedera, Fatsia, Ferns, Ficus pumila, Fittonia, Hedera helix, Helxine, Howea, Maranta, Neanthe, Philodendron scandens, Sansevieria, Scindapsus, Tolmiea
BRIGHT BUT SUNLESS On a sunless windowsill or near a bright window		Anthurium, Asparagus, Azalea, Begonia rex, Bromeliads, Chlorophytum, Columnea, Cyclamen, Dieffenbachia, Dizygotheca, Fuchsia, Garden Bulbs, Hedera, Monstera, Peperomia, Philodendron, Pilea, Schefflera, Scindapsus, Spathiphyllum, Vines, Zygocactus
SOME DIRECT SUNLIGHT On or very close to an east- or west-facing windowsill. May need protection from hot summer sun		Beloperone, Capsicum, Chlorophytum, Chrysanthemum, Codiaeum, Cordyline terminalis, Cuphea, Ficus elastica decora, Gynura, Hoya, Impatiens, Nertera, Plumbago, Poinsettia, Saintpaulia, Sansevieria, Solanum, Sparmannia, Tradescantia, Zebrina
SUNNY WINDOW On or very close to a south-facing windowsill. Light shading may be necessary in midsummer		Acacia, Agapanthus, Bougainvillea, Bouvardia, Cacti & Succulents, Callistemon, Celosia, Citrus, Coleus, Garden Annuals, Heliotropium, Hibiscus, Hippeastrum, Iresine, Jasminum, Lantana, Nerine, Nerium, Oxalis, Passiflora, Pelargonium, Rosa, Zebrina
NO HEAT IN WINTER		Araucaria, Aspidistra, Beloperone, Cacti & Succulents, Chlorophytum, Cineraria, Clivia, Cyclamen, Fatshedera, Fatsia, Grevillea, Hedera helix, Helxine, Hydrangea, Nertera, Rosa, Saxifraga sarmentosa, Setcreasea, Streptocarpus, Tolmiea
CENTRAL HEATING IN WINTER		Increase humidity to counteract desert-dry air (see page 107). Otherwise choose Aechmea, Billbergia, Cacti & Succulents, Chlorophytum, Dracaena godseffiana, Eucalyptus, Ficus elastica decora, Grevillea, Nerium, Peperomia, Zebrina

11% of indoor plant owners grow them in the BEDROOM

The experts are divided on this subject. Some believe that bedrooms are used far too infrequently during the waking hours to make a house plant display worthwhile. Others feel that the bedroom is an important spot for greenery, to see foliage on waking and to smell the fragrance of Jasmine, Stephanotis or Hyacinths before going to sleep. Whatever your view, you need not worry about the old wives' tale that plants are unhealthy in a bedroom.
If your bedroom is heated at night during winter you can use it as a pot plant 'hospital'. Off-colour plants can be kept out of general view in an environment where the temperature will be fairly constant and where draughts are not usually a problem.
The window of an unheated bedroom is an excellent home for plants which need cool conditions in winter.

34% of indoor plant owners grow them in the HALL/LANDING

Indoor plants are a vital feature of the well-furnished hall, for it is here that visitors gain their first impression of your house. Beautiful leaves and flowers are an immediate indication of a properly cared-for home.
The favourite site is a table near the front door, and here the conditions are usually poor. Light is deficient, there is often no winter warmth and cold draughts can be a problem. Flourishing but unexciting plants will look better than struggling exotics, so choose from the 'easy' group on page 5.
A well-lit spot near the hall window or at the top of the stairs is often a better environment for indoor plants. Bulbs, Azalea, Chrysanthemum and Cyclamen will be happier here than in a warm living room. If the hall is well-lit and heated in winter then you can choose from a vast range of plants.

12% of indoor plant owners grow them in the BATHROOM

A plant display in the bathroom is more likely to be seen in a magazine than in the home, but it can so easily be used to add a touch of luxury. The best display for an unheated bathroom is a Pot Group of glossy-leaved plants such as Cissus antarctica and Fatsia. Philodendron scandens is ideal – in the U.S. it is known as the Bathroom Plant.
The moist air will keep the plants flourishing, and steamy conditions provide a tonic for many varieties. The absence of clear glass windows means that no direct sunlight will fall on tender leaves, and with these conditions the bathroom makes an ideal 'hospital' for ailing plants. If the room is heated in winter you can grow delicate varieties, such as Anthurium, Calathea, Maranta and many Ferns which do so badly downstairs. Wash leaves regularly; talcum powder and hair lacquer aerosols are the enemies in the bathroom.

79% of indoor plant owners grow them in the LIVING ROOM

This is the area where the family gathers. The adults relax, the children play and everyone seeks comfort. Most living rooms have indoor plants to provide splashes of leafy green or flower colour, but they must not obstruct.
If the room is comfortably warm in winter then you have created a problem for some plants. It may be too warm for most flowering pot plants and the air will be too dry for many house plants. Don't worry – there are still many plants which will flourish with proper care in the centrally-heated home.
The windowsill remains the favourite spot, but be a little more adventurous… try a floor-standing specimen plant, an Indoor Garden or a Bottle Garden. Decorate a dark corner or unused fireplace with Ferns or Philodendron. The most spectacular display is the Plant Window, where a trough replaces the windowsill.

28% of indoor plant owners grow them in the DINING ROOM

The dining room can provide a good home for indoor plants, so it is surprising that only a quarter of them are used in this way. There are plenty of horizontal surfaces such as a sideboard, table, trolley and windowsills to support containers and the kitchen is nearby to make watering convenient. Proper maintenance is important here – dust and greenfly on the leaves are distinctly distasteful.
Plants make an excellent centrepiece for the table. Choose low-growing plants so as not to interfere with conversation – good examples are Saintpaulia, Begonia semperflorens, Peperomia, Pilea and small-leaved Ivy.
Many homes have a combined living/dining area and plants make an excellent room divider. They can be grown in pots set in a waterproof trough at ground level, or stood on a sideboard or shelf unit. Vigorous climbers growing up a framework of vertical supports are popular.

51% of indoor plant owners grow them in the KITCHEN

The kitchen is second only to the living room as the most popular place for indoor plants. The housewife spends much of her day here, and the windowsill is often the home of a favourite collection of small plants – Saintpaulia, Primula, Cacti, Succulents, Pelargoniums, Hyacinths etc. A Pebble Tray (see page 15) will increase the range and quality of the display.
The environment is good for most plants. Lighting is usually bright and the air is moister than in any other area. The gas cooker is no longer a problem; natural gas is much kinder than coal gas to indoor plants.
Windowsill plants above the sink can pose one or two problems—the varieties chosen must be unobtrusive and the foliage is in danger of being splashed with hot, soapy water. Try an alternative display on the top of a work surface or in a well-lit corner.

Buying indoor plants

Indoor plants are raised in glasshouses in which the air is warm and humid. The world outside is far less accommodating, so always buy from a reputable supplier who will have made sure that the plants have been properly hardened off. In this way the shock of moving into a new home will be reduced to a minimum.

House plants can, of course, be bought at any time of the year, but it is preferable to purchase delicate varieties between late spring and mid-autumn. But some plants can only be bought in winter, and you should be extra careful at this time of the year. Plants stood outside the shop or on a market stall will have been damaged by the cold unless they are hardy varieties — avoid buying delicate plants which are stood in the open as 'bargain' offers.

Now you are ready to buy. If you are shopping for flower seeds, choose F_1 hybrids if available. If you are picking bulbs, make sure that they are firm, rot-free and without holes or shoots. When buying house plants, ensure that the specimen is not too big for the space you have in mind and then look for the danger signs. None present? Then you have a good buy.

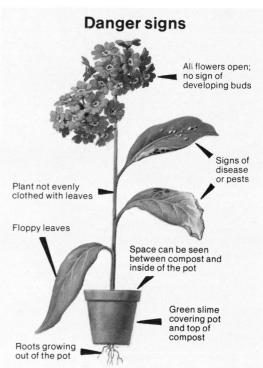

Danger signs

All flowers open; no sign of developing buds

Signs of disease or pests

Plant not evenly clothed with leaves

Floppy leaves

Space can be seen between compost and inside of the pot

Green slime covering pot and top of compost

Roots growing out of the pot

Taking plants home

Make sure the plant is properly wrapped before leaving the shop or nursery. The purpose of this wrapping is twofold — to protect stray leaves from damage and to keep out draughts. In winter the protecting cover should be closed at the top.

Much has been written about the danger of walking home with a delicate house plant in the depths of winter, but just as much damage is done by putting plants in the boot of a car in the height of summer... plants can be killed by baking as well as freezing. When taking a plant home by car the best plan is to secure it in a box and place it on a seat.

Once your new plant is home it will need a period of acclimatisation. For a few weeks keep it out of direct sunlight and draughts, and be careful not to give it too much heat or water. It is quite normal for a delicate variety to lose a leaf or two during this settling-in period, and the worst thing you can do is to keep on moving it from one spot to another in order to find the 'proper' home. Just leave it alone in a moderately warm spot out of the sun.

Flowering pot plants (such as Azalea, Chrysanthemum and Cyclamen) which are purchased in flower during the winter months require different treatment; put them in their permanent quarters immediately and give them as much light as possible.

Displaying indoor plants

Take the average indoor plant. It sits on the windowsill or sideboard, providing a green shape or a splash of colour. The small pot hangs on the wall, the large plant stands on the floor.

These single specimens have an important part to play in the art of decorating rooms with indoor plants, but there is no need to regard house plants solely as green pets, to be stood apart from each other in their pots and treated as individuals.

Look out of the window. The garden is brought alive by its contrasting shapes and colours. The individual bedding plant is insignificant but when massed in the flower bed the display is bold and colourful.

The same thing can be true indoors. Grouping plants together brings the added pleasure of making your own arrangement and even small plants can materially change the appearance of the room when treated in this way. There are also hidden benefits from grouping—the air humidity is raised, the effect of draughts is lowered and the damaged part of a plant can be hidden.

There are very few firm rules to tell you how to arrange plants correctly. They should be in keeping with their surroundings—large architectural specimens in spacious rooms, small pots on tiny windowsills. Let dramatic plants stand on their own as specimens, but always hide below-par plants in a group. Pick up ideas from magazines, TV and films but, most important of all, create a display which pleases *you*.

This section will tell you some of the secrets of interior decorating with pot plants. The first step is to learn the four basic ways in which they can be displayed in your home:

Stand it on its own

A Specimen Plant is a flowering or foliage plant grown as a solitary feature. It may be retained in its pot or transplanted into a container.

THE
Specimen Plant

see page 12

Place it alongside several other pots

A Pot Group is a collection of plants in pots, closely grouped to create a massed effect. The pots remain visible as separate units.

THE
Pot Group

see page 14

Arrange it with other plants in a container

An Indoor Garden is a container filled with several plants, in which no pots can be seen. The pots may have been removed or merely hidden from sight.

THE
Indoor Garden

see page 16

Place it with other plants inside a glass container

A Terrarium is a glass or transparent plastic container inside which plants are grown. The top is either naturally restricted or covered with transparent material.

THE
Terrarium

see page 19

THE
Specimen Plant

The purpose of a plant display is to provide an attractive focal point in the room. Most ordinary plants need to be grouped together to achieve this effect, but some are best seen on their own in a prominent place. These are the Specimen Plants. Of course, correct plant choice is all-important, but you must also pay attention to the position, container, lighting and background provided for the plant if you want to achieve the maximum effect.

You may want a large specimen which will cover an area of several square feet. Unfortunately the cost of a mature floor-standing house plant which can dominate a corner or wall could well be prohibitive. A good plan is to buy a young plant, repot regularly and then place it in its permanent position once it has reached the required height. Alternatively stand a hanging plant on a pedestal or grow a vigorous climber to clothe the required area.

As shown below, it makes good design sense to display fine examples of dramatic plants as solitary specimens. Small and medium-sized foliage types, however, are usually best grouped together and not kept as a collection of isolated pots on shelves and windowsills.

ARCHITECTURAL PLANTS

Foliage plants with a distinctly architectural shape are the most popular choice for bold effects. They are used to clothe empty spaces, divide living areas and form eye-catching accents to the decor of the room.
Trees and false palms are the types most frequently used, and interior decorators usually choose tall specimens from the following list:

Abutilon striatum thompsonii
Araucaria heterophylla
Beaucarnea recurvata
Dieffenbachia
Dracaena
Fatsia japonica
Ficus benjamina
Ficus elastica decora
Ficus lyrata
Grevillea robusta
Monstera deliciosa
Palms
Philodendron bipinnatifidum
Schefflera actinophylla
Yucca

CLIMBING PLANTS

Many climbers make excellent Specimen Plants, and the more vigorous ones can be used to provide a large, leafy specimen at the lowest possible cost. You can choose a foliage type (Philodendrons, Vines, etc.) or a flowering climber (Hoya, Thunbergia, etc.). Good examples are

Cissus
Monstera
Passiflora
Philodendron hastatum
Philodendron panduraeforme
Rhoicissus
Scindapsus
Stephanotis

HANGING PLANTS

Some hanging plants are showy enough to be displayed on their own in hanging baskets or on pedestals rather than as part of a plant group. Good examples are

Chlorophytum
Columnea
Nephrolepis
Zygocactus

MULTICOLOURED FOLIAGE PLANTS

Many popular house plants have multicoloured foliage, and the most dramatic varieties are frequently used as Specimen Plants. Good examples are

Begonia rex
Caladium
Codiaeum
Cordyline terminalis
Nidularium
Rhoeo

FLOWERING POT PLANTS

Some flowering pot plants are so colourful that they are best displayed on their own. Good examples are

Azalea indica
Begonia tuberhybrida
Cyclamen
Garden Bulbs
Gloxinia
Hydrangea
Pelargonium
Poinsettia

The Right Position

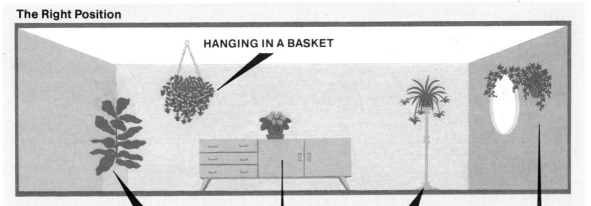

HANGING IN A BASKET

STANDING ON THE FLOOR The place for the large Specimen Plant is on the floor — placing a heavy pot on a table can make it look unsafe. Bold architectural plants are the usual choice, but there are other possibilities. Flowering standards (see page 86) should be displayed in this way, and tall climbers make excellent floor-standing specimens; use a moss stick (see page 43) to support climbers with aerial roots.
A floor-standing display can be used to divide areas in a room, provide a focal point or bring the garden indoors by being stood near a window. It is important to choose the right container; remember it can damage the carpet so place a piece of wood or cork below it.

STANDING ON FURNITURE Small Specimen Plants need to be raised off the ground so that they can be enjoyed at close range. The usual way to do this is to place the pot on a windowsill, shelf or piece of furniture. If the pot has drainage holes you must use a drip tray which is deep enough to protect the surface of the furniture; mop up any spillage immediately.

STANDING ON A PEDESTAL A number of indoor plants produce long pendulous stems or arching leaves and the display is often spoilt if the pot is stood on a sideboard or windowsill. The place for such plants is in a hanging basket or on a pedestal. You can buy a reproduction antique pedestal if your home is decorated in this style, but for modern surroundings it is extremely simple to make a plain wooden pillar.

GROWING AGAINST A WALL The plants most usually grown against a wall are flowering types (to provide a splash of colour against a pastel wall) and trailers (to frame windows, pictures, etc.). There are a number of difficulties — it is not easy to create moist conditions, the pot is often small which means that constant watering is essential and it is difficult to tell when the plant requires watering in a high-mounted display. Choose a container which is soundly made, not too ornate and with a saucer which is large and deep.

The Right Background

Light-coloured walls without a pattern are the ideal backcloth, although strongly variegated specimens are best displayed against a dark wall. If the background is highly coloured and intricately patterned, choose a plant with all-green, simple leaves. Deeply cut leaves (such as Monstera) and delicate flowers (such as Stephanotis) need a plain background.

The Right Lighting

For life-giving illumination the plants must rely on daylight or fluorescent lighting. For display purposes the light of an ordinary bulb directed on to the foliage or flowers will greatly enhance the appearance of a Specimen Plant in the evening. The best type of bulb to use is a spotlight or floodlight, but overheating can be a problem. Switch on the light and place your hand just above the leaves nearest the bulb. If you can feel the warmth then the plant is too close.

The Right Container

Some people enjoy the natural look of a clay pot, but most Specimen Plants are improved by being placed in an outer container. This pot holder should be taller than the pot and the space between them should be filled with damp peat. Containers come in many forms — you can buy ones made of wire, plastic, pottery or metal and you can use ordinary household objects, such as copper bowls and pans. Make sure that the size of the container is in keeping with the plant, a large palm in a small pot would look distinctly top-heavy. Never use multicoloured pot holders for multicoloured plants and remember that mobility is important — large floor-standing containers should have castors.

THE
Pot Group

The simple step of bringing together several isolated plants to make a Pot Group can add a new dimension to your indoor display. There are three basic reasons for this transformation:

- The overall effect is much bolder than can be achieved with individual pots. Plants at the rear of the group can be raised to give added height.
- Small-leaved plants such as Ficus pumila, Adiantum, Helxine and Tradescantia can seem insignificant and uninteresting when grown in isolated pots, but when grouped with large-leaved varieties they suddenly come to life and add an important ingredient to the overall effect.
- Individual perfection, so important with the Specimen Plant, is not vital. Bare stems, lop-sided growth and damaged leaves can all be easily hidden by surrounding them with other plants.

The advantage of grouping is not just a matter of appearance; there are also cultural benefits. Watering is an easier task when plants are collected together rather than scattered around the room. The close proximity of other plants and a large expanse of moist compost means that the air humidity around the foliage is increased, and this can be vitally important for a delicate variety.

The house plant owner has the satisfaction of creating an individual arrangement. Various groupings are shown on these two pages, but there are no hard and fast rules except that plants should, wherever possible, have the same basic light and warmth requirements. At first glance the Pot Group would seem to be less desirable than the more natural-looking Indoor Garden, where the pots are either removed or hidden. But the groupings on this page have an important advantage—pots can be treated separately which means that water-loving plants such as Chlorophytum can be grown alongside desert plants such as Cacti and Succulents.

THE STANDARD GROUP

Between four and a dozen clay or plastic pots are closely grouped together to produce a pleasing arrangement in which both shapes and tints are varied. In the most usual grouping foliage plants are used to provide the permanent framework and flowering pot plants are used to provide splashes of colour. The taller plants, the darker greens and the larger leaves are placed at tne back of the group. It is a basic error to assume that you *must* create a riot of different colours and a wide variety of shapes in order to give your Pot Group a professional touch. The skilled interior decorator will sometimes use only foliage plants, relying on different leaf forms and variegation to produce an attractive display.

THE PROFESSIONAL GROUP

This type of display, much loved by interior designers, is the big brother of the Standard Group. Although it is usually found in public buildings, a simple version is worth considering for a bare corner in your home. Pot hiders are an important feature of the Professional Group—they are decorative and of different heights. The container at the back of the group is either much taller than the others or is raised on a block of wood to display to the maximum the pinnacle plant it contains—a Kentia Palm in the illustration above. The pot hider at the front of the group holds a large flowering pot plant which is replaced when its display is finished. A trailing plant is grown in one of the middle containers and its stems are allowed to drape over the base unit.

THE PEBBLE TRAY

Grouping plants within a shallow tray is a useful technique for maintaining plants which need high humidity in a centrally-heated room. If you have difficulty in growing African Violets then try them in a Pebble Tray. The tray should be about 2in. high, and can be made of any waterproof material. The dimensions are up to you, but avoid a dangerously wide overhang if the tray is to be stood on a windowsill.

Place 1in. of gravel in the bottom of the tray and keep the bottom of this layer wet at all times. The water level, however, must not be allowed to cover the top of the gravel. Group the plants on the surface.

A favourite place for a Pebble Tray is on the radiator shelf below a windowsill. In this situation the humidity around the plants in winter will be trebled. Watering plants is a simple matter—allow excess water to run out of the pots and into the gravel.

THE COLLECTION

A group of pots containing closely related plants can be found in the homes of people at both ends of the house plant knowledge scale. The young beginner often starts with a collection of Succulents and Cacti, grouped neatly on a windowsill . . . in the home of the keen indoor gardener you will often find a prized collection of his or her speciality—Ferns, African Violets, Orchids, etc. In the U.K. collections are usually housed in a spot exposed to natural light; in the U.S. the fluorescent-lit Plant Table is popular—see page 103.

Collections, big and small, have one feature in common. Unlike the Standard Group where the overall decorative effect is all-important, the basic purpose of the Collection is to highlight the individuality, rarity or beauty of each plant.

Living Furniture

There is nothing new about Living Furniture. For hundreds of years it has been common practice for housewives to cover or fill a standard piece of furniture with pot plants. The original purpose of the object is generally lost, and it is transformed from a thing of utility to a thing of beauty. A small, fern-covered mahogany table in a Victorian villa, or a double-glazed, thermostatically-controlled Plant Window in an ultra-modern apartment—both are Living Furniture.

A table-top is an obvious surface to house a Pot Group, and the Plant Table is the most popular of all Living Furniture items. Use a Pebble Tray as described above or choose a glass-topped table in order to avoid water stains. The most useful piece of Living Furniture is the Plant Trolley. It can be wheeled into the kitchen for watering and maintenance, moved away from the window in summertime and wheeled into a sunnier spot in winter.

THE
Indoor Garden

Find a container which is large enough to hold several indoor plants—it should be attractive in shape, colour and design. Now plant out the specimens into potting compost you have placed inside the container; alternatively stand the pots on a layer of peat, sand, gravel or pebbles and surround each pot with damp peat so that the clay or plastic is no longer visible. You now have an Indoor Garden.

Your Indoor Garden may be five small plants in a bowl or it may be a forest of greenery and flowers in a multi-tiered Planter, but the basic advantages and principles of construction remain the same.

Some of the advantages of the Indoor Garden are similar to those of the Pot Group—the creation of a bold effect, the proper utilisation of insignificant foliage and flowers, the hiding of ugly bare stems and damaged leaves, the ease of watering and the creation of moist conditions around the foliage. But the 'natural' effect is much more dramatic than with the Pot Group—here you are truly gardening.

Surprisingly, indoor gardening remains an unusual concept because there is still a strange reluctance to growing house plants in groups rather than as individual specimens. Colourful plants such as Begonia semperflorens and Coleus can be bedded out in the home as they are in the garden, but they are nearly always grown indoors as single plants in solitary pots. As every gardener knows, most ordinary shrubs, perennials and roses look best when grown with other plants in a bed or border, but very rarely do we find a bed or border indoors. The Multiple Planter (see page 18) undoubtedly offers the greatest scope for a bold display, but any large Planter will do. The fact remains that many house plants look better and thrive better when grown in the company of others.

There are several reasons why most plants grow much better in an Indoor Garden than in a solitary pot. Higher humidity, insulation of the roots from sudden changes in temperature and the water reservoir below each pot are amongst the most important benefits. But there are dangers, and you should be on your guard against them. Close planting means reduced ventilation, and so the chance of pest and disease attack is increased. Prune or remove plants to avoid overcrowding and cut off mouldy leaves or flowers immediately they are seen.

The Ingredients of the Indoor Garden

PLANT
All the plants in a container will receive approximately the same conditions of moisture and warmth. Light conditions will also be similar across a small Indoor Garden, but the plants at the back of a corner unit or in the centre of a large square unit may receive appreciably less light than the unshaded plants at the edges. For planting suggestions see page 18—the standard pattern is to have a permanent foliage background with splashes of colour provided by flowering plants.

POT
It is much better to leave the plants in their pots rather than planting them directly into the compost. In this way plants can be occasionally turned to prevent one-sided growth and to stop them rooting into the surrounding peat. Plants can also be easily removed when flowering is over or when repotting is necessary. The individual pots must have drainage holes.

PEAT
Make sure that the peat reaches to the rim of each pot and keep it moist but not saturated. This damp peat will provide a moisture reserve beneath each pot, which means that a plant will survive much better in an Indoor Garden than in an isolated pot if regular watering is interrupted at holiday time.

CONTAINER
There is an almost limitless range of watertight containers from which you can take your choice—plastic tubs, ornate jardinières, old copper steamers, home-made boxes and so on. If the container is made of wood, the inner surface and corners must be waterproof. You can use polyurethane varnish, good quality sealant, a polythene liner but never creosote.

SOAKAWAY
A soakaway is not essential but it is a good idea to place a layer of gravel, small pebbles or coarse sand at the bottom of the container before adding peat. Include lumps of charcoal if you have this material available.

THE MIXED BOWL

One of the simplest of all Indoor Gardens, in which a small selection of foliage plants and one or two flowering plants are removed from their pots and planted in a peat-based compost. The traditional pattern is to have a large pinnacle plant towards the back of the bowl, several compact bushy plants in the middle and a trailing plant at the front. The container is usually a bulb bowl, but any waterproof bowl will do.

A Mixed Bowl is always a welcome present to receive, but it is not a *permanent* Indoor Garden. When the flowers fade the best plan is to break up the arrangement and repot the individual plants before the roots become hopelessly intertwined. Explain to the donor, if necessary, that you are not destroying her present—you are preserving it.

THE PLANTER

The single Planter is the most popular of all Indoor Gardens. Until recently long troughs of metal, wood or plastic were the only popular containers, but there is now a wide range of cylindrical and cubic containers in every shade of tough plastic. A black or white Planter is recommended for modern decor.

Water carefully so that the surrounding peat does not become waterlogged. If the pots are stood on a thick layer of peat, the roots can be allowed to grow through the drainage holes and into the moist peat so that the Planter becomes a self-watering one. The usual recommendation where the pots stand on a shallow layer of gravel or peat is to lift or turn the pots occasionally to prevent rooting.

THE POT-ET-FLEUR

The Pot-et-Fleur is essentially a small Planter in which a group of foliage house plants is grown. During its construction a glass tube or metal florist tube is sunk into the peat between the pots. Subsequently this tube is filled with water and used for arranging cut flowers. In this way flowers from the garden or florist can be used to produce ever-changing and colourful displays. Seasonal arrangements with holly at Christmas and Daffodils in early spring can be easily created, with the added attraction of a background of living plants.

THE MINIATURE GARDEN

This special type of Indoor Garden is an attempt to reproduce an outdoor garden on a small scale. Paths, pools, figurines, etc., are used for decoration and mossy turf plus tiny-leaved plants are used for landscaping. Japanese styles are popular, and the Miniature Garden is usually kept on a trolley so that it can be wheeled outside in fine weather and into the kitchen for watering. This style of Indoor Garden is really for the keen hobbyist, as upkeep is difficult and without a high degree of artistry the result can appear distinctly amateurish.

THE DISH GARDEN

A small Indoor Garden made in a shallow dish using carefully-chosen Succulents. Unlike other Indoor Garden containers the dish usually has drainage holes. For further details see page 54.

THE *Indoor Garden* continued

THE MULTIPLE PLANTER

Foliage
House
Plants

Flowering
Pot Plants

Bedding
with one variety
of flowering plants

The simplest form consists of two or more ordinary containers pushed together to form a Multiple Planter. The best form is a tailor-made garden designed to fit the allotted space. The average handyman can quite easily construct a Multiple Planter from plastic-coated board—for maximum effect the planting units should be on different levels. The cracks between the boards must be sealed.

Each planting unit can be treated individually from both the planting and cultural standpoint. In the illustration flowering pot plants are grown in the unit closest to the window, the lowest unit is used for indoor bedding (Wax Begonia, Coleus, Crocus, etc.) which changes with the season and finally the tallest units provide a permanent back-cloth of foliage house plants. An added advantage is that each unit can be individually watered so that moisture-lovers can be grown alongside Cacti and Succulents.

Planting Suggestions for an Indoor Garden

You will be able to make your selection from scores of different varieties—let the A-Z sections later in this book be your guide. Aim for closely-matched requirements for heat, light and water whenever you can. Remember that you have to live with the Indoor Garden, so choose colour and form which you find pleasing.

The next step is to make sure that the height and shape of the plants are in keeping with the size of the container. Aim for a variation in height, a contrast in leaf shape and texture, and a controlled use of colour.

First of all, the tall plant or plants ('pinnacle' plants) which give height to the display. Be careful in small Indoor Gardens that you don't choose a wide-spreading giant which dwarfs and shades all others. Sansevieria provides height without spread, and feathery-leaved plants such as Grevillea and Dizygotheca avoid the shading effect of large leaves. The choice of pinnacle plants for a large Planter is of course much easier—Palms, Dracaena, Ficus, Monstera and Philodendron are all widely used.

For most displays it is the medium-sized range of plants which form the basic framework. If you don't want to rely on flowering pot plants for colour you can use some non-green foliage varieties—red-leaved Cordyline terminalis, yellow Scindapsus, variegated Chlorophytum and Ivies, and the multicoloured Croton, Coleus and Begonia rex.

Finally, don't forget the trailers which are needed to soften the hard line of the edge of the container. The popular four are Ivy, Tradescantia, Ficus pumila and Zebrina, but there are others—Gynura, Asparagus sprengeri, Plectranthus or Pelargonium peltatum can be used as alternatives.

THE HANGING BASKET

A group of attractive indoor plants in a hanging basket will indeed provide a beautiful display, but do not rush into hanging a container from a hook in the ceiling or a bracket on the wall until you have carefully studied the difficulties.

The air will be warmer and drier than at floor or windowsill level. The height of the display usually makes watering difficult, and when water is applied too liberally the basket may drip on to the floor. To avoid problems choose either a hanging pot which has a built-in drip tray or put the pots of plants inside a larger, waterproof container. In the latter case fill the space between the pots and the outer container with moist peat before suspending the 'basket' from ceiling or wall. Choosing the right type of hanging container for indoors will remove the drip problem associated with wire baskets; to make watering and misting an easier task place the display at eye-level or if you must suspend it over head-high then have a pulley arrangement instead of an ordinary hook. Ensure that the hook is securely fixed to a ceiling joist or the bracket is firmly attached to the wall, and finally make sure that your choice of plants is suited to the light available—flowering plants and variegated foliage house plants will need a spot near a window.

Good hanging basket plants:

Aporocactus	Episcia	Scindapsus
Asparagus	Fuchsia	Setcreasea
Begonia	Hoya	Tradescantia
Campanula	Lobelia	Zebrina
Chlorophytum	Pelargonium	Zygocactus

THE Terrarium

The reason why the Terrarium has remained the Cinderella of indoor plant displays is hard to understand. It cannot be a matter of cost, because suitable containers are to be found in most homes. All you need is a goldfish bowl, fish tank, large bottle, brandy snifter or even a glass mixing bowl. Anything, in fact, which has transparent sides and has either a restricted neck or can be covered with a sheet of glass or transparent plastic.

The essential point of a Terrarium is that the plants are *surrounded* by the container, and access to the outside air is limited. As a result the air around the leaves remains moist at all times, and plant-killing draughts are excluded. So for the first time you will be able to grow delicate varieties which would fail in ordinary pots in most rooms, and yet the maintenance work involved is much less. Watering takes place every few weeks or even not at all because the system is enclosed and the moisture re-circulates.

There are danger points—waterlogging is fatal and the container must be kept well away from direct sunlight. Misting-over can be a nuisance; remove the cork or cover until the glass is clear.

THE FISHTANK GARDEN

Begin by placing a layer of gravel and charcoal at the bottom of the container and then add Baby Bio Seed & Cutting Compost. In most cases it is a good idea to landscape the 'ground' into hills and valleys. Use small rocks and pebbles, but do not incorporate wood which will rot and may contain pests. After planting cover the top with a sheet of glass with bevelled edges or with transparent plastic.

Planting Suggestions for a Terrarium

The range of plants you can grow in a Terrarium with a restricted or closed top is strictly limited. Do not use flowering plants, quick-growing foliage plants, Cacti or Succulents. Choose from the following list and buy small specimens:

Acorus	Hedera helix (small-leaved var.)
Begonia rex (small-leaved var.)	Maranta
Calathea	Neanthe bella
Cryptanthus	Pellionia
Dracaena sanderiana	Peperomia
Ferns	Pilea
Ficus pumila	Saxifraga sarmentosa
Fittonia	Selaginella

THE BOTTLE GARDEN

It is curious that the only type of Terrarium to become popular in Britain is the Carboy or Bottle Garden. It is difficult to make, requiring special tools and some dexterity. First of all, make sure that the bottle is clean and dry. Insert a stiff paper cone in the mouth and pour in a 2 in. layer of gravel. Add a thin layer of charcoal and finally a thick layer of Baby Bio Seed & Cutting Compost. Firm the compost with a tamper (a cotton reel at the end of a bamboo cane) and then build up the compost to form the back of the garden.

Now introduce the plants. You will need about six, including one tree-like specimen and at least one trailer. The planting tools are a dessert spoon at the end of one cane and a fork at the end of another. Firm the compost around each plant with the tamper.

Your Bottle Garden is now finished and is ready for watering. Use a long-necked watering can and train a gentle stream of water against the glass. Use very little water–just enough to clean the glass and moisten the surface. Insert the stopper; if the glass clouds over later, then remove the stopper until the condensation disappears. Re-insert the stopper — you will probably never have to water again.

CHAPTER 2

FOLIAGE HOUSE PLANTS

Foliage house plants make up the permanent framework of an indoor plant collection. Here are the plants which remain green throughout the year, their attraction arising from the beauty of each individual leaf (e.g. Monstera deliciosa and Begonia rex) or from the overall effect of the foliage (e.g. Asparagus and Chlorophytum).

A few of these plants, such as Zebrina and Sansevieria occasionally produce small flowers, but it is for their leaves and general growth habit that specimens of this group are grown. This does not mean that they can only provide a dull green background — Coleus, Croton, Gynura, Begonia, Maranta and many others offer a multicoloured display. Even more types have foliage which is lined, splashed or spotted with white or cream — Tradescantia, Dieffenbachia, Chlorophytum, Scindapsus and Ivy are just a few examples.

These plants *belong* indoors. Some of them appreciate a winter holiday in an unheated room away from the family but not for them the fate of flowering pot plants — the end-of-season dustbin, the enforced summer outdoors or a stemless winter indoors. With proper care many varieties are capable of outliving their owners, but a few do deteriorate with age. Coleus tends to become unattractive after a year or two and so do Gynura and Hypoestes. The answer is to raise cuttings and replace the parent plant. The only 'temporary' foliage house plant is Caladium, which spends each winter as a dormant tuber.

It is impossible to generalise about the proper care of foliage house plants; a few are extremely delicate and some have cast-iron constitutions. The popular types which have all-green, large, shiny leaves are usually extremely tolerant of poor conditions. Variegated types need more care; fleshy-leaved varieties need less frequent watering. But each plant has its own personality, and in the following A-Z guide you will find your plant and a list of its needs.

ABUTILON

The Spotted Flowering Maple is an excellent shrub for a large room, where its vigorous stems and yellow-splashed leaves can be allowed to spread. Orange blooms appear in summer as an extra bonus.

There are no special cultural problems, and mealy bug is the only pest which is likely to be a nuisance. Prune the shoots in spring to encourage bushiness and cut back the shrub to half its size in autumn. Weeping Chinese Lantern (A. megapotamicum) is grown for its red and yellow flowers as well as its foliage.

A. striatum thompsonii
Spotted Flowering Maple

SECRETS OF SUCCESS

Temperature: Average warmth; keep cool in winter (50° – 60°F).

Light: Choose a partially shady spot.

Water: Water liberally from spring to late autumn. Water sparingly in winter.

Air Humidity: Mist leaves occasionally.

Repotting: Repot in spring.

Propagation: Stem cuttings or seeds in spring.

ACALYPHA

It is difficult to overwinter Copper Leaf in the average room. The problem is the high humidity requirement, which can be readily satisfied in the greenhouse but not in the home. For this reason it is more usual to raise new plants from cuttings each year rather than to try to maintain a permanent shrub.

Keep in a well-lit spot or the red and brown mottling of the leaves will be lost. Watch for red spider mite, do not keep the plant in an unheated room in winter, and do not overwater.

A. wilkesiana
Copper Leaf

SECRETS OF SUCCESS

Temperature: Keep the shrub warm; 65° – 75°F during the day, minimum 60°F at night.

Light: Bright, indirect light or some sun.

Water: Keep the compost fairly dry at all times.

Air Humidity: Moist air is vital. Surround pot with damp peat and mist leaves frequently.

Repotting: Repot annually in spring.

Propagation: Stem cuttings in spring or summer.

AGLAONEMA

leathery, bluish-green leaves; arum-like flowers occasionally appear

A. pseudobracteatum
Golden Evergreen

A. modestum
Chinese Evergreen

A. crispum
Silver Queen

A. treubii
Silver Spear

A. pictum

BASIC FACTS

The spear-shaped decorative leaves of Aglaonema, the Chinese Evergreen, have the virtue of thriving in poorly lit locations. A. modestum is the most tolerant of shade; A. pseudobracteatum and A. crispum are perhaps the most attractive.

According to some European authorities the shade tolerance of this slow-growing plant is its *only* virtue — it has even been described as being far too difficult for growing in the home. In the United States, however, it is regarded as one of the most tolerant and reliable of house plants.

The best advice is to treat it as a moderately easy plant with a few special needs. Grow it in a shallow pot and keep it well away from draughts and smoky air. In winter it requires warm and moist air.

SECRETS OF SUCCESS

Temperature: Warm in summer; at least 60°F in winter.

Light: Semi-shade. Keep well away from direct sunlight.

Water: From November to March water sparingly. For the rest of the year water thoroughly.

Air Humidity: Moist air is necessary. Mist leaves regularly, but never use a coarse spray. Surround pot with damp peat.

Repotting: Every 3 years transfer to a larger pot in spring.

Propagation: In spring or summer pot up basal shoots with a few leaves and roots attached. Air layering is an alternative.

SPECIAL PROBLEMS

LEAVES SHRIVELLED. BROWN TIPS
Cause: Air too dry.

LEAVES CURLED. BROWN EDGES
Cause: Air too cool, or cold draughts.

INSECTS
Mealy bugs at the base of the leaf stalks can be a serious problem; so can red spider mite if the light is too bright. See Chapter 9.

ACORUS

The white-striped leaves of this grassy plant form fan-shaped tufts. It is not particularly showy, but it is a useful addition to the bottle garden or terrarium. Its great advantage as a background plant among more spectacular specimens is that it will withstand poor conditions— it is not affected by waterlogging, draughts or cold winter nights. It suffers from few problems, but leaf tips will turn brown if the compost is short of water. Watch for red spider mite if the air is warm and dry.

SECRETS OF SUCCESS

Temperature: Prefers cool conditions —keep in an unheated room in winter.

Light: Bright light or semi-shade; not direct sun.

Water: Keep compost wet at all times.

Air Humidity: Misting is not necessary.

Repotting: Repot, if necessary, in spring.

Propagation: Divide plants at any time of the year.

A. gramineus variegatus

Sweet Flag

ASPIDISTRA

A Victorian favourite, now regaining a little of its former popularity. The common name of Cast Iron Plant indicates its ability to withstand neglect, draughts and shade. The all-green type is illustrated here; the cream-striped variegated variety is more attractive but less hardy. The leaves are both slow growing and long lasting. The plant can withstand periods of dryness at the roots if the temperature is not too high, but it does have two strong dislikes – it will die if the soil is constantly saturated and it will be harmed by frequent repotting.

SECRETS OF SUCCESS

Temperature: Average warmth; keep cool but frost-free in winter.

Light: Extremely tolerant, but not of direct sun.

Water: Water regularly from spring to autumn. Water sparingly in winter.

Air Humidity: Wash leaves occasionally, but can stand dry air.

Repotting: Repot every 4-5 years in spring.

Propagation: Divide plants in spring or summer.

A. elatior

Cast Iron Plant

ARAUCARIA

A handsome and easy-to-grow conifer with many uses—seedlings for the terrarium, small plants for table display and tall trees as bold specimens in halls or large rooms.

The Norfolk Island Pine is best grown on its own where its tiered branches bearing green needle-like leaves can develop symmetrically. It flourishes in cool and light conditions, and will grow steadily to reach about 5 ft. Keep it pot-bound to restrict the rate of growth.

The major problem is leaf drop and loss of lower branches. The main cause is either hot, dry air or drying out of the compost. Too much sun or waterlogging can also be the culprit, but even with expert care the loss of lower branches will occur with age.

A. heterophylla (A. excelsa)

Norfolk Island Pine

SECRETS OF SUCCESS

Temperature: Average warmth; keep cool in winter (night temperature 50°F).

Light: Bright light or semi-shade; avoid direct sun in summer.

Water: Water regularly from spring to autumn. Water sparingly in winter.

Air Humidity: Mist leaves occasionally, especially if room is heated in winter. Ventilate in summer.

Repotting: Repot every 3-4 years in spring.

Propagation: Difficult —— best to buy plants. Try sowing seed in spring or using tip of an old plant (not branches) as a cutting.

AUCUBA

The Spotted Laurel is a useful plant for rooms and hallways which are not heated in winter and where adequate light is a problem. It is not suitable for hot and dry locations as serious leaf fall is almost bound to occur.

This plant is grown for its large yellow-spotted leaves which are borne in profusion; brown edges in summer mean that you are not watering frequently enough. When small, the Spotted Laurel can be stood on a windowsill or table. If allowed to grow it will produce a woody shrub reaching 5 ft or more, but it can be kept in check by pruning in the spring.

A. japonica variegata

Spotted Laurel (Gold Dust Plant)

SECRETS OF SUCCESS

Temperature: Average warmth; keep cool in winter (night temperature 40° – 45°F).

Light: Bright light or shade; avoid direct sun in summer.

Water: Water regularly from spring to autumn. Water sparingly in winter.

Air Humidity: Mist plant frequently, especially in winter. Wash leaves occasionally.

Repotting: Repot annually in spring.

Propagation: Stem cuttings root easily. Late summer is the best time.

FOLIAGE HOUSE PLANTS

ASPARAGUS

BASIC FACTS

The two popular Asparagus Ferns (A. plumosus and A. sprengeri) are grown for their graceful feathery foliage, which is often used in flower arrangements. But all is not what it seems; they are not ferns, and the 'leaves' are really needle-like branches.

Asparagus Fern is an easy plant to grow, much easier than most true ferns, because it will adapt to wide variations in light, heat and frequency of watering. It does not demand a humid atmosphere and can be easily propagated. For maximum effect make sure that the arching or trailing branches are not impeded by other plants—a hanging basket is the ideal home.

The flat-leaved variety called Smilax by florists is A. asparagoides. It is more difficult to grow indoors than the ferny varieties, but it is sometimes recommended for hanging displays.

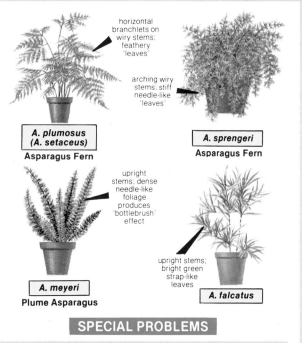

horizontal branchlets on wiry stems; feathery 'leaves'

arching wiry stems; stiff needle-like 'leaves'

A. plumosus (A. setaceus)
Asparagus Fern

A. sprengeri
Asparagus Fern

upright stems; dense needle-like foliage produces 'bottlebrush' effect

upright stems; bright green strap-like leaves

A. meyeri
Plume Asparagus

A. falcatus

SECRETS OF SUCCESS

Temperature: Average warmth; not less than 50°F at night. Constantly high temperature can be harmful.

Light: Can adapt to bright or semi-shady conditions. Keep away from direct sunlight.

Water: Water regularly from spring to autumn. Occasionally water from below (see page 105). In winter water sparingly.

Air Humidity: Mist occasionally, especially in winter if room is heated.

Repotting: Repot annually in spring.

Propagation: Divide plants at any time of the year. Sow seeds in spring.

SPECIAL PROBLEMS

YELLOWING FOLIAGE, BROWN-EDGED OR SCORCHED. LEAF DROP
Cause: Too much sun, or compost has been allowed to dry out.

YELLOWING FOLIAGE, NO SCORCH. LEAF DROP
Cause: Temperature too high or not enough light.

PLANT DEATH
Cause: Root rot disease is the likely culprit, caused by faulty watering. For more details see page 121.

ANTHURIUM

The Crystal Anthurium is neither easy to care for nor easy to obtain, yet it is one of the most spectacular of all foliage house plants. The velvety leaves can be 2 ft long, dark green with prominent ivory veins. It is not impossible to keep this jungle plant in an ordinary room for years, but it will need careful attention. Don't plant too deeply, keep the air moist and warm, and learn to satisfy its special watering needs. Finally a vital tip—make sure that the aerial roots are placed in damp moss or peat.

SECRETS OF SUCCESS

Temperature: Average warmth; minimum temperature 60°F in winter.

Light: Bright in winter; away from direct sun in summer.

Water: Give a little water every few days to keep the compost moist at all times but not waterlogged.

Air Humidity: Mist leaves very frequently.

Repotting: Repot annually in spring.

Propagation: Divide plants at repotting time.

A. crystallinum
Crystal Anthurium

BEAUCARNEA

A curiosity rather than a thing of beauty, the Pony Tail Plant is still very useful if you want a tall specimen plant which will not require a lot of attention. The swollen bulb-like base stores water, so occasional dryness at the roots will do no harm. The plume of long strap-like leaves gives the plant its common name. It is a rarity in Britain but is popular in the U.S., where it flourishes and reaches ceiling height in the warm, dry atmosphere of centrally heated rooms.

SECRETS OF SUCCESS

Temperature: Average warmth; minimum temperature 50°F in winter.

Light: Brightly lit spot; some sun is beneficial.

Water: Water thoroughly, then leave until compost is moderately dry. Avoid overwatering.

Air Humidity: Misting not necessary.

Repotting: Repot, when necessary, in spring.

Propagation: Plant up offsets at repotting time. Not easy; best to buy plants.

B. recurvata
Pony Tail Plant

BROMELIADS

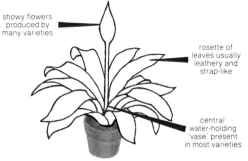

showy flowers
produced by
many varieties

rosette of
leaves usually
leathery and
strap-like

central
water-holding
'vase' present
in most varieties

The bromeliads are full of surprises. Interior designers look upon them as almost essential for their modern decor schemes, yet beginners often feel that these spectacular and often brightly-coloured plants must be too difficult for them to grow. The first surprise is that few plants are easier to care for.

Another surprise is the method of watering — into the central rosette rather than into the compost. Then there is the flowering habit — as the flower head opens the parent rosette begins to die, although it may survive for a further year or two. So propagation after flowering is necessary to preserve your collection.

The native home of the bromeliads is the American jungle, where they dwell among the orchids in the trees or on the forest floor. A novel way of growing and showing your plants is to build a bromeliad tree. Otherwise keep them in small pots with drainage holes and a peat-based compost. Remember that they all have a tiny root system so overpotting or overwatering can be fatal.

Some bromeliads, such as Aechmea, Vriesia and Guzmania, are grown for the beauty of their flower heads as well as for the attractiveness of their foliage. Two others (Tillandsia and Billbergia) are grown mainly for their colourful blooms. For details of the flowering bromeliads, see page 63.

HOW TO MAKE A BROMELIAD TREE

Bromeliad —
Choose plants with a well pronounced 'cup' in the heart of the rosette. Remove from pot, wrap roots with sphagnum moss and then tightly attach with plastic-covered wire to branch

Tillandsia usneoides (Spanish Moss) — a unique bromeliad which grows as grey-green strands in moist air.
No watering required

Keep cup filled with water and syringe sphagnum moss weekly

Pebbles

Branch set in Plaster of Paris and stones

Bromeliad

Bromeliad

Sphagnum moss

Container

SECRETS OF SUCCESS

Temperature: High temperatures (above 75°F) may be required to bring plants into flower, but average warmth (minimum 50°F) is satisfactory for foliage types or plants in flower.

Light: Most bromeliads require a brightly–lit spot away from direct sunlight. Pineapple and the Earth Stars will thrive in full sun.

Water: Never overwater, and ensure that there is good drainage. Keep the 'vase' filled with water — use rainwater in hard water areas. Empty and refill 'vase' every 1–2 months. Water the compost only when it dries out. With non-vase varieties keep the compost moist, but never wet.

Air Humidity: Mist the leaves in summer. Feeding through the leaves is the natural method of nutrition, so occasionally use dilute Fillip instead of water in the sprayer.

Repotting: Rarely, if ever, necessary.

Propagation: Offsets appear at the base of the plant. When the offset is several months old remove it with some roots attached and plant shallowly in Baby Bio Seed & Cutting Compost. Keep warm until established.

SPECIAL PROBLEMS

LEAVES WITH PALE BROWN PATCHES
Cause: Sun scorch. Move plant away from direct sunlight.

LEAVES WITH BROWN TIPS
Cause: Dry air is a likely reason — mist during the summer months. Other possibility is failure to fill 'vase' with water or use of hard water.

PLANT DEATH
Cause: Overwatering if plant has not yet flowered. If it has flowered then rotting and death of the rosette which bore the flower stalk is natural.

INSECTS
Scale and mealy bug can be troublesome — see page 120.

TYPES

Aechmea

large saw-edged leaves

A. fulgens discolor

A. macracantha

A. fasciata (A. rhodocyanea)
Urn Plant (Vase Plant)

A. chantinii

Ananas

narrow saw-edged leaves

A. comosus (A. sativus)
Common Pineapple

A. comosus variegatus
Ivory Pineapple

A. bracteatus striatus

Cryptanthus

small wavy-edged leaves

C. bivittatus

C. zonatus

C. acaulis
Earth Star (Starfish Plant)

C. bromelioides tricolor
Rainbow Star

C. fosterianus
Pheasant Leaf

Guzmania

large smooth-edged leaves

very wide rosette base

G. lingulata

Neoregelia

N. carolinae marechalii

large saw-edged leaves

N. carolinae tricolor
Blushing Bromeliad

N. spectabilis
Fingernail Plant

Nidularium

large saw-edged leaves

N. innocentii
Bird's Nest Bromeliad

Tillandsia

small bristle-covered leaves

T. ionantha

Vriesia

V. hieroglyphica
King of the Bromeliads

large smooth-edged leaves

V. splendens
Flaming Sword

V. fenestralis

FOLIAGE HOUSE PLANTS

BEGONIA

large lop-sided leaves. hairy leaf stalks

B. rex
Rex Begonia

TYPES

● **REX TYPES**

B. rex Silver Queen

B. rex Yuletide

B. rex Merry Christmas

B. rex Her Majesty

● **OTHER TYPES**

puckered surface; distinct central cross

glistening surface; chocolate areas near margin

brown markings near hairy margin

B. masoniana
Iron Cross Begonia

B. boweri
Eyelash Begonia

B. Cleopatra

BASIC FACTS

Begonias are an essential part of any worthwhile house plant collection, but the range of types available is bewildering. Most are grown for their floral display (see pages 62 and 81), and these varieties may also have attractive leaves. The Begonias shown on this page are displayed for their foliage. Rex Begonias dominate this group and they all require similar treatment — no summer sun, careful watering, warm days and fairly cool nights. Even with care these foliage varieties usually last for only a year or two under ordinary room conditions.

SECRETS OF SUCCESS

Temperature: Average warmth; not less than 55°F.

Light: A bright spot away from direct sunlight. A few hours of morning or evening sun in winter are beneficial. Turn pots occasionally.

Water: The compost should be kept moist from spring to autumn; allow surface to dry between waterings. Water sparingly in winter.

Air Humidity: Moist air needed — surround pots with damp peat. Mist surrounding air, but never wet the leaves.

Repotting: Repot annually in spring. Leaves of pot-bound plants lose colour.

Propagation: Leaf cuttings root easily (see page 115). Plants can be divided at repotting time.

SPECIAL PROBLEMS

Diseases are a menace. See page 121.

BUXUS

B. sempervirens
Box

Box is a favourite shrub outdoors, but only recently has it been accepted as a house plant. Both the Common Box (B. sempervirens) and the Small-leaved Box (B. microphylla) are extremely useful for indoor decoration. They are tolerant of cool conditions and draughts, producing a dense screen of shiny small leaves which have few problems and require little attention. These shrubs can be clipped and trained at any time of the year. The only danger is overwatering — the compost must be kept on the dry side.

SECRETS OF SUCCESS

Temperature: Average or below average warmth; keep cool in winter.

Light: A well-lit spot; some direct sunlight is beneficial.

Water: Water thoroughly but let compost become dryish between waterings — do not keep compost constantly moist.

Air Humidity: Mist leaves occasionally.

Repotting: Repot, if necessary, in spring.

Propagation: Stem cuttings in late summer.

CAREX

C. morrowii variegata
Japanese Sedge

From the vast family of Sedges only one or two are suitable as house plants. The Japanese Sedge is not often seen but is extremely easy to look after indoors. Its arching, foot-long, white-striped leaves make it a useful specimen for a terrarium or for growing among other plants in an indoor garden. It is one of the most durable of foliage plants, growing happily in sun or shade, low temperatures and in wet or dryish compost. Producing more specimens is a simple job as divided-up plants root very easily.

SECRETS OF SUCCESS

Temperature: Average or below average warmth; keep cool in winter.

Light: Not fussy; semi-shade, well-lit or sunny.

Water: Keep the compost moist but it should not be kept waterlogged.

Air Humidity: Ventilate on warm days.

Repotting: Repot every 2 years in spring.

Propagation: Divide plants at any time of the year.

CALADIUM

A unique foliage house plant, both in appearance and cultivation. The striking arrow-shaped leaves are spectacular — paper thin and beautifully marked and coloured. Long stalks bear these foot-long leaves above the pots, which are best set amongst other plants. The dazzling foliage, however, is not permanent and lasts only from late spring to early autumn.

Plant Caladium tubers in Potting Compost during March and keep moist at 75°F or more. When shoots appear mist daily and slowly adjust to living room temperature. Warmth at all times is vital — at no stage should the temperature fall below 60°F. If you buy a Caladium plant, protect from cold on the way home.

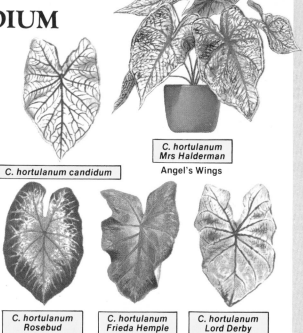

C. hortulanum candidum

C. hortulanum Mrs Halderman
Angel's Wings

SECRETS OF SUCCESS

Temperature: Warm; above 70°F whenever possible, never below 60°F.

Light: Moderately well-lit but away from direct sunlight.

Water: Water freely during the growing season.

Air Humidity: Mist frequently, especially in spring.

After Care: Foliage dies down in September. Stop watering; keep tubers at about 60°F in pots or in peat. Replant tubers in March — small 'daughter' tubers can be potted up separately.

C. hortulanum Rosebud

C. hortulanum Frieda Hemple

C. hortulanum Lord Derby

CHLOROPHYTUM

The Spider Plant has been grown indoors for 200 years, and it is now one of the most popular of all house plants. This popularity is not surprising — it is quick-growing with attractive arching leaves, and in spring and summer the cascading wiry stems produce small white flowers followed by tiny plantlets. Left on the mother plant, these plantlets grow to give an attractive display, especially in a hanging basket. Removed from the mother plant they can be used to produce new plants. Above all the Spider Plant has the prime requirement for popularity — it is extremely adaptable. It will grow in hot or cool rooms, sunny windows or shady corners and it doesn't mind dry air.

SECRETS OF SUCCESS

Temperature: Average warmth; not less than 45°F in winter.

Light: Not fussy; a well-lit spot away from direct sunlight is best.

Water: Water liberally from spring to autumn; sparingly in winter.

Air Humidity: Misting occasionally in summer is beneficial.

Repotting: Repot in spring if plant has started to lift out of the pot.

Propagation: Peg down plantlets in compost — cut stem when rooted. Alternatively divide plants at repotting time.

C. comosum variegatum
Spider Plant
(St. Bernard's Lily)

SPECIAL PROBLEMS

INSECTS
Chlorophytum is virtually pest-free. Aphid may attack if plants are weak.

LEAVES WITH BROWN TIPS
Cause: Most likely reason is underfeeding — don't forget to use Baby Bio with every watering. Other possible causes are bruising and excessively hot air. Cut off damaged tips and correct the fault.

LEAVES PALE & LIMP IN WINTER. SOME YELLOWING & LEAF FALL
Cause: Too much heat and too little light.

LEAVES WITH BROWN STREAKS IN WINTER
Cause: Too much water under cool conditions when the plant is not growing. Water sparingly in winter.

LEAVES CURLED WITH BROWN SPOTS & EDGES. SOME YELLOWING & LEAF FALL
Cause: The soil around the roots has dried out. Chlorophytum needs a plentiful supply of water when it is actively growing.

NO STEMS
Cause: The plant is too young; stems bearing plantlets will not form until the plant is mature. If it is mature, then lack of space is the most likely cause; avoid overcrowding.

CLEYERA

**C. japonica tricolor
(Eurya japonica)**

In contrast to the many universal favourites in this book, Cleyera japonica tricolor is a rarity in Britain. It deserves to be more popular as it is easy to grow and does not drop its leaves at the first change in conditions — an annoying habit of some other variegated-leaved shrubby plants. It is slow growing and it can be kept compact by occasionally removing the tips of the leading shoots. The leaves are edged with cream and are reddish when young.

SECRETS OF SUCCESS

Temperature: Average warmth; keep cool in winter (minimum temperature 50°F).
Light: Well-lit but away from direct sunlight.
Water: Keep the compost moist at all times. Use rainwater if tap water is hard.
Air Humidity: Mist leaves occasionally.
Repotting: Repot, when necessary, in spring.
Propagation: Stem cuttings in summer. Bio Roota and bottom heat are necessary.

CODIAEUM (CROTON)

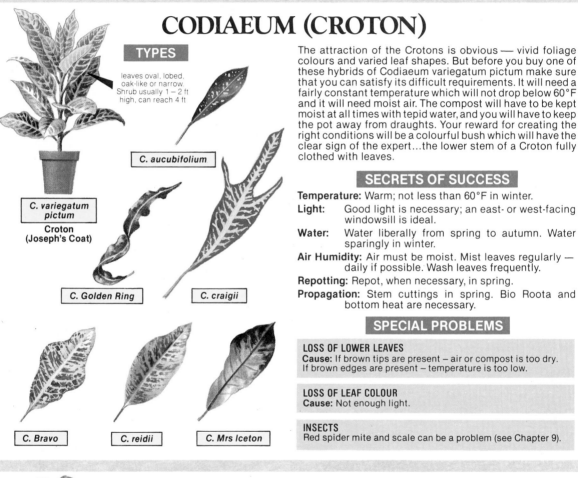

TYPES

leaves oval, lobed, oak-like or narrow. Shrub usually 1 – 2 ft high, can reach 4 ft

C. aucubifolium

C. variegatum pictum
Croton (Joseph's Coat)

C. Golden Ring

C. craigii

C. Bravo

C. reidii

C. Mrs Iceton

The attraction of the Crotons is obvious — vivid foliage colours and varied leaf shapes. But before you buy one of these hybrids of Codiaeum variegatum pictum make sure that you can satisfy its difficult requirements. It will need a fairly constant temperature which will not drop below 60°F and it will need moist air. The compost will have to be kept moist at all times with tepid water, and you will have to keep the pot away from draughts. Your reward for creating the right conditions will be a colourful bush which will have the clear sign of the expert...the lower stem of a Croton fully clothed with leaves.

SECRETS OF SUCCESS

Temperature: Warm; not less than 60°F in winter.
Light: Good light is necessary; an east- or west-facing windowsill is ideal.
Water: Water liberally from spring to autumn. Water sparingly in winter.
Air Humidity: Air must be moist. Mist leaves regularly — daily if possible. Wash leaves frequently.
Repotting: Repot, when necessary, in spring.
Propagation: Stem cuttings in spring. Bio Roota and bottom heat are necessary.

SPECIAL PROBLEMS

LOSS OF LOWER LEAVES
Cause: If brown tips are present – air or compost is too dry. If brown edges are present – temperature is too low.

LOSS OF LEAF COLOUR
Cause: Not enough light.

INSECTS
Red spider mite and scale can be a problem (see Chapter 9).

COFFEA

C. arabica
Coffee Plant

The Coffee Plant won't disappoint you if you expect an attractive bush with dark, shiny, wavy-edged leaves for decoration. It will disappoint you if you expect coffee beans for breakfast, as the white fragrant flowers and red berries rarely appear under ordinary room conditions. It is an undemanding plant, but the compost must never be allowed to dry out, and draughts are positively harmful. It can reach 4 ft or more in height, but you can keep it in check by pruning in spring.

SECRETS OF SUCCESS

Temperature: Average warmth; minimum winter temperature 50°F.
Light: Well-lit but away from direct sunlight.
Water: Keep the compost moist at all times.
Air Humidity: Mist leaves occasionally.
Repotting: Repot every 2 years in spring.
Propagation: Stem cuttings in summer; Bio Roota and bottom heat are necessary. Plants can be raised from unroasted coffee beans.

COLEUS

The poor man's Croton. Coleus thoroughly deserves this nickname as it is the cheapest and easiest way to add brightly-coloured foliage to a house plant collection. The soft-stemmed bush should be kept at about 1 ft high by pinching the tips, and flower stalks should be removed as they appear. Plants are obtained by sowing seed, taking cuttings or buying nursery-grown stock. They can be over-wintered, but Coleus soon becomes leggy and defoliated. The best plan is to treat it as an annual by sowing seed or taking cuttings each spring. Care is easy; just remember to keep it in a sunny spot, use soft water and never let the compost dry out.

TYPES

● UPRIGHT, FRILLED   ● TRAILING
small leaf, pendent stems

C. blumei
Coleus
(Flame Nettle)

C. blumei
Firebird

C. pumilus
Trailing Queen

SECRETS OF SUCCESS

Temperature: Average warmth; not less than 50°F.
Light: Give as much light as possible, but shade from summer noonday sun.
Water: Keep compost moist at all times; reduce watering in winter. Use rainwater if tap water is hard.
Air Humidity: Keep air moist; mist leaves in winter and summer.
Repotting: Cut back and repot in February.
Propagation: Stem cuttings in spring or summer. Alternatively sow seeds in February or March.

● UPRIGHT, NETTLE-LEAVED

C. blumei Klondyke | C. blumei candidum | C. blumei Salmon Lace | C. blumei Volcano

SPECIAL PROBLEMS

LEGGY STEMS
Cause: Young plants – not enough light or failure to pinch out tips. Old plants – normal effect, nothing can be done.

LEAF DROP
Cause: Not enough water; in summer it may be necessary to water every day.

CYPERUS

There is just one golden rule for success with the Umbrella Plant — keep the roots constantly wet. Place the pot in a saucer or outer container which should always contain water. This plant is grown for its overall shape rather than the beauty of its foliage — thin stems topped by radiating strap-like leaves, with small grass-like flowers in summer. It is best grouped with other plants or grown in a bottle garden; choose the dwarf-growing C. diffusus if space is limited. Cut out yellowing stems to encourage new growth and watch for brown tips — the sign of dry air or water shortage.

C. diffusus
Umbrella Plant

SECRETS OF SUCCESS

Temperature: Not fussy, but keep at 50°F or above in winter.
Light: Well-lit or shade, but avoid direct summer sunlight.
Water: Keep it soaked and restrict free drainage.
Air Humidity: Mist leaves frequently.
Repotting: Repot every year in spring.
Propagation: Divide plants at repotting time.

C. alternifolius
Umbrella Plant

DIZYGOTHECA

A graceful plant with leaves divided into finger-like serrated leaflets which are dark green or almost black. The bush has a splendid lacy effect when well grown. It has the usual problems of so many delicate plants — it detests soggy compost but it drops its leaves if the soil ball is allowed to dry out. It does not like sudden changes in temperature and the air must be moist. If lower leaves fall, cut off the stem in spring and the stump will shoot again.

SECRETS OF SUCCESS

Temperature: Average warmth; minimum temperature 60°F in winter.
Light: Bright, but away from direct sunlight.
Water: Water moderately from spring to autumn; sparingly in winter.
Air Humidity: Mist leaves frequently.
Repotting: Repot every 2 years in spring.
Propagation: Difficult. Try stem cuttings in spring; use Bio Roota and bottom heat.

D. elegantissima
(Aralia elegantissima)
Finger Aralia

The DRACAENA Group

HOW TO GROW A TI TREE

Ti Trees are grown by planting pieces of mature cane cut from Dracaena, Cordyline or Yucca. The crown of leaves which appears at the top of the cane gives an 'instant palm' effect. Nursery-raised Ti Trees can be obtained but you can also grow your own — Ti Canes (cut from outdoor tropical plants and dried before shipment) are becoming increasingly available.

Crown of leaves appears at the side of the cane once rooting has taken place

Dry cane planted firmly in Seed and Cutting Compost. Keep compost moist but not wet

An old Dracaena, after its top has been removed and used as a cutting, will grow as a Ti Tree.

SPECIAL PROBLEMS

LEAVES WITH BROWN TIPS AND YELLOW EDGES
Cause: The most likely reason is dry air. Most Dracaenas need high air humidity – surround pot with moist peat and mist regularly. Cold draughts can have a similar effect, and so can underwatering. If dryness at the roots is the cause there will also be brown spotting on the foliage – see below.

LEAVES SOFT & CURLED WITH BROWN EDGES
Cause: Temperature too low. Delicate Dracaenas will quickly show these symptoms if kept close to a window on cold winter nights.

YELLOWING LOWER LEAVES
Cause: If this effect occurs slowly it is the natural and unavoidable process of old age. Dracaenas are false palms, with a characteristic crown of leaves on top of a bare stem. This growth habit is due to the limited life span of the foliage, each leaf turning yellow and dying after about 2 years.

LEAVES WITH BROWN SPOTS
Cause: Underwatering. The soil ball must be kept moist.

PLANT DEATH
Cause: One of 2 fatal faults – either too much water has been given in winter or the plant has been kept too cold.

LEAVES WITH BLEACHED DRY PATCHES
Cause: Too much sun. Move to a shadier spot.

BASIC FACTS

Dracaena is becoming increasingly popular as a specimen plant, providing a bold and attractive focal point for a living room or hallway. Tall specimens are much in demand for public buildings, and the choice is much larger than it was a few years ago.

There is some confusion over the naming of plants in this group. Some are species of Cordyline, but are frequently described as Dracaenas. As a general rule Cordyline roots are white when cut, Dracaena roots are orange. There is also some confusion over the ease (or difficulty) of growing these false palms, with their cane-like stems and crown of leaves. The simple answer is that they can be easy or difficult; it all depends on which variety you choose.

There are three easy ones — Dracaena marginata, D. draco and Cordyline australis. These will stand some shade, some neglect and quite low winter temperatures. The remainder of the group need more care — higher winter temperatures, careful watering to ensure moist but not soggy compost, and frequent misting of the leaves.

Not all the Dracaenas are false palms — D. godseffiana is a shrub which bears no similarity to its relatives. It is a robust plant, withstanding lower winter temperatures than the delicate varieties, and unlike them it should not be misted with water.

SECRETS OF SUCCESS

Temperature: Average warmth; not less than 55°F in winter. The easy types, listed in Basic Facts, can withstand lower temperatures.

Light: Light shade is the best general position — close to an east or west window is an ideal spot. Some varieties, such as C. terminalis, must have good light; but two — D. marginata and D. fragrans — will grow in shade.

Water: Keep the compost moist at all times. Reduce watering in winter but do not let it dry out.

Air Humidity: Mist leaves regularly. Only D. draco and D. godseffiana can grow happily in dry air.

Repotting: Every 2 years transfer to a larger pot in spring.

Propagation: There are several methods to choose from. Remove crown from old leggy canes and plant in Potting Compost; use Bio Roota and bottom heat. Alternatively, air layer the crown before potting up. Pieces of stem, 2 or 3 inches long, can be used as cane cuttings (see page 115).

HOW TO CHOOSE A DRACAENA

Easiest to grow	**C. australis** **D. marginata** **D. draco**
Smallest leaves	**D. sanderiana**
Largest leaves	**D. fragrans massangeana**
Most attractive leaves	**C. terminalis** **D. marginata tricolor** **D. deremensis bausei**
Tallest stems	**D. fragrans**

TYPES

● CORDYLINE TYPES

leaves green flushed with red; compact — 3 ft high

C. terminalis tricolor

leaves and stem smaller than ordinary Ti Plant

C. terminalis Rededge

tall and slender, reaching 6 ft high

long, narrow arching leaves

C. terminalis (Dracaena terminalis)

Ti Plant (Flaming Dragon Tree)

C. stricta

C. australis (Dracaena indivisa)

Cabbage Tree (Grass Palm)

● DRACAENA – FALSE PALM TYPES

narrow leaves, red margins

narrow stem, often branched and twisted

broad leaves

tough, sword-shaped leaves; resin ('dragon's blood') exudes from trunk

D. marginata tricolor

D. fragrans massangeana

Corn Palm

D. fragrans lindenii

D. marginata

Madagascar Dragon Tree

D. fragrans

Corn Palm

D. draco

Dragon Tree

D. deremensis bausei

D. deremensis Janet Craig

small leaves; suitable for restricted space

D. deremensis warneckii

D. deremensis rhoersii

D. deremensis

D. sanderiana

Ribbon Plant

● DRACAENA – SHRUBBY TYPE

yellow-blotched leaves; thin wiry stems

D. godseffiana

Gold Dust Dracaena

● PLEOMELE TYPES

P. thalioides

P. reflexa variegata

Song of India

P. angustifolia honorariae

FOLIAGE HOUSE PLANTS

DIEFFENBACHIA

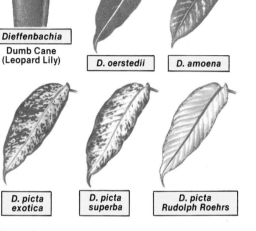

large leaves borne on a stout, upright stem

Dieffenbachia
Dumb Cane
(Leopard Lily)

D. oerstedii   *D. amoena*

D. picta exotica   *D. picta superba*   *D. picta Rudolph Roehrs*

A splendid plant, much beloved by interior decorators on both sides of the Atlantic. Its common name, Dumb Cane, is derived from the unpleasant effect of its poisonous sap on the mouth and throat. Wash hands after taking cuttings.

A well-grown Dieffenbachia will reach 5ft or more, but under ordinary room conditions some of the lower leaves will fall to give a false palm effect. It is not an easy plant to grow; it will not tolerate low winter temperatures or cold draughts. Dry air and fluctuating temperatures can be fatal to some delicate varieties, but the most popular type (D. picta exotica) is fairly tolerant and not at all difficult to grow in the centrally heated home. With age or bad management the plant may become leggy and unattractive. Cut off the cane, leaving a 4in. stump. The crown of leaves can be used as a cutting; the stump will resprout to produce a new plant.

SECRETS OF SUCCESS

Temperature: Average or above average warmth. Not below 60°F in winter.

Light: Partial shade in summer; bright light in winter.

Water: Water regularly from spring to autumn; sparingly in winter. Let soil surface dry between waterings.

Air Humidity: Mist frequently. Surround pot with damp peat. Wash leaves occasionally.

Repotting: Repot annually in spring.

Propagation: There are several methods to choose from. Remove and pot up top crown of leaves; use Bio Roota and bottom heat. Pieces of stem, 2 or 3in. long, can be used as cane cuttings (see page 115). Some varieties produce daughter plants at the base; remove and use as cuttings.

SPECIAL PROBLEMS

INSECTS
Keep watch for scale and red spider mite; see Chapter 9.

STEM BASE SOFT & DISCOLOURED
Cause: Stem rot disease. This condition is encouraged by overwatering and low temperatures. If damage is slight – cut out diseased area, spray with Benlate and repot. If damage is severe – discard plant; use top as a cutting.

LOWER LEAVES YELLOW & WILTED
Cause: Low winter temperatures or cold draughts are the most likely reason. Plants will survive at 50° – 55°F but lower leaves will suffer.

LOSS OF COLOUR
Cause: Direct sunlight or excessive brightness will give leaves a washed-out appearance. Move to a shadier spot.

LOSS OF LEAVES
Cause: Most likely reasons are temperature too cool, dry air or cold draughts if leaves are young. Old leaves tend to drop naturally with age.

LEAVES WITH BROWN EDGES
Cause: Compost has been allowed to dry out; it should be kept moist but not soggy at all times. Cold air can have a similar effect.

EUCALYPTUS

E. globulus
Blue Gum

Young plants of these giant Australian trees have attractive grey-green leaves which produce a distinctive aroma when crushed. Three species are grown as indoor shrubs—E. gunnii (Cedar Gum), E. globulus (Blue Gum) and E. citriodora (Lemon-scented Gum). These shrubs will flourish under ordinary room conditions if they are kept well-lit and cool. Pots can be stood outdoors during the summer months. Pinch out tips to keep growth in check and to maintain the production of juvenile foliage—old leaves are much less attractive.

Eucalyptus is a fast-growing plant—seeds sown in spring will produce a large shrub in autumn. Plants are usually discarded after a couple of years.

SECRETS OF SUCCESS

Temperature: Cool or average warmth; keep at 45° – 50°F in winter.

Light: Bright light; some direct sun is beneficial.

Water: Water regularly from spring to autumn. Water sparingly in winter.

Air Humidity: Misting is not essential.

Repotting: Repot annually in spring.

Propagation: Sow seeds in spring or early summer – keep at 65°F.

EUONYMUS

E. japonicus medio-pictus

Several variegated types are available; two popular varieties are illustrated here. These shrubby plants have oval, leathery leaves — an inch or more long except for the small leaves of E. japonicus microphyllus. Small white flowers may appear in late spring. Euonymus is a useful specimen for a bright unheated room, and will happily spend the summer outdoors. In a heated room, however, it will probably shed its leaves in winter and red spider mite attack is likely. Keep the plant in check by pruning in spring, and remove all-green shoots as soon as they appear.

SECRETS OF SUCCESS

Temperature: Average warmth; keep cool in winter.

Light: Bright, indirect light or some sun.

Water: Water regularly from spring to autumn; sparingly in winter.

Air Humidity: Mist the leaves occasionally.

Repotting: Repot every year in spring.

Propagation: Stem cuttings in summer.

E. japonicus microphyllus

FATSHEDERA

F. lizei
Fat-headed Lizzie (Ivy Tree)

This easy-to-grow hybrid of Hedera and Fatsia deserves its popularity. It prefers cool conditions, but it can be grown in a heated room as long as the winter temperature is kept below 70°F and the light is reasonably bright. It can be grown as a shrub, like its Castor Oil Plant parent — all you have to do is to pinch out the growing tips each spring. Or you can grow it as a climber like its Ivy parent — train it to a stake or trellis. For maximum effect grow about three plants in each pot and occasionally wash the attractive, dark green leaves. The variegated form is more unusual but it is less easy to grow.

SECRETS OF SUCCESS

Temperature: Average warmth; not less than 35°F in winter.

Light: Bright or light shade; keep well-lit in winter.

Water: Water regularly from spring to autumn; sparingly in winter.

Air Humidity: Mist the leaves frequently.

Repotting: Repot every year in spring.

Propagation: Stem cuttings in summer.

F. lizei variegata
Variegated Ivy Tree

FATSIA

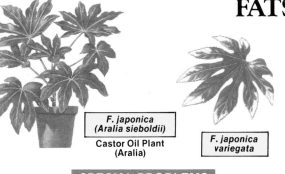

F. japonica (Aralia sieboldii)
Castor Oil Plant (Aralia)

F. japonica variegata

The Castor Oil Plant makes an excellent specimen for living room or hallway, reaching a height of 4ft or more with large, deeply lobed and shiny green leaves. It prefers a cool, well-ventilated and bright situation but it is extremely durable, accepting a wide range of conditions. For economy buy a small plant — it will grow quickly, especially if it is fed regularly and repotted annually. Cut back the growing tips each spring to keep it bushy.

For a top quality plant follow the simple rules listed in Secrets of Success. In addition, wash the leaves occasionally and remove the flower buds which may appear in the mature plant. If despite all your care the leaves become disfigured, cut back the stalk and the plant will quickly sprout again.

SPECIAL PROBLEMS

LEAVES SHRIVELLED
Cause: The air is too dry or the leaves have been exposed to hot summer sun. Remember to mist the foliage regularly and to provide some shade in summer.

LEAVES TURN YELLOW AND THEN DROP
Cause: Two quite separate culprits can cause this trouble; look for other symptoms. If leaves are wilted and soft – overwatering is the reason. If leaves are dry and brittle – too much heat is the cause.

LEAVES PALE & SPOTTED, LEAF EDGES BROWN & BRITTLE
Cause: Underwatering. A large plant will need frequent watering in summer.

SECRETS OF SUCCESS

Temperature: Average warmth; if possible keep cool in winter. Avoid temperatures above 70°F.

Light: Bright or light shade. Keep well-lit in winter.

Water: Water regularly from spring to autumn; sparingly in winter.

Air Humidity: Mist leaves frequently.

Repotting: Repot every year in spring.

Propagation: Stem cuttings in summer. Alternatively sow seeds in spring.

FERNS

SECRETS OF SUCCESS

Temperature: Average warmth; cool but not cold nights are desirable. The best temperature range is 60°-70°F; the minimum for most types is about 50°F and ferns may suffer at more than 75°F.

Light: Despite popular opinion, ferns are not shade lovers indoors as most varieties originated in the dappled brightness of tropical woodland. Good indirect light is the proper location; an east- or north-facing windowsill is ideal.

Water: Compost must be kept moist at all times and never allowed to dry out. This does not mean constantly soggy compost — waterlogging will lead to rotting. Reduce watering in winter.

Air Humidity: Moist air is necessary for nearly all ferns. Spray plants regularly and use one or other of the techniques described on page 107.

Repotting: Repot in the spring when the roots fill the pot — most young specimens will probably require annual repotting. Do not bury the crown of the plant.

Propagation: The simplest way is to divide the plant into 2 or 3 pieces in early spring if it produces rhizomes. Some ferns produce young plants at the ends of runners (example — Boston Fern) or on fronds (example — Mother Fern). It is possible, but not always easy, to raise plants from spores obtained from the underside of mature fronds — see page 116.

BASIC FACTS

Ferns are making a comeback. In Victorian times they were extremely popular and large collections were grown in conservatories and in specially constructed glass cases. But very few varieties were grown as ordinary living room plants, because gas fumes and coal fire smoke are extremely toxic to nearly all ferns. It was the advent of central heating with its freedom from fumes which led to the revival of interest, but radiators in turn have their problems. Few ferns can tolerate hot dry air, so air humidity has to be artificially increased (see Secrets of Success).

Most ferns are not really difficult to grow in the modern home, but they will not tolerate neglect. The compost must never be allowed to dry out, and the surrounding air needs to be kept moist.

There is a bewildering choice of varieties. Nearly two thousand are suitable for growing indoors, but comparatively few are available commercially. The classical picture of a fern is a rosette of much divided, arching leaves (correctly referred to as 'fronds') but there are also ferns with spear-shaped leaves, holly-like leaflets and button-like leaflets. There is also a wide choice of ways to display your collection. Many of them are ideal for a hanging basket and some, such as Boston Fern and Bird's Nest Fern, are large enough and bold enough to be displayed as specimen plants on their own. Delicate ferns, such as Delta Maidenhair, are best planted in a terrarium. When grouping ferns with other plants make sure that they are not crushed — the fronds are fragile and need room to develop. In addition ensure that all dead and damaged fronds are removed so that new ones can grow.

SPECIAL PROBLEMS

BROWN DOTS OR LINES REGULARLY ARRANGED ON UNDERSIDE OF FRONDS
Cause: These are spore cases — an indication that the frond is mature and healthy. The spores produced inside these spore cases can be used for propagation — see page 116.

BROWN SHELLS IRREGULARLY SCATTERED ON FRONDS
Cause: Scale — the Bird's Nest Fern is particularly susceptible to this pest. For control, see page 120.

YELLOWING FRONDS, BEGINNING AT BASE OF PLANT. MATURE FRONDS DEVELOP BROWN SPOTS AND FALL
Cause: Air too warm – a common complaint when ferns are stood too close to radiators. Few ferns can tolerate very high temperatures. If the plant is also limp and wilting, then the cause is incorrect watering.

YELLOWING FRONDS, BROWN TIPS. NO NEW GROWTH
Cause: Air too dry. See Secrets of Success.

PALE FRONDS, SCORCH MARKS ON SURFACE
Cause: Too much sun. Ferns must be protected from midday sunshine in summer.

PALE FRONDS, WEAK GROWTH
Cause: Not enough fertilizer. Ferns need feeding, little and often, during the growing season.

FRONDS DYING BACK
Cause: Two most likely culprits are dry air and dry compost.

HOW TO CHOOSE A FERN

Easiest to grow	*Cyrtomium* *Davallia* *Pteris cretica* *Nephrolepis* *Asplenium nidus* *Pellaea rotundifolia*
For hanging baskets	*Nephrolepis* *Adiantum*
For bold display as a specimen plant	*Nephrolepis* *Asplenium nidus* *Blechnum gibbum*

TYPES

Adiantum

small filmy leaflets

young fronds coppery pink

fronds forked at base

A. raddianum (A. cuneatum)
Delta Maidenhair

A. hispidulum
Rose Maidenhair

Asplenium

feathery fronds

large spear-shaped fronds with dark midribs

wiry stems

small plantlets ('bulbils') develop on mature fronds

wavy margins

A. bulbiferum
Mother Spleenwort

A. nidus
Bird's Nest Fern

Blechnum

large palm-like crown of stiff fronds; trunk develops with age

B. gibbum

Cyrtomium

holly-shaped leaflets, glossy dark green

C. falcatum
Holly Fern
(Fishtail Fern)

Davallia

tiny leaflets on small fronds

wiry stems

creeping rhizome ('rabbit's foot')

D. canariensis
Rabbit's Foot Fern

Didymochlaena

leathery brownish-green fronds

D. truncatula
Cloak Fern

Nephrolepis

plain leaf edges

graceful arching foliage

ruffled leaf edges

feathery leaf edges

erect foliage

N. exaltata
Sword Fern

N. exaltata bostoniensis
Boston Fern

N. exaltata Fluffy Ruffles
Feather Fern

N. exaltata whitmannii
Lace Fern

Phyllitis

bright green, wavy-edged fronds

brown stalks

eared base

P. scolopendrium (Scolopendrium vulgare)
Hart's Tongue Fern

Pellaea

round, leathery leaflets on low-growing fronds

fronds darken with age, up to 2ft long

black leaf stalks

P. rotundifolia
Button Fern

P. viridis
Green Brake Fern

FERN LEAF LANGUAGE

sorus ('spore case')

rachis ('leaf stalk')

pinna ('leaflet')

frond ('leaf')

petiole ('leaf stalk')

rhizome

FOLIAGE HOUSE PLANTS

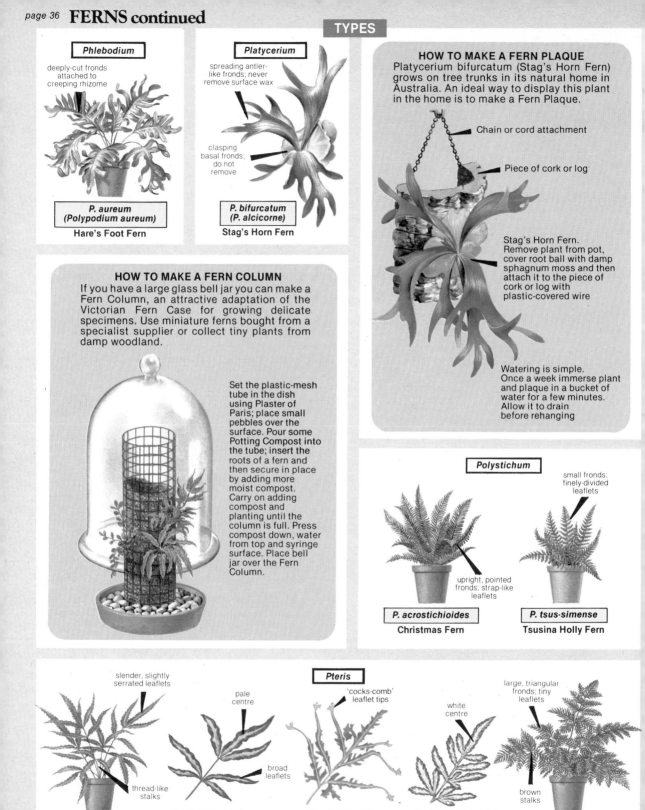

Phlebodium

deeply-cut fronds attached to creeping rhizome

P. aureum (Polypodium aureum)

Hare's Foot Fern

Platycerium

spreading antler-like fronds; never remove surface wax

clasping basal fronds; do not remove

P. bifurcatum (P. alcicorne)

Stag's Horn Fern

HOW TO MAKE A FERN PLAQUE

Platycerium bifurcatum (Stag's Horn Fern) grows on tree trunks in its natural home in Australia. An ideal way to display this plant in the home is to make a Fern Plaque.

Chain or cord attachment

Piece of cork or log

Stag's Horn Fern. Remove plant from pot, cover root ball with damp sphagnum moss and then attach it to the piece of cork or log with plastic-covered wire

Watering is simple. Once a week immerse plant and plaque in a bucket of water for a few minutes. Allow it to drain before rehanging

HOW TO MAKE A FERN COLUMN

If you have a large glass bell jar you can make a Fern Column, an attractive adaptation of the Victorian Fern Case for growing delicate specimens. Use miniature ferns bought from a specialist supplier or collect tiny plants from damp woodland.

Set the plastic-mesh tube in the dish using Plaster of Paris; place small pebbles over the surface. Pour some Potting Compost into the tube; insert the roots of a fern and then secure in place by adding more moist compost. Carry on adding compost and planting until the column is full. Press compost down, water from top and syringe surface. Place bell jar over the Fern Column.

Polystichum

small fronds; finely-divided leaflets

upright, pointed fronds; strap-like leaflets

P. acrostichioides

Christmas Fern

P. tsus-simense

Tsusina Holly Fern

slender, slightly serrated leaflets

pale centre

'cocks-comb' leaflet tips

white centre

large, triangular fronds; tiny leaflets

thread-like stalks

broad leaflets

brown stalks

P. cretica

Ribbon Fern (Table Fern)

P. cretica albolineata

Variegated Table Fern

P. cretica cristata

Cristate Table Fern

Pteris

P. ensiformis Victoriae

Silver Lace Fern

P. tremula

Trembling Fern

FICUS

TYPES

● TREE TYPES

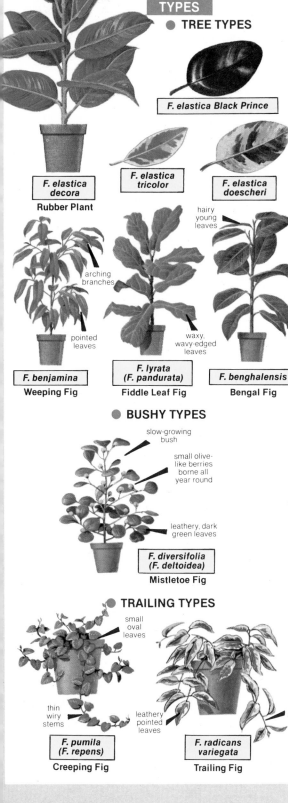

F. elastica Black Prince

F. elastica
decora
Rubber Plant

F. elastica
tricolor

F. elastica
doescheri

hairy young leaves

arching branches

pointed leaves

waxy, wavy-edged leaves

F. benjamina
Weeping Fig

F. lyrata
(F. pandurata)
Fiddle Leaf Fig

F. benghalensis
Bengal Fig

● BUSHY TYPES

slow-growing bush

small olive-like berries borne all year round

leathery, dark green leaves

F. diversifolia
(F. deltoidea)
Mistletoe Fig

● TRAILING TYPES

small oval leaves

thin wiry stems

leathery pointed leaves

wiry stems

F. pumila
(F. repens)
Creeping Fig

F. radicans
variegata
Trailing Fig

In the Ficus or Ornamental Fig family are found house plants which vary from stately trees to lowly creepers, and since Victorian times the unchallenged head of the family has been the Rubber Plant. Once only the narrow-leaved F. elastica was grown, but this old-fashioned variety has now been replaced by the much more attractive F. elastica decora and F. elastica robusta. The all-green Rubber Plants are much easier to grow than the variegated ones, and by far the most important danger is overwatering. Wash leaves occasionally.

The Weeping Fig is increasing in popularity because it is a splendid specimen plant for the modern home. Its leaves are not large, but it is so much more tree-like and graceful than the Rubber Plant.

At the other end of the scale are the trailing types, which are much smaller...and more difficult to grow. This is because they need moist air and are fussy about their requirement for evenly moist compost.

SECRETS OF SUCCESS

Temperature: Average warmth; not less than 55°F in winter.

Light: A bright spot for tree types, a partially shaded site for others. A Rubber Plant will adapt to a few hours' sunshine each morning, but this would be fatal to a Creeping Fig.

Water: Water with care. With tree types the compost must dry out to some extent between waterings. Use tepid water and apply very little in the winter months. The trailing types require more frequent watering than tree types during the growing season.

Air Humidity: Mist occasionally in summer. Misting is essential for trailing types.

Repotting: Avoid frequent repotting. Repot every 2 years in spring until the plant is too large to handle.

Propagation: Stem cuttings in summer if stems are non-woody; Bio Roota and bottom heat are necessary. Air layer woody varieties. (See page 114).

SPECIAL PROBLEMS

SUDDEN LOSS OF LEAVES
Cause: The most likely reason depends on the type of Ficus. Rubber Plant — overwatering is the usual culprit; carry out standard remedial treatment (see page 122). Other possibilities are low winter temperatures, too little light, too much fertilizer and cold draughts. Weeping Fig — most likely cause is too little light or movement of the plant from one environment to another.

LOSS OF LOWEST LEAF
Cause: The bottom leaf of tree types will turn yellow and drop with age—this is a natural process and some degree of legginess is usual after a few years.

YELLOWING LEAF EDGES, SOME LOSS OF LOWER FOLIAGE
Cause: An early sign of more serious trouble, or the effect of underfeeding. Use Baby Bio at the recommended rate throughout the growing season.

DRY SHRIVELLED LEAVES
Cause: A common problem with trailing types—the most likely reason is exposure to direct sunlight, failure to mist the leaves regularly and allowing the compost to dry out.

INSECTS
Both red spider mite and scale can be troublesome. See Chapter 9.

FITTONIA

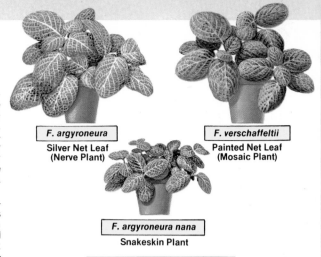

F. argyroneura
Silver Net Leaf
(Nerve Plant)

F. verschaffeltii
Painted Net Leaf
(Mosaic Plant)

F. argyroneura nana
Snakeskin Plant

BASIC FACTS

Fittonia is a low-growing creeper with extremely attractive leaves. Prominent white or red veins form a delicate network over the green surface, and many people have bought a specimen to add novelty to their collection... only to find that the plant has died within weeks. Unfortunately the standard large-leaved types are very difficult to grow under ordinary room conditions; they demand constant warmth and abundant moisture around the leaves. The usual advice is to grow them in a terrarium or bottle garden.

A dwarf-leaved variety of F. argyroneura has been introduced and the textbooks will have to be changed. This Fittonia (F. argyroneura nana) is quite easy to grow in the living room. It is just as attractive as its large-leaved parent, but it will flourish in dry air provided it is kept away from sunlight, given some winter heat and occasionally misted with water.

SECRETS OF SUCCESS

Temperature: Average warmth; not less than 60°F in winter.

Light: Choose a partially shaded spot. Direct sunlight must be avoided.

Water: Water liberally from spring to autumn; sparingly in winter. Use tepid water.

Air Humidity: Moist air is vital. Surround pot with damp peat and mist leaves frequently.

Repotting: Repot annually in spring.

Propagation: Creeping stems will root in surrounding compost — remove and pot up rooted cuttings. Divide plants in spring.

SPECIAL PROBLEMS

SUDDEN DEATH IN WINTER
Cause: Cold and wet conditions are always fatal. The plant needs winter warmth and the compost should be kept slightly moist but never soggy at this season of the year.

SHRIVELLED LEAVES
Cause: Air too dry or too much light. See Secrets of Success.

STRAGGLY GROWTH
Cause: Fittonia is a creeping plant and straggly growth is natural. Cut back stems in spring.

YELLOWING, WILTING LEAVES
Cause: Overwatering. Carry out standard remedial treatment (see page 122).

GREVILLEA

Large indoor trees are expensive to buy, but with nearly all suitable varieties buying a seedling will mean a wait of several years before it becomes a shoulder-high specimen tree. Grevillea may be the answer for a cool and bright spot — it can be grown easily from seed and will reach 1ft high in the first season and reach the ceiling in four or five years. The lacy fern-like effect of the foliage tends to disappear with age, so it is more usual to discard plants once they reach 2-3ft. Grevillea is an easy and reliable plant to grow with no special requirements.

SECRETS OF SUCCESS

G. robusta
Silk Oak

Temperature: Cool or average warmth; not less than 45°F in winter.

Light: Brightly lit spot; some sun is acceptable but protect from midday summer sunlight.

Water: Water liberally from spring to autumn; sparingly in winter.

Air Humidity: Mist leaves occasionally.

Repotting: Repot annually in spring.

Propagation: Raised easily from seed. Sow in spring or summer.

GYNURA

An extremely useful climber or trailer for a well-lit spot. It grows quickly, it has no special needs and its foliage is covered with shiny purple hairs. This attractive colouring requires good light for development. There are two species available — the popular climber/trailer G. sarmentosa and the upright G. aurantiaca. Both Gynuras produce small dandelion-like flowers in spring; these should be removed at the bud stage as most people find the flower scent offensive. Pinch out the tips occasionally to stimulate new leaf production; after a couple of years discard the plant and replace by rooted cuttings.

SECRETS OF SUCCESS

G. sarmentosa
Purple Passion Vine
(Velvet Plant)

Temperature: Average warmth; not less than 50°F in winter.

Light: Brightly lit spot; some direct sunlight is beneficial.

Water: Water liberally from spring to autumn; sparingly in winter.

Air Humidity: Mist leaves occasionally.

Repotting: Repot in spring, but not usually necessary.

Propagation: Stem cuttings root very easily.

HEDERA (IVY)

TYPES

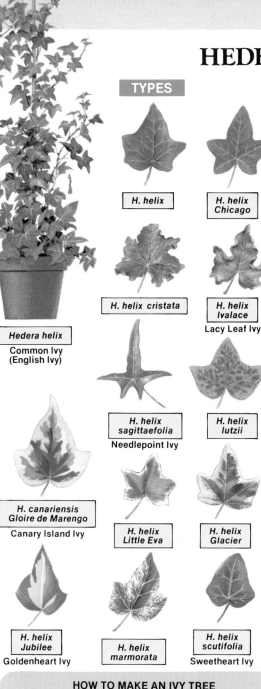

H. helix

H. helix Chicago

H. helix cristata

H. helix Ivalace
Lacy Leaf Ivy

Hedera helix
Common Ivy
(English Ivy)

H. helix sagittaefolia
Needlepoint Ivy

H. helix lutzii

H. canariensis Gloire de Marengo
Canary Island Ivy

H. helix Little Eva

H. helix Glacier

H. helix Jubilee
Goldenheart Ivy

H. helix marmorata

H. helix scutifolia
Sweetheart Ivy

BASIC FACTS

The Ivies thoroughly deserve their high reputation as decorative plants. As climbers they can quickly clothe bare surroundings, provided you choose a vigorous Hedera helix variety. The stems bear aerial roots which cling to wallpaper, woodwork etc. The larger leaved, slower growing Canary Island Ivy does not possess these clinging aerial roots, so adequate support is necessary.

Ivies are just as useful as trailers in hanging baskets or as ground cover between larger plants, and it is here that the smaller bushy varieties come into their own. Examples of suitable types are Little Eva, Glacier and Needlepoint Ivy.

On the other hand the Ivies no longer deserve their past reputation as easy plants. They flourished in the unheated rooms of yesterday, but they do suffer in the hot, dry air of the centrally heated homes of today.

SECRETS OF SUCCESS

Temperature: Cool but frost-free. Ideally the room should be unheated in winter. Night temperatures above 60°F can lead to problems.

Light: Bright conditions in winter. Avoid direct sunlight in summer.

Water: Keep compost moist in summer by regular watering. In winter water sparingly, but never let the compost dry out.

Air Humidity: Mist frequently in summer, especially if the room is warm and dry. Mist in winter if the room is heated. Wash leaves occasionally.

Repotting: Every 2 years transfer to a larger pot in spring.

Propagation: Occasional removal of tips is necessary to promote bushiness. Use these trimmings as stem cuttings.

SPECIAL PROBLEMS

LEAF EDGES BROWN & DRY. BARE SPINDLY GROWTH
Cause: Too warm. Look for red spider mite (see page 120). Cut back bare stems. Move to a cooler site.

LEAVES UNDERSIZED. BARE SPINDLY GROWTH
Cause: Too little light, although it is natural for mature leaves at stem base to drop with age. Cut back bare stems.

LEAVES ALL GREEN
Cause: Too little light. Variegated types revert to all-green habit in shady conditions. Another possibility is the need for repotting.

LEAF TIPS BROWN & DRY. STUNTED GROWTH
Cause: Air too dry. Look for red spider mite (see page 120). Remove dead growth. Mist leaves regularly.

HOW TO MAKE AN IVY TREE
Cut the side shoots from a specimen of Fatshedera lizei and stake the stem. When it has reached 3 ft. high remove the top growth with a horizontal cut. Make crossed cuts on stem top as shown below.

4 Ivy cuttings inserted into cut stem and bound with raffia

1 inch-deep cuts

HEMIGRAPHIS

A climbing plant, popular in some parts of the U.S. for hanging baskets but a rarity in Britain. Red Ivy (H. colorata) has coloured leaves — silvery in the absence of sunshine, metallic purple when exposed to a few hours' sunshine. The Waffle Plant (H. exotica) has puckered leaves. Hemigraphis is not an easy plant to grow, but it is not quite as difficult as indicated by some text books. It needs winter warmth, occasional misting, and pruning when stems become straggly. Small white flowers occasionally appear.

SECRETS OF SUCCESS

Temperature: Average warmth; not less than 55°F in winter.

Light: Bright light or semi-shade; some direct sun will enhance colour.

Water: Water liberally from spring to autumn; sparingly in winter.

Air Humidity: Mist leaves regularly.

Repotting: Repot annually in spring.

Propagation: Stem cuttings in late spring or summer.

H. colorata
Red Ivy

HEPTAPLEURUM

A fast-growing tree-like plant with about ten leaflets radiating from each leaf stalk. The Parasol Plant is a fairly recent introduction, and it is still relatively unknown compared with its popular and much larger close relative, Schefflera actinophylla. Its main advantage over Schefflera is that it will happily grow as a bush if the growing point of the main stem is removed. Heptapleurum is quite easy to grow if you provide winter warmth, good light and mist regularly when the room is centrally heated. Leaf fall may occur if there is a sudden change in conditions; blackened tips indicate overwatering.

SECRETS OF SUCCESS

Temperature: Average warmth; not less than 60°F in winter.

Light: Bright light; not direct sun.

Water: Water liberally from spring to autumn; sparingly in winter.

Air Humidity: Wash leaves occasionally. Mist plant frequently.

Repotting: Repot annually in spring.

Propagation: Take stem cuttings or sow seeds in spring.

H. arboricola
Parasol Plant

HELXINE

Unlike nearly all other house plants, new pots of Helxine are raised at home rather than on professional nurseries. A small clump is removed from an established plant and placed on the surface of moist compost in a pot; in a short time tiny green leaves start to cover the surface.

Helxine is a carpeting plant, and is excellent for covering the soil around tall plants or in hanging baskets. But a word of warning — low-growing delicate plants in an indoor garden can easily be smothered and if used in a bottle garden the leaves of Helxine wither in the stuffy atmosphere.

This undemanding plant is easy to grow and extremely adaptable, but it does not like temperatures over 75°F and it cannot stand dryness around its roots.

H. soleirolii
Mind Your Own Business
(Baby's Tears)

SECRETS OF SUCCESS

Temperature: Average warmth; not less than 45°F in winter.

Light: Extremely adaptable; bright indirect light is best but will survive almost anywhere.

Water: Keep the compost evenly moist at all times.

Air Humidity: Mist the leaves frequently.

Repotting: Repot, if necessary, in spring.

Propagation: Very easy — pot up small clumps at any time of the year.

HYPOESTES

Freckle Face is grown solely for the colourful nature of its leaves — irregular pink spots on a dull green downy background. In a well-lit spot with some direct sunshine the leaf colouring will be vivid; in a shady site the foliage will be all-green.

Young plants make attractive small bushes, but they must be regularly pruned to keep them 1-2 ft high. Hypoestes is best treated as an annual as new plants are so easy to raise and old plants become leggy and unattractive.

Lavender flowers appear in summer, but they are insignificant and should be pinched out. After flowering, the plant sometimes becomes dormant and watering should be reduced until new growth starts.

H. sanguinolenta
Freckle Face
(Polka Dot Plant)

SECRETS OF SUCCESS

Temperature: Average warmth; not less than 55°F in winter.

Light: Bright light; some direct sun will enhance colour.

Water: Keep soil evenly moist. Water liberally from spring to autumn; more sparingly in winter.

Air Humidity: Mist the leaves frequently.

Repotting: Repot annually in spring.

Propagation: Sow seeds in spring or take stem cuttings in spring or summer.

IRESINE

The Iresines are unusual plants. Chicken Gizzard has a most unusual common name and Blood Leaf has remarkable wine-red leaves and stems. They are rarities in Britain but are quite widely grown in the U.S.

Iresines are sun-lovers —away from a south-facing window the colours tend to fade and growth becomes lank and straggly. Even under ideal conditions the plants become leggy with age and they are therefore usually grown as annuals. Nip out growing tips occasionally to maintain bushiness. Pots can be stood outdoors in summer.

I. herbstii
Blood Leaf
(Beefsteak Plant)

SECRETS OF SUCCESS

Temperature: Average warmth; not less than 55°F in winter.

Light: Give as much light as possible; shade from summer noonday sun.

Water: Keep compost moist at all times; reduce watering in winter.

Air Humidity: Mist leaves regularly.

Repotting: Repot, if necessary, in spring.

Propagation: Stem cuttings in spring or summer.

I. herbstii aureoreticulata
Chicken Gizzard

JACARANDA

An elegant plant, lacy-leaved and tree-like. It is an excellent choice for a pedestal or plant table in a sunny position, but specimens are not easy to obtain. Under good conditions it grows rapidly and will reach 3 ft high, but Jacaranda cannot be expected to produce its beautiful blooms outside the greenhouse or conservatory. It is therefore grown as a foliage house plant, and despite its rarity it is by no means difficult to grow in a heated sunny room. Remember to use tepid soft water and to mist the leaves when the air is dry.

SECRETS OF SUCCESS

Temperature: Average or above average warmth; not less than 55°F in winter.

Light: Bright light; some direct sun is beneficial.

Water: Water moderately from spring to autumn; sparingly in winter.

Air Humidity: Mist leaves frequently.

Repotting: Repot, when necessary, in spring.

Propagation: Stem cuttings in summer. Sow seeds in spring.

J. mimosifolia
Jacaranda

LAURUS

The Laurel or Bay Tree is not often referred to in house plant books, but it was first grown inside Roman villas more than 2,000 years ago. This popular patio shrub will thrive under ordinary room conditions if it is kept in a sunny spot, given plenty of fresh air (it doesn't mind draughts) and watered with care. Overwatering in winter is the usual cause of failure. Keep the shrub trimmed to 3 – 4 ft high and the pot can be stood outdoors in summer. The dark green, leathery leaves are the 'bay leaves' sold for kitchen use.

SECRETS OF SUCCESS

Temperature: Cool or average warmth; keep cool but frost-free in winter.

Light: Bright light; some direct sunlight is beneficial.

Water: Water moderately from spring to autumn; sparingly in winter.

Air Humidity: Mist leaves regularly.

Repotting: Repot, when necessary, in spring.

Propagation: Stem cuttings in spring or autumn.

L. nobilis
Bay Tree
(Laurel)

MIMOSA

The Sensitive Plant will grow to about 2 ft high, its delicate branches bearing feathery foliage. Although this plant makes an attractive feature, its main claim to fame is its peculiar habit of rapidly folding up its leaves and drooping its branches when touched during the day — at night the leaves fold naturally. It is an easy plant to raise from seed or cuttings and it is easy to care for, with the added benefit of bearing ball-like pink flower heads during the summer months. Mimosa is usually raised in the spring from seed and grown as an annual, as older plants soon become woody and unattractive.

SECRETS OF SUCCESS

Temperature: Average warmth; not less than 60°F in winter.

Light: Bright light; some direct sunlight is beneficial.

Water: Keep compost moist at all times; reduce watering in winter.

Air Humidity: Mist leaves regularly.

Repotting: Not usually necessary.

Propagation: Stem cuttings in spring or summer. Sow seeds in early spring; pour hot water over seeds before sowing.

M. pudica
Sensitive Plant
(Touch-me-not)

The MARANTA Group

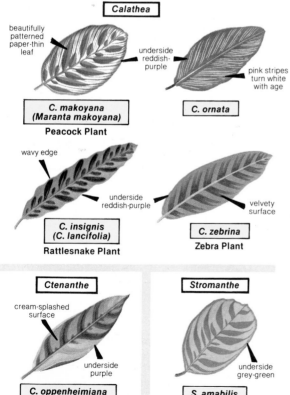

TYPES

Maranta

brown blotches turn dark green with age

prominent red veins

blackish-green leaf, silvery veins

M. leuconeura kerchoveana
Prayer Plant (Rabbit Tracks)

M. tricolor (M. leuconeura erythrophylla)
Herringbone Plant

M. leuconeura massangeana

Calathea

beautifully patterned paper-thin leaf

underside reddish-purple

pink stripes turn white with age

C. makoyana (Maranta makoyana)
Peacock Plant

C. ornata

wavy edge

underside reddish-purple

velvety surface

C. insignis (C. lancifolia)
Rattlesnake Plant

C. zebrina
Zebra Plant

Ctenanthe

cream-splashed surface

underside purple

C. oppenheimiana tricolor
Never Never Plant

Stromanthe

underside grey-green

S. amabilis

BASIC FACTS

The Maranta group contains four closely-related members — Maranta, Calathea, Ctenanthe and Stromanthe. The outstanding feature of all of these plants is their spectacular foliage, bearing coloured veins or prominent blotches on a background which ranges from near white to almost black. The plants in the Maranta group have a number of requirements in common — protection from the direct rays of the sun, a need for high air humidity, a hatred of cold draughts and a vital need for warmth in winter.

The true Marantas and Stromanthe are low-growing, rarely exceeding 8 in. high. The two popular varieties — M. leuconeura kerchoveana and M. tricolor are not at all difficult to grow, although in general the Maranta group is not for the beginner. The common name of Prayer Plant describes their curious habit of folding and raising their leaves at night.

The Calatheas and Ctenanthe are generally taller and more difficult to care for. In expert hands they can be grown as uncovered specimens but they are much more suitable for the terrarium or bottle garden.

SECRETS OF SUCCESS

Temperature: Average warmth — sudden fluctuations can harm delicate varieties. Maintain minimum winter temperature of 50°F for Maranta, 60°F for Calathea.

Light: Partial shade — colours fade in bright light. Do not expose to direct sunlight. Move to a well-lit but sunless spot in winter.

Water: Keep compost moist at all times; reduce watering in winter. Use tepid soft water.

Air Humidity: Mist leaves regularly. Surround pot with damp peat.

Repotting: Repot every 2 years in spring.

Propagation: Divide plants at repotting time. Cover pots with polythene and keep warm until new plants are established.

SPECIAL PROBLEMS

LEAF TIPS BROWN & DRY. STUNTED GROWTH
Cause: Air too dry. Look for red spider mite (see page 120). Remove dead growth. Mist leaves regularly.

LEAVES CURLED & SPOTTED. LOWER LEAVES YELLOW
Cause: Underwatering. Compost should be kept moist at all times — unlike many house plants it should not be allowed to dry out slightly between waterings when the plant is actively growing.

LEAF FALL
Cause: Air too dry. The plant is particularly sensitive to low air humidity and should be surrounded with damp peat or planted in a bottle garden.

LIMP, ROTTING STEMS
Cause: Air too cool and compost too wet in winter. See Secrets of Success.

LEAVES DISCOLOURED OR SCORCHED
Cause: Too much light, especially direct sunlight. The plant should be moved immediately; delay could be fatal.

MONSTERA

BASIC FACTS

Monstera deliciosa has been a favourite for many years. With proper care young specimens (sometimes mistakenly sold as Philodendron pertusum) soon develop large adult leaves (perforated and deeply cut). Sturdy support is essential, and stems can reach a height of 20ft or more. If your aim is to grow a tall plant with giant leaves you must care for the aerial roots — push them into the compost or use a moss stick. For average room conditions choose M. deliciosa borsigiana which is smaller and more compact.

The Monsteras are easy to grow and have no special requirements. However, the white lily-like flowers and edible fruits are only likely to appear on conservatory or greenhouse plants.

SECRETS OF SUCCESS

Temperature: Average warmth; not less than 50°F in winter. Active growth starts at 65°F.

Light: Keep out of direct sunlight. Choose a spot in light shade or moderate brightness.

Water: From November to March keep the soil just moist — make sure it is not waterlogged. For the rest of the year water thoroughly, but allow compost to become dryish between waterings.

Air Humidity: Mist if room is heated. Occasionally wash and polish mature leaves.

Repotting: Every 2 years transfer to a larger pot in spring.

Propagation: When too tall remove tip in summer at a point just below an aerial root. Plant the cutting — the severed parent will continue to grow. Air layer as an alternative.

HOW TO MAKE A MOSS STICK

A moss stick (U.S. name — totem pole) is a valuable aid for growing Monstera, Philodendron, Ivies and Vines. It serves a double purpose for Monstera — it provides support for the weak stem and it provides moisture through the aerial roots to the upper leaves.

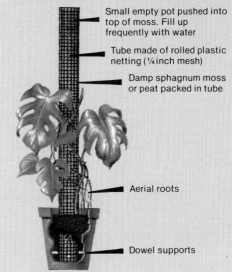

Small empty pot pushed into top of moss. Fill up frequently with water

Tube made of rolled plastic netting (¼ inch mesh)

Damp sphagnum moss or peat packed in tube

Aerial roots

Dowel supports

M. deliciosa
Swiss Cheese Plant
(Split Leaf Philodendron)

SPECIAL PROBLEMS

LEAVES WEEPING AT EDGES
Cause: Compost too wet. Allow to dry out and increase time between waterings.

ROTTING STEMS
Cause: Stem rot disease. This is usually a winter problem as the fungus is encouraged by too much moisture and too little heat. It may be possible to save the plant by repotting and keeping the compost dry and warm.

YELLOWING LEAVES
Cause: Overwatering is the most likely reason if many leaves are affected and if there are signs of wilting and rotting. If there is no wilting or rotting, underfeeding is the probable cause. If only lower leaves are affected, look for brown spots and for small and dark new leaves — the signs of underwatering. Pale leaves with straw — coloured patches indicate too much sunlight.

LOSS OF LEAVES
Cause: It is normal for the lowest leaves to drop with age. If there is abnormal leaf fall then any serious upset in conditions could be the cause — always look for other symptoms on upper leaves. If the leaves turn brown and dry before falling then too much warmth is the cause. This is a common winter problem when the pot is kept near a radiator.

LEGGY GROWTH, SMALL PALE LEAVES
Cause: Too little light is the first thing to look for. Monstera will not thrive in deep shade.

BROWN SPOTS ALONG VEINS ON UNDERSIDE OF LEAVES
Cause: Red spider mite – see page 120.

LEAVES WITH BROWN AND PAPERY TIPS & EDGES
Cause: Dry air is the most probable cause. Mist the leaves or surround the pot with damp peat. A pot-bound plant will show similar symptoms. Brown tips are also a symptom of overwatering, but general yellowing will also be present if waterlogging is the cause.

NO HOLES IN LEAVES
Cause: It is normal for the leaves in young plants to be uncut and not perforated. In mature leaves the most likely causes are lack of light, cold air, too little water and underfeeding. In tall plants the most likely reason is failure of water and food to reach the uppermost leaves. Aerial roots should be pushed into the compost or allowed to grow into a moist support.

NICODEMIA

The Indoor Oak is a rarity in Europe, but it is gaining popularity in the U.S. where it was introduced from Africa some years ago. The common name relates to the shape of its leaves, but the similarity with the familiar oak tree ends there. Nicodemia foliage is dark green and glossy with a quilted surface; the growth habit is shrubby and definitely not tree-like. This indoor plant would add an unusual note to any house plant collection, but it is no more attractive than many of the popular shrubs described elsewhere in this book. It is not difficult to care for, but winter warmth is essential. Pinch out tips occasionally to maintain bushiness.

SECRETS OF SUCCESS

Temperature: Average warmth; not less than 55°F in winter.

Light: Bright light or semi-shade; avoid direct sun in summer.

Water: Keep compost moist at all times; reduce watering in winter.

Air Humidity: Mist leaves occasionally.

Repotting: Repot if necessary in spring.

Propagation: Stem cuttings in spring or summer.

N. diversifolia
Indoor Oak

OPHIOPOGON

Lily Turf is not often seen indoors, but it is an undemanding durable plant for an unheated room. It will grow in sun or shade and has the added benefit of producing small white or purple flowers in summer. Lily Turf is an apt name for Ophiopogon — although a member of the Lily family its long green, green-and-white striped, or purplish-black leaves are distinctly grass-like and spread quite rapidly to form a turf. The variety illustrated is the smallest Lily Turf, its dark green leaves growing only 8 in. high. Brown leaf tips indicate too much heat in winter or too little water in summer.

SECRETS OF SUCCESS

Temperature: Average warmth; keep cool but frost-free in winter.

Light: Bright light or semi-shade; avoid direct sun in summer.

Water: Keep compost moist at all times; reduce watering in winter.

Air Humidity: Mist leaves frequently.

Repotting: Repot every year in spring.

Propagation: Divide plants at repotting time.

O. japonicus
Lily Turf
(Mondo Grass)

OPLISMENUS

Basket Grass is an excellent alternative to the ever-popular Tradescantia in hanging baskets and wall pots. Its slender stems spread rapidly and trail gracefully, bearing wavy-edged striped leaves. The variegated form, with its white, pink and green colouring, is the one to grow. Oplismenus is sometimes recommended as a ground cover for use between other plants, but it can be a menace if allowed to get out of hand. One of the main blessings of this useful trailer is the simplicity of raising new plants — just snip off a piece and plant in Bio Potting Compost. It is not usually worthwhile keeping old plants — plant several cuttings in a pot each spring to maintain the display of fresh young plants.

O. hirtellus variegatus
Basket Grass
(Panicum)

SECRETS OF SUCCESS

Temperature: Average warmth; not less than 45°F in winter.

Light: Bright light, but avoid direct sun.

Water: Water liberally from spring to autumn; sparingly in winter.

Air Humidity: Mist leaves occasionally.

Repotting: Not usually necessary. If plant is to be retained, repot in spring.

Propagation: Very easy. Divide plants or take stem cuttings between spring and autumn. Self-rooted cuttings may be found around the plant; remove and pot up.

PANDANUS

The spiny-edged narrow leaves are quite similar to those of the Pineapple plant and they are arranged spirally around the stem — hence the common name Screw Pine. It is a slow-growing plant, but with proper treatment it will develop into a showy false palm several feet high, with a corkscrew-like trunk and leaves 2 or 3 ft long. Thick aerial roots will appear; these should not be removed.

Grow Pandanus as a specimen plant, away from other plants and away from easy contact with people — the spines are sharp! Winter warmth is necessary and so is moist air. Keep the compost almost dry in winter — the most common cause of death is water standing at the base of the leaves when the air is cold.

P. veitchii
Screw Pine

SECRETS OF SUCCESS

Temperature: Average warmth; not less than 55°F in winter.

Light: Bright light; avoid direct sun in summer.

Water: Water liberally from spring to autumn; very sparingly in winter. Use tepid water.

Air Humidity: Mist leaves frequently.

Repotting: Repot every 2 or 3 years in spring. Use thick gloves.

Propagation: Remove basal suckers when they are about 6 in. long and treat as stem cuttings. Use Bio Roota and bottom heat.

PALMS

BASIC FACTS

Palms are attractive...and expensive. It is not the nurseryman's fault; they are difficult and costly to raise. They are still well worth the investment for two special purposes. For a bottle garden or terrarium the Parlour Palm is unrivalled as a centrepiece, and the old 'Palm Court' favourite, the Kentia Palm, is ideal if you want an elegant specimen plant with a cast-iron constitution.

Both of these well-known palms are remarkably easy to look after in an average room, provided you don't regard them as lovers of tropical sunshine and desert-dry air. In fact they require cool winters, moist summers and protection from direct sunlight. The Parlour Palm produces tiny ball-like flowers while the plant is still quite small.

SECRETS OF SUCCESS

Temperature: Average warmth; not less than 50°F in winter. Winter night temperature should not exceed 60°F for Parlour and Kentia Palms.

Light: A few delicate palms revel in sunshine, but the popular varieties should be kept in partial shade. Both Parlour and Kentia Palms can thrive in low light conditions.

Water: The first need is for good drainage; all palms detest stagnant water at the roots. During winter keep the soil slightly moist. Water more liberally in spring and summer.

Air Humidity: Mist if room is heated. Occasionally sponge mature leaves. Avoid draughts.

Repotting: Only repot when the plant is thoroughly pot-bound, as palms dislike disturbance. Compact the compost around the soil ball.

Propagation: From seed. A temperature of 80°F is required, so propagation is difficult.

SPECIAL PROBLEMS

LEAVES WITH BROWN TIPS
Cause: Dry air is the most likely reason. Mist the plants regularly during hot weather. Other possibilities are underwatering, cold air and damage by touching.

LEAVES WITH BROWN SPOTS
Cause: Usual reason is leaf spot disease, due to overwatering or sudden chilling. Remove affected foliage and improve growing conditions. Another possible cause is use of very hard water.

YELLOWING LEAVES
Cause: Underwatering. Roots should not be allowed to dry out during the summer months.

BROWN LEAVES
Cause: It is natural for the lowest leaves to turn brown and droop. Remove by cutting, not pulling. If browning is general and accompanied by rotting, the problem is overwatering. Carry out standard remedial treatment (see page 122).

INSECTS
Red spider mite, scale and mealy bug can be troublesome. See page 120.

TYPES

● BAMBOO PALMS
Chamaedorea seifrizii — Reed Palm — cane-like stems

● SAGO PALMS
Cycas revoluta — Sago Palm — ball-like base

● FAN PALMS
Rhapis excelsa — Lady Palm — small leaflet fan
Chamaerops humilis — European Fan Palm — large leaflet fan
Livistona chinensis — Chinese Fan Palm

● FEATHER PALMS
Howea forsteriana (Kentia forsteriana) — Kentia Palm — popular in U.K. — wide leaflets
Howea belmoreana (Kentia belmoreana) — Sentry Palm — popular in U.S. — arching leaflets
Neanthe bella (Chamaedorea elegans) — Parlour Palm — fairly wide leaflets
Phoenix canariensis — Canary Date Palm — narrow leaflets
Phoenix roebelinii — Pygmy Date Palm — very narrow leaflets
Cocos weddeliana — Coconut Palm

FOLIAGE HOUSE PLANTS

PEPEROMIA

These compact slow-growing plants are easy to care for under average room conditions, and they are frequently included in bowls and bottle gardens. There are scores of different species and varieties, but only four or five are readily available. P. caperata, P. hederaefolia and P. magnoliaefolia have been popular for many years.

The original home of most Peperomias was the mossy floor of the S. American jungle, so it is not surprising that they prefer peat-based composts to soil.

TYPES

● BUSHY TYPES

rat-tail flower heads

red stalk

P. caperata
Emerald Ripple

P. caperata variegata

fleshy leaf

heart-shaped leaves

P. hederaefolia (P. griseo-argentea)
Ivy Peperomia (Silver Ripple)

P. argyreia (P. sandersii)
Watermelon Peperomia (Rugby Football Plant)

● UPRIGHT TYPES

fleshy stems

fleshy leaf

P. magnoliaefolia
Desert Privet

fine hairs cover leaf surface

red stem

purple edge

fleshy leaf

P. obtusifolia
Baby Rubber Plant (Pepper Face)

P. verticillata
Whorled Peperomia

● TRAILING TYPES

tiny all-green succulent leaves

green stem

red stem

succulent leaves

tiny silver-marked leaves

P. rotundifolia

P. prostrata
Creeping Peperomia

P. scandens variegata
Cupid Peperomia

SECRETS OF SUCCESS

Temperature: Average warmth; not less than 50° – 55°F in winter.

Light: A bright or semi-shady spot, away from direct sunlight. Peperomias will thrive in fluorescent light.

Water: Water with care. The compost must dry out to some extent between waterings, but never wait until the leaves wilt. Use tepid water and apply very little in the winter months.

Air Humidity: Mist occasionally in summer; never in winter.

Repotting: Avoid frequent repotting. If necessary after several years transfer to a slightly larger pot in spring.

Propagation: Cuttings root easily. Between spring and late summer take stem cuttings from upright and trailing varieties; leaf cuttings from bushy varieties.

SPECIAL PROBLEMS

LEAVES WITH BROWN TIPS & EDGES
Cause: Sudden drop in temperature. Remove all damaged leaves; keep plants out of draughts and away from cold windowsills.

SUDDEN LOSS OF LEAVES FROM SUCCULENT VARIETIES
Cause: Foliage has been allowed to wilt before watering. Remember to water when the compost is dryish but *before* leaves wilt.

LEAVES WILTED & DISCOLOURED. STEM OR LEAF ROT PRESENT. CORKY SWELLINGS UNDER LEAVES
Cause; Overwatering, especially in winter. Carry out standard remedial treatment (see page 122).

SUDDEN LOSS OF LEAVES IN WINTER
Cause: Temperature too cool. Move to a spot where a minimum of 50°F can be maintained.

PELARGONIUM

P. capitatum
Rose-scented
Geranium

P. crispum
Lemon-scented
Geranium

P. graveolens
Rose-scented
Geranium

P. tomentosum
Peppermint
Geranium

P. odoratissimum
Apple-scented
Geranium

Pelargoniums, commonly known as Geraniums, are among the most popular of all house plants. It is, of course, the flowering varieties which are responsible for this popularity, but there is a small group which are grown for their foliage rather than their indifferent flowers. These are the Scented-leaved Geraniums, and the common names describe the aroma when the leaves are gently crushed. Keep the plants cool and fairly dry in winter and prune back the stems in spring to maintain bushiness.

SPECIAL PROBLEMS

See Flowering Geraniums, page 75.

SECRETS OF SUCCESS

Temperature: Average warmth; keep cool (45° – 55°F) in winter.

Light: Bright with some direct sunlight, but protect from midday summer sun.

Water: Water liberally from spring to autumn; sparingly in winter.

Air Humidity: Do not mist the leaves.

Repotting: Repot, when necessary, in early spring.

Propagation: Stem cuttings in summer. Do not use a rooting hormone and do not cover the pot containing cuttings.

PELLIONIA

P. daveauana (P. repens)

There are two varieties of this creeping plant – P. pulchra with dark brown veins; P. daveauana with dark brown leaf edges. Both make useful additions for the terrarium or bottle garden, but when used in a hanging basket or as ground cover between other plants they are more demanding than easy trailers like Tradescantia. The Pellionias require moist air and winter warmth. They are not too fussy about the amount of light they receive but they are unusually sensitive to draughts. In its native home Pellionia is a jungle creeper and the low-growing stems root into the compost as they grow over the surface.

SECRETS OF SUCCESS

Temperature: Average warmth; not less than 55°F in winter.

Light: Semi-shade or bright indirect light. Protect from direct sunlight.

Water: Keep compost moist at all times; reduce watering in winter. Use soft water.

Air Humidity: Mist leaves frequently.

Repotting: Repot every 2 years in spring.

Propagation: Divide plants at repotting time. Stem cuttings root easily.

P. pulchra

PIPER

Several varieties of Ornamental Pepper are grown as house plants, but they are not easy to obtain. They are climbers, and with support they will reach 5 ft high. Their leaves are several inches long and highly decorative, but the plants do not bear fruit. Piper is often described as a difficult plant to grow under ordinary room conditions, but its culture should not be a problem if the winter temperature can be maintained at 55°F or more and if you are prepared to mist the leaves regularly. Leaf fall is the sign that conditions are wrong; pearly drops of liquid under the leaves are quite normal.

SECRETS OF SUCCESS

Temperature: Average warmth; not less than 55°F in winter.

Light: Bright light; not direct sun.

Water: Keep compost moist at all times; reduce watering in winter.

Air Humidity: Mist leaves regularly.

Repotting: Repot every 2 years in spring.

Propagation: Stem cuttings in spring or summer. Use Bio Roota and bottom heat.

P. crocatum
Ornamental Pepper

PHILODENDRON

TYPES

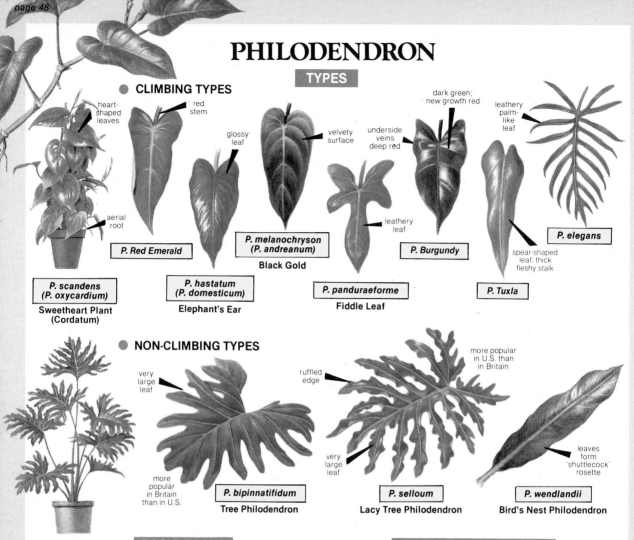

● CLIMBING TYPES

heart-shaped leaves

red stem

glossy leaf

velvety surface

dark green; new growth red

underside veins deep red

leathery palm-like leaf

aerial root

leathery leaf

spear-shaped leaf; thick fleshy stalk

P. Red Emerald

P. melanochryson (P. andreanum)
Black Gold

P. Burgundy

P. elegans

P. scandens (P. oxycardium)
Sweetheart Plant (Cordatum)

P. hastatum (P. domesticum)
Elephant's Ear

P. panduraeforme
Fiddle Leaf

P. Tuxla

● NON-CLIMBING TYPES

very large leaf

ruffled edge

more popular in U.S. than in Britain

very large leaf

leaves form 'shuttlecock' rosette

more popular in Britain than in U.S.

P. bipinnatifidum
Tree Philodendron

P. selloum
Lacy Tree Philodendron

P. wendlandii
Bird's Nest Philodendron

BASIC FACTS

Philodendrons have been used as house plants since Victorian times, and their popularity has increased in recent years. The conditions they need for healthy growth are those which they enjoyed in their ancestral home within the American tropical forests – no direct sunlight and moist surroundings when the air is warm.

There are two basic types of Philodendron. The first group, the climbers, are well suited to the average room, as long as you provide firm support for the stems. The Sweetheart Plant is the smallest and it is also the easiest to look after, with its ability to withstand both neglect and poor conditions. A feature of many climbing Philodendrons is the production of aerial roots from the stems, and these roots have an important part to play. Push them into the compost to provide moisture for the upper leaves.

Most of the second group, the non-climbers, are capable of growing into immense plants with large, deeply-lobed leaves. They are therefore more suitable for public buildings than for the average home.

SPECIAL PROBLEMS

See Monstera, page 43.

SECRETS OF SUCCESS

Temperature: Average warmth; not less than 55°F in winter. P. scandens will endure lower temperatures (minimum 50°F) but P. melanochryson needs higher than average warmth (minimum 65°F).

Light: All Philodendrons should be kept out of direct sunlight. P. scandens will succeed in shady conditions, but the usual requirement is light shade or moderate brightness. Both P. melanochryson and variegated-leaved forms should be kept in a well-lit spot.

Water: From November to March keep the soil just moist – make sure it is not waterlogged. For the rest of the year water thoroughly and regularly.

Air Humidity: Keep the air moist in summer and in heated rooms in winter — surround pots with damp peat or mist leaves regularly.

Repotting: Every 2 or 3 years transfer to a larger pot in spring.

Propagation: Cuttings require warm conditions. In summer take stem cuttings or air layer the climbing varieties. With a non-climbing variety, shoots taken from the base of the stem should be used as cuttings.

PILEA

A wide variety of bushy and trailing Pileas are available, and they are generally quite easy to grow, even for a beginner. Easiest of all is the popular Aluminium Plant with its white-splashed leaves. The list of dangers is a small one — move pots off window-sills on frosty nights, pinch out growing tips occasionally to keep plants bushy, and keep pots away from draughts. Even in expert hands the bushy Pileas tend to become leggy and unattractive with age. As cuttings root easily it is a good idea to start new plants each spring rather than retaining old specimens. Nearly all of the bushy varieties are grown for the beauty of their individual leaves, but the Artillery Plant is grown for its ferny effect and for the novelty of its puffs of smoke-like pollen when disturbed in summer.

SECRETS OF SUCCESS

Temperature: Average warmth; not less than 50°F in winter.

Light: Bright light or semi-shade; protect from direct sun in summer.

Water: Water liberally from spring to autumn, allowing compost to dry out slightly between waterings. Water sparingly in winter. Use tepid water.

Air Humidity: Mist leaves regularly.

Repotting: Repot in spring if the plant is to be retained.

Propagation: Stem cuttings in late spring or summer.

SPECIAL PROBLEMS

LEAVES WILTED & DISCOLOURED. STEM ROT PRESENT. SOME LEAF FALL
Cause: Overwatering, especially in winter. Carry out standard remedial treatment (see page 122).

LEAVES DISCOLOURED WITH BROWN TIPS & EDGES
Cause: Too much shade is the most likely reason. Move to a brighter spot. If the plant is well-lit, the probable cause is a sudden drop in temperature.

INSECTS
Red spider mite can be troublesome; see page 120.

LEAF FALL IN WINTER
Cause: Cold air and wet compost can cause serious leaf fall, but even a healthy plant may shed a few leaves in winter. Cut back affected stems in spring to induce new healthy growth.

TYPES

● BUSHY TYPES

silvery patches on quilted surface

P. cadierei
Aluminium Plant

reddish brown when grown in sunlight, green when grown in shade

underside purple

P. involucrata (P. spruceana)
Friendship Plant (Panamiga)

deeply quilted surface

P. Moon Valley

dull bronze green, silver centre

P. Bronze

glossy surface dark green or brown

P. repens
Black Leaf Panamiga

tiny pale green leaves

underside purple

P. microphylla (P. muscosa)
Artillery Plant

● TRAILING TYPES

circular, fleshy ¼ in. leaves

green stems

P. depressa
Creeping Jenny

circular, quilted ¾ in. leaves

reddish stems

P. nummulariifolia
Creeping Charlie

PLECTRANTHUS

Three species are known as Swedish Ivy — two are pictured here, the white-veined P. oertendahlii is not illustrated. This common name indicates their popularity in Scandinavia, where they are found in hanging baskets or on windowsills.

It is a pity that Swedish Ivy is not more popular in other countries as it has many good points. It will survive in dry air, it will withstand occasional dryness at the roots and it will sometimes flower. Pinch out the stem tips occasionally to keep the plant bushy, and use these tips as cuttings which will root very easily.

P. australis
Swedish Ivy

SECRETS OF SUCCESS

Temperature: Average warmth; not less than 50°F in winter.

Light: Bright light or semi-shade; avoid direct sunlight.

Water: Keep compost moist at all times; reduce water in winter.

Air Humidity: Mist leaves occasionally.

Repotting: Repot every 2 or 3 years in spring if plant is retained, but best grown as an annual.

Propagation: Very easy. Take stem cuttings or divide plant in spring or summer.

P. coleoides marginatus
White-edged Swedish Ivy

PODOCARPUS

Many plants suffer if they are not kept moderately warm on cold winter nights, but Podocarpus demands an unheated room if it is to live successfully for many years indoors. This durable plant does not mind a draughty situation, and there are few better trees for a cold hallway. The upright stems bear narrow, glossy strap-like leaves about 3 in. long, and if not pruned the stems will reach 6 ft or more. Buddhist Pine can be kept as a compact shrub by regular pruning, but its slow-growing habit means that it requires little attention. Hard to obtain, but well worth looking for.

SECRETS OF SUCCESS

Temperature: Average warmth, but prefers cool conditions. Minimum temperature 40°F in winter.

Light: Brightly lit spot, some sun is beneficial.

Water: Keep compost fairly moist at all times; reduce watering in winter. Do not overwater.

Air Humidity: Mist leaves occasionally.

Repotting: Repot, when necessary, in spring.

Propagation: Stem cuttings in summer. Use Bio Roota and bottom heat.

P. macrophyllus
Buddhist Pine

POLYSCIAS

P. balfouriana
Dinner Plate Aralia

Varieties of Polyscias are attractive oriental trees with twisted stems and decorative foliage. Large specimens are prohibitively expensive; buy a small plant if you can and look after it carefully. The leaves are usually ferny, but the most popular Polyscias is the Dinner Plate Aralia with large rounded leaflets. Unfortunately Polyscias is not easy to grow under room conditions, and it will readily drop its leaves if the environment is wrong. It will need good light, moist air, even moisture at the roots, and warmth in winter.

SECRETS OF SUCCESS

Temperature: Warm or average temperature; minimum temperature 55° – 60°F in winter.

Light: Bright, but away from direct sun. Will adapt to light shade.

Water: Water moderately from spring to autumn; sparingly in winter.

Air Humidity: Mist leaves frequently.

Repotting: Repot every 2 years in spring.

Propagation: Not easy. Take stem cuttings in spring; use Bio Roota and bottom heat.

P. fruticosa
Ming Aralia

RHOEO

The short stem bears fleshy lance-shaped leaves which grow about 1 ft long. Their colouring is unusual — glossy green or green-and-white above, purple below. An added feature of interest is the presence of small white flowers in purple 'boats' at the base of the lower leaves. Remove side shoots if Boat Lily is to be grown as a specimen plant; retain them if it is planted in a hanging basket. Rhoeo is not a difficult plant but it is more temperamental than its relatives in the Tradescantia family. It needs winter warmth, freedom from draughts and moist air. Remove dead leaves and flowers.

SECRETS OF SUCCESS

Temperature: Average warmth; not less than 50° – 55°F in winter.

Light: Bright or semi-shade, no direct sun in summer.

Water: Keep compost moist at all times; reduce watering in winter.

Air Humidity: Mist leaves frequently.

Repotting: Repot every year in spring.

Propagation: Use side shoots as cuttings in spring or summer. Alternatively bushy plants can be divided at repotting time.

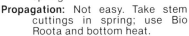

R. discolor
Boat Lily
(Moses in the Cradle)

SAXIFRAGA

The outstanding feature of Mother of Thousands is the production of long, slender red runners which bear miniature plants at their ends. These runners should be allowed to hang freely, so the plant is best grown in a hanging basket or wall display. Clusters of insignificant flowers appear in summer. You can choose from two varieties — S. sarmentosa has green leaves and white veins, is easy to care for and is easy to propagate. S. sarmentosa tricolor is more attractive and more colourful, with red-edged green-and-white leaves, but it is unfortunately slow growing and more tender.

SECRETS OF SUCCESS

Temperature: Cool or average warmth; not less than 40° – 45°F in winter.

Light: Brightly lit spot, away from direct sunlight.

Water: Water liberally from spring to autumn; sparingly in winter. Allow surface to dry out slightly between waterings.

Air Humidity: Mist leaves occasionally.

Repotting: Repot every year in spring.

Propagation: Very easy. Peg down plantlets in compost — cut stem when rooted.

S. sarmentosa tricolor
Mother of Thousands
(Strawberry Geranium)

SANSEVIERIA

S. trifasciata laurentii
Mother-in-Law's Tongue
(Snake Plant)

S. trifasciata (S. zeylanica)
Mother-in-Law's Tongue
(Snake Plant)

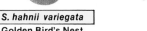

S. hahnii
Bird's Nest Sansevieria

S. hahnii variegata
Golden Bird's Nest

BASIC FACTS

If all else fails, grow Sansevieria. This tough and universally popular plant, known as Mother-in-Law's Tongue in Britain, and Snakeskin Plant in the U.S., deserves its reputation for near-indestructibility. It will grow in bright sunshine or shade, withstand dry air, draughts and periods without water, and it rarely needs repotting. It can, however, be quite easily killed by prolonged overwatering in winter and prolonged exposure to near freezing temperatures.

The most popular variety is S. trifasciata laurentii. Its erect, fleshy, sword-like leaves may reach 3ft or more, and its cross-banded foliage with distinct golden edges is a common sight everywhere. Grow this plant in a clay pot and treat it properly — under good conditions sprays of small, fragrant flowers will appear. The low-growing rosette varieties are much less popular, but are useful for a sunny or shady windowsill.

SECRETS OF SUCCESS

Temperature: Average warmth; not less than 50°F in winter.

Light: Bright light with some sun preferred, but will grow in shade.

Water: From spring to autumn water moderately, allowing compost to dry out slightly between waterings. In winter water every 1-2 months. Avoid wetting the heart of the plant.

Air Humidity: No need to mist the leaves.

Repotting: Seldom required—repot when growth cracks the pot.

Propagation: Remove offset by cutting off at base; allow to dry before inserting in compost. Alternatively divide up plant. Leaf cuttings can be used for all-green varieties (see page 115).

SPECIAL PROBLEMS

ROT AT BASE, LEAVES YELLOW AND DYING BACK
Cause: Basal rot disease. The cause is generally overwatering in winter. If the whole of the base is affected, use the upper foliage as leaf cuttings and then discard the plant. If only part of the plant is affected, remove it from the pot and chop off the diseased section. Dust cut surface with sulphur and repot. Keep dry and move to a warmer spot.

ROT AT BASE IN WINTER; NOT OVERWATERED
Cause: Cold damage. Sansevieria can be quickly damaged at 40°F or below; 50°F is the minimum temperature for safe winter care.

BROWN BLOTCHES ON LEAVES
Cause: A non-infectious disorder which starts at the tips and works downwards along the leaf. The cause is unknown and there is no cure.

SCHEFFLERA

S. actinophylla (Brassaia actinophylla)
Umbrella Tree

A fine indoor tree, much used by interior decorators on both sides of the Atlantic. In subtropical gardens it is known as the Octopus Tree because of its spectacular tentacle-like flowers. Unfortunately it does not bloom under room conditions and the indoor plant form is known as the Umbrella Plant, which refers to the finger-like glossy leaflets radiating like umbrella spokes from each leaf stalk. There are four or five leaflets per stalk on young plants, twelve or more on mature specimens.

Schefflera is not a difficult plant to grow, provided it is kept moderately warm and protected from cold draughts. With time it will reach 6 ft or more, but it becomes lanky with age due to the loss of lower leaves. Scale insect may be a problem.

SECRETS OF SUCCESS

Temperature: Average warmth; not less than 55°F in winter. If possible avoid temperatures above 70°F.

Light: Bright light, away from direct sunshine. Will adapt to light shade.

Water: Water liberally from spring to autumn; sparingly in winter.

Air Humidity: Mist leaves frequently.

Repotting: Repot every 2 years in spring.

Propagation: Difficult. Stem cuttings in summer; use Bio Roota and bottom heat. Alternatively sow fresh seeds in spring.

SCINDAPSUS

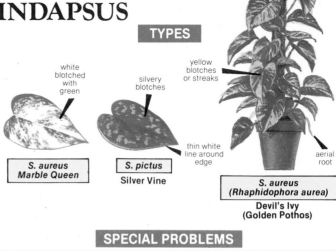

The most common variety of Scindapsus is S. aureus — the Devil's Ivy or Golden Pothos. It is similar to but more colourful than the popular Sweetheart Plant (page 48), and although it is sometimes described as a difficult plant to grow there is no reason why it should not do well if you follow the Secrets of Success. The other two types illustrated on this page — the near-white S. aureus Marble Queen and the silver-spotted S.pictus are unquestionably difficult and are best confined to the conservatory or greenhouse.

Scindapsus is a climber with aerial roots and stems which can reach 6 ft or more; a moss stick makes an ideal support. The stems are sometimes allowed to trail from a hanging basket or wall display. Pinch out tips to induce bushiness; keep the plant well away from draughts.

TYPES

white blotched with green

S. aureus Marble Queen

silvery blotches

S. pictus
Silver Vine

yellow blotches or streaks

thin white line around edge

aerial root

S. aureus (Rhaphidophora aurea)
Devil's Ivy (Golden Pothos)

SECRETS OF SUCCESS

Temperature: Average warmth; not less than 50°–55°F in winter (60°F for S.pictus).

Light: Well-lit but sunless spot. Variegation will fade in poor light.

Water: Water liberally from spring to autumn; let compost dry out slightly between waterings. Water sparingly in winter.

Air Humidity: Mist leaves frequently.

Repotting: Repot, when necessary, in spring.

Propagation: Stem cuttings in spring or summer; use Bio Roota. Keep compost rather dry and leave in dark until rooted.

SPECIAL PROBLEMS

YELLOWING & FALLING LEAVES; ROTTING STEMS
Cause: Overwatering, especially in winter. Scindapsus cannot survive in waterlogged soil. Carry out standard remedial treatment (see page 122).

BROWN & SHRIVELLED LEAF TIPS
Cause: Air too dry. Mist the leaves regularly.

BROWN LEAF EDGES; BROWN SPOTS ON LEAF SURFACE
Cause: Underwatering during the growing season. Surface of compost should become dry between waterings, but root ball must not be allowed to dry out.

CURLED LIMP LEAVES; ROTTING STEMS
Cause: Cold air damage. Scindapsus is extremely sensitive to a sudden drop in temperature below 50°F.

SENECIO

S. macroglossus variegatus
Cape Ivy

At first glance both the Cape Ivy and German Ivy can be mistaken for the Common Ivy. On closer inspection the lobes of Senecio leaves will be found to be fleshier and generally more pointed, and when the small daisy-like flowers appear the difference becomes immediately obvious. There are also cultural differences — Senecios are less affected by warm and dry winter conditions than the Common Ivies. Pinch out tips to maintain bushiness.

SECRETS OF SUCCESS

Temperature: Average warmth; not less than 50°F in winter.

Light: Bright; some direct sun is beneficial in winter. Will tolerate semi-shade.

Water: Keep compost moist at all times; reduce watering in winter.

Air Humidity: Mist leaves frequently.

Repotting: Repot every 2 years in spring.

Propagation: Easy. Take stem cuttings in spring or summer.

S. mikanioides
German Ivy

SELAGINELLA

S. uncinata
Peacock Fern

Selaginella, or Creeping Moss, was a Victorian favourite. Today it has lost much of this early popularity, but it is still an excellent choice for the bottle garden or terrarium. It is much less happy away from this protection, the tiny leaves shrivelling in hot rooms, draughty rooms or in dry air. To increase your chance of success grow it in a shallow, well-drained pot in semi-shade some distance away from the window. Surround the pot with damp peat and use soft water for watering and misting.

SECRETS OF SUCCESS

Temperature: Average warmth; not less than 55°F in winter.

Light: Semi-shade.

Water: Keep compost moist at all times; reduce watering in winter. Use soft water.

Air Humidity: Moist air is essential. Mist leaves regularly; avoid soaking leaves.

Repotting: Repot, when necessary, in spring.

Propagation: Stem cuttings in spring or summer; use Bio Roota.

S. martensii
Creeping Moss

SONERILA

A low-growing plant from Java which will provide colour in a bottle garden — coppery green leaves with purple below and silvery spots above, red stems and small pink flowers in summer. It will grow quite happily in a carboy or terrarium, but Sonerila is a real challenge to your skill under ordinary room conditions without glass protection. It is a hot house plant, needing warmth, constant moisture around the leaves and careful watering. Surround the pot with damp peat and mist the leaves each day with tepid water. Dry leaf tips indicate that the air is too dry; leaf drop means that the air is too cold.

SECRETS OF SUCCESS

Temperature: Warm or average warmth; not less than 60°F in winter.

Light: Semi-shade; keep away from direct sunlight.

Water: Keep compost moist at all times; reduce watering in winter. Avoid overwatering.

Air Humidity: High air humidity essential. Mist leaves regularly.

Repotting: Repot every 2 years in spring.

Propagation: Stem cuttings in spring or summer. Use Bio Roota and bottom heat.

S. margaritacea
Frosted Sonerila

SYNGONIUM

Syngonium, the Goose Foot Plant, is closely related to the climbing Philodendrons, and like them it requires warmth, moist air and protection from direct sunlight. Aerial roots are produced by the adult plant and a moss stick (see page 43) makes an excellent support for this attractive climbing plant.

An unusual feature of the Goose Foot Plant is the dramatic change in leaf shape which takes place as the plant gets older. The young leaves are arrow-shaped and borne on erect stalks. At this stage the variegation is boldest and brightest. With age the stems acquire a climbing habit and need support; at the same time the leaves become lobed. The juvenile form can be retained by cutting off the climbing stems as they form.

SECRETS OF SUCCESS

Temperature: Average warmth; at least 60°F in winter.

Light: Well-lit but sunless spot for variegated types, semi-shade for all-green varieties.

Water: Keep compost moist at all times; reduce watering in winter. Avoid overwatering.

Air Humidity: Mist leaves regularly.

Repotting: Every 2 years in spring.

Propagation: Take stem cuttings bearing aerial roots in spring or summer. Use Bio Roota.

TYPES

S. podophyllum Green Gold

S. podophyllum Imperial White

S. podophyllum Emerald Gem

S. podophyllum
Goose Foot Plant
(Arrowhead Vine)
(Nephthytis)

JUVENILE LEAF FORM → → → ADULT LEAF FORM

TOLMIEA

This easy-to-grow novelty plant gets its common name from the plantlets which form at the base of mature leaves. It forms a compact mound of downy, bright green leaves about 6 in. high, and has the virtue of standing up to poor conditions. Tolmiea is one of the hardiest of all house plants and actually relishes a cold, well-ventilated and sunless environment. Its enemy is hot, dry air which can quickly lead to red spider mite attack and plant deterioration. It prefers a brightly lit spot but will adapt to shade. An excellent plant for a child's collection as it is easy to propagate by planting the 'babies'.

SECRETS OF SUCCESS

Temperature: Cool to average warmth; not less than 40°F in winter.

Light: Bright light preferred, but will grow in shade.

Water: Keep compost moist at all times; reduce watering in winter.

Air Humidity: Mist leaves occasionally.

Repotting: Repot every year in spring.

Propagation: Peg down plantlets in compost — cut stems when rooted. For full instructions see page 114.

T. menziesii
Piggyback Plant

FOLIAGE HOUSE PLANTS

SUCCULENTS

BASIC FACTS

Three or four tiny pots of succulents and a small cactus or two are the usual starting point for a life-long interest in house plants.

The succulents are indeed a good starting point for children as these plants are easy to care for, can withstand a great deal of neglect and mismanagement, and are amongst the easiest of all plant groups to propagate.

Succulents are easily defined as plants with fleshy leaves or stems which can store water; the cacti (page 96) are a distinct group of succulents. Much less distinct is the dividing line between 'succulents' and 'house plants with fleshy leaves'. Sansevieria and other fleshy-leaved types which have different requirements to other succulents are treated as ordinary house plants in this book. Those succulents which are grown mainly for their blooms (Hoya, Rochea, Kalanchoe blossfeldiana etc.) are treated as flowering house plants or flowering pot plants.

Hundreds of succulents with widely differing shapes and sizes are commercially available. Most of them have a rosette shape, as the tightly-packed leaf arrangement helps to conserve water in their desert habitat. With age some of these types become 'rosette trees' with leaf clusters at the ends of woody stems. The remainder grow as trailing or bushy plants.

Despite the wide variety of shapes, the succulents are remarkably consistent in their needs. They evolved in the dry areas of the world and their general requirements are related to this habitat — free-draining compost, sunshine, fresh air, water in the growing season and a cold and dry resting period. Winter dormancy is vital if you want your plants to bloom and last for many years; another requirement for top quality plants is a period outdoors in summer.

HOW TO MAKE A DISH GARDEN

Succulents are ideal plants for a dish garden. Choose carefully and aim for an attractive landscape. Once made it will require very little attention and should last for a number of years on a windowsill.

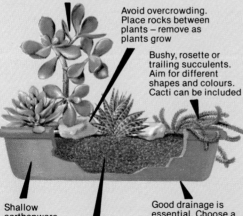

Tree-like succulent at rear or centre

Avoid overcrowding. Place rocks between plants – remove as plants grow

Bushy, rosette or trailing succulents. Aim for different shapes and colours. Cacti can be included

Shallow earthenware or glazed dish

Peat-based Seed & Cutting Compost

Good drainage is essential. Choose a container with holes in the base, or add a thick layer of charcoal

SECRETS OF SUCCESS

Temperature: Average warmth from spring to autumn; succulents (unlike most house plants) relish a marked difference between night and day temperatures. Keep cool in winter; 50° – 55°F is ideal but no harm will occur at 40°F.

Light: A windowsill is the right spot, as some sunshine is vital. Choose a south-facing windowsill if you can, but some shade in summer may be necessary. Haworthia and Gasteria need a bright but sunless site.

Water: Treat as an ordinary house plant from spring to autumn, watering thoroughly when the compost begins to dry out. In winter water very infrequently, once every 1 – 2 months.

Air Humidity: No need to mist the leaves. The main requirement is for fresh air; open windows in summer.

Repotting: Only repot when essential — then transfer to a slightly larger container in spring. Use a shallow pot rather than a deep one.

Propagation: Cuttings root easily. Take stem cuttings, offsets or leaf cuttings in spring or summer. It is vital to let the cuttings dry for a few days (large cuttings for 1 – 2 weeks) before inserting in compost. Water very sparingly and do not cover with polythene or glass. Another propagation method is seed sowing — germination temperature 70° – 80°F.

SPECIAL PROBLEMS

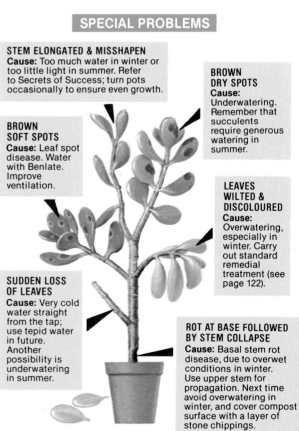

STEM ELONGATED & MISSHAPEN
Cause: Too much water in winter or too little light in summer. Refer to Secrets of Success; turn pots occasionally to ensure even growth.

BROWN DRY SPOTS
Cause: Underwatering. Remember that succulents require generous watering in summer.

BROWN SOFT SPOTS
Cause: Leaf spot disease. Water with Benlate. Improve ventilation.

LEAVES WILTED & DISCOLOURED
Cause: Overwatering, especially in winter. Carry out standard remedial treatment (see page 122).

SUDDEN LOSS OF LEAVES
Cause: Very cold water straight from the tap; use tepid water in future. Another possibility is underwatering in summer.

ROT AT BASE FOLLOWED BY STEM COLLAPSE
Cause: Basal stem rot disease, due to overwet conditions in winter. Use upper stem for propagation. Next time avoid overwatering in winter, and cover compost surface with a layer of stone chippings.

TYPES

Aeonium

tightly packed waxy leaves

shiny leaves

A. tabulaeforme
Saucer Plant

A. arboreum atropurpureum

Aloe

white tubercles

saw-edged leaves

toothed leaves

white-edged leaves

A. aristata

A. humilis
Hedgehog Aloe

A. variegata
Partridge Breast

A. arborescens
Tree Aloe

fine threads

black spines at leaf ends

Agave

saw-edged leaves

A. filifera
Thread Agave

A. victoriae-reginae

A. americana
Century Plant

A. americana mediopicta

Ceropegia

purple stems

C. woodii
Rosary Vine

Bryophyllum

plantlets on leaves

B. tubiflorum

B. daigremontianum
Good Luck Plant

paired leaves surrounding stem

Crassula

tiny scale-like leaves

propeller-shaped leaves

green shiny leaves

furry surface

red edge

C. perforata
String of Buttons

C. lycopodioides
Rat Tail Plant

C. falcata (Rochea falcata)

C. argentea
Jade Plant

surface covered with fine hairs

red-tipped leaves

Echeveria

flat-topped leaves

brown-tipped pointed leaves

waxy leaves

pink bronzy leaves

fine white hairs

E. harmsii
Mexican Snowball

E. setosa

E. derenbergii
Painted Lady

E. agavoides

E. glauca
Blue Echeveria

E. gibbiflora metallica

TYPES

Cotyledon

ribbed leafless stem

wavy-edged leaves

silvery surface

C. undulata
Silver Ruffles

Euphorbia

milky sap (poisonous!)

leafless stems

E. obesa
Turkish Temple

E. tirucalli
Milk Bush

Faucaria

sharply toothed 'jaws'

F. tigrina
Tiger's Jaws

Gasteria

white warts on leaves

G. verrucosa
Cape Hart's Tongue

Graptopetalum

grey-green leaves

G. paraguayense
Ghost Plant

Haworthia

white warts on leaves

almost transparent upper surface

white warts on leaves

finely pointed leaves

H. reinwardtii
Wart Plant

H. tessellata
Star Window Plant

H. margaritifera
Pearl Plant

H. fasciata
Zebra Haworthia

Kleinia

grey-green stems

K. articulata
Candle Plant

Kalanchoe

velvety leaves covered with brown hairs

brown-edged leaves

furry surface

K. beharensis
Velvet Leaf

K. tomentosa
Panda Plant

Lithops

pebble-like plants ('living stones')

L. fulleri

L. pseudo-truncatella

L. salicola

Pachyphytum

silvery-white bloom

P. oviferum
Sugar Almond Plant

Senecio

globular leaves

S. rowleyanus
String of Beads

Sempervivum

dark red tips

dense cover of threads

S. tectorum
Hens & Chickens

S. arachnoideum
Cobweb Houseleek

Sedum

boat-shaped waxy leaves

red tips

pale green leaves

leaves turn red in sun

waxy leaves

cream-centred leaves

S. pachyphyllum
Jelly Bean Plant

S. adolphii
Golden Sedum

S. rubrotinctum
Jelly Bean Plant

S. morganianum
Burro's Tail

S. sieboldii mediovariegatum

The TRADESCANTIA Group

BASIC FACTS

By far the most important members of this group are the Inch Plants or Wandering Jews — Tradescantia, Zebrina and Callisia. Their 1-3 in. oval, striped leaves clasp the creeping or trailing stems and this group are perhaps the most popular of all hanging basket plants, with Z. pendula as the most colourful. All of them are easy to propagate, and home-raised plants far outnumber shop-bought specimens. Pinch out the growing tips regularly to encourage bushiness, and remove all-green shoots as soon as they appear. Winter warmth is not essential.

Purple Heart is also easy to grow and trails like a Wandering Jew, but its leaves are much longer. The Teddy Bear Vine has succulent leaves, densely covered with fur. All members of the Tradescantia family may occasionally flower indoors, but the blooms are generally insignificant.

As with most families there is one difficult member. Brown Spiderwort has broad, colourful leaves borne in a rosette and this plant needs skill and a great deal of air humidity.

SECRETS OF SUCCESS

Temperature: Average warmth; not less than 45° – 50°F in winter (Siderasis – 55°F).

Light: Bright light is essential for variegated types. Some direct sunlight is beneficial for Zebrina, Setcreasea and Cyanotis. Grow Siderasis in semi-shade.

Water: Water liberally from spring to autumn; sparingly in winter.

Air Humidity: Mist leaves occasionally. Mist Siderasis regularly.

Repotting: Repot, when necessary, in spring.

Propagation: Very easy; stem cuttings in spring, summer or autumn. Propagate Siderasis by division.

SPECIAL PROBLEMS

BARE SPINDLY GROWTH
Cause: Too little light, too little water or too little fertilizer. All stems become straggly and bare with age. Cut back spindly growth; replace old plants.

LEAVES ALL GREEN
Cause: Too little light. Variegated types revert to all-green form in shady conditions.

STEMS LIMP, LEAVES YELLOW & SPOTTED
Cause: Underwatering. Water liberally during the growing season; allow surface to dry between waterings.

LEAF TIPS BROWN & SHRIVELLED
Cause: Air too dry. Look for red spider mite (see page 120). Remove dead growth. Mist leaves frequently.

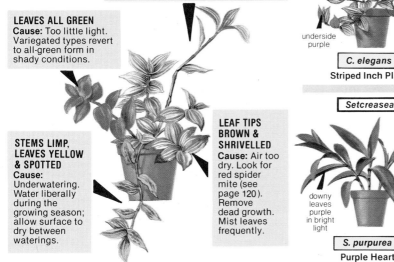

TYPES

Tradescantia

T. fluminensis variegata

T. fluminensis tricolor

Tradescantia
Wandering Jew (Inch Plant)

hairy stems

underside purple

T. blossfeldiana variegata

T. albovittata

Zebrina

Z. pendula
Silvery Inch Plant

underside purple

Zebrina
Wandering Jew (Inch Plant)

Z. purpusii
Bronze Inch Plant

Callisia

underside purple

C. elegans
Striped Inch Plant

Cyanotis

fleshy leaves covered with hair

underside purple

C. kewensis
Teddy Bear Vine

Setcreasea

downy leaves purple in bright light

S. purpurea
Purple Heart

Siderasis

leaves covered with brown hair

underside red

S. fuscata
Brown Spiderwort

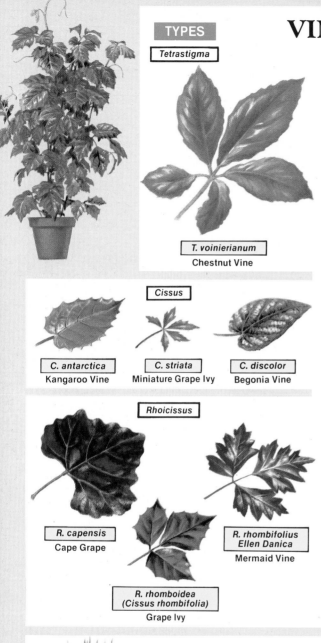

VINES

Tetrastigma

T. voinierianum
Chestnut Vine

Many climbers are commonly referred to as 'vines' but the true vines are all members of the Grape family. They cling to supports by means of tendrils and two of them (Grape Ivy and Kangaroo Vine) are extremely popular and easy to grow.

The most important use of the popular vines is to clothe poles, screens and trellis work. Chestnut Vine is useful for covering large areas, Vines can also be employed for hanging baskets and as ground cover. The general requirement is for semi-shade or good light (without direct sunshine), cool conditions and occasional misting; but individual requirements vary. At one end of the scale Grape Ivy is one of the most tolerant of all house plants, surviving sun or shade, hot or cold air, dry or moist surroundings. Kangaroo Vine is a little less tolerant, suffering in bright sun and in hot, stuffy rooms. At the other end of the scale Cissus discolor is a delicate plant needing warmth and constant moisture around the leaves. All vines need good drainage; pinch out stem tips to induce bushy growth.

Cissus

C. antarctica
Kangaroo Vine

C. striata
Miniature Grape Ivy

C. discolor
Begonia Vine

Rhoicissus

R. capensis
Cape Grape

R. rhombifolius Ellen Danica
Mermaid Vine

R. rhomboidea (Cissus rhombifolia)
Grape Ivy

SECRETS OF SUCCESS

Temperature: Cool or average warmth; not less than 45° – 55°F in winter (Cissus discolor – 60°F).

Light: Brightly lit spot away from direct sunlight. Semi-shade for Cissus discolor and C. capensis.

Water: Water liberally from spring to autumn; sparingly in winter.

Air Humidity: Mist leaves occasionally.

Repotting: Repot, when necessary, in spring.

Propagation. Stem cuttings in spring or summer; use Bio Roota.

SPECIAL PROBLEMS

GLASSY BLOTCHES ON LEAVES WHICH LATER FALL
Cause: Direct sunlight; move plant away from the window.

LEAF TIPS BROWN & SHRIVELLED
Cause: Air too dry; mist leaves occasionally. If other symptoms (wilting, rotting, leaf fall) are present, the cause is overwatering.

SPOTTED & CURLED LOWER LEAVES WHICH LATER FALL
Cause: Underwatering. Compost must not be allowed to dry out.

MILDEW ON LEAVES
Cause: Poor drainage. Remove diseased leaves, spray with Benlate and repot into a container with adequate drainage. Improve ventilation.

YUCCA

Y. elephantipes
Spineless Yucca

A mature Yucca bears a crown of sword-like leaves on top of a stout trunk — a fine false palm for a hallway or large room. Choose the Spineless Yucca rather than the more popular but sharp-pointed Spanish Bayonet (Y. aloifolia). A large Yucca is expensive and should be treated properly. It will need a deep, well-drained container which can be moved outdoors in summer. In winter it will need an unheated and well-lit spot. At all times it should be kept in a sunny spot when indoors. White bell-shaped flowers may appear after a number of years.

SECRETS OF SUCCESS

Temperature: Average warmth; keep cool in winter (minimum 45°F).

Light: Provide as much light as possible, a south-facing windowsill is ideal.

Water: Water liberally from spring to autumn; sparingly in winter.

Air Humidity: Misting is not necessary.

Repotting: Repot every 2 years in spring.

Propagation: Remove and pot up offsets growing at the base.

CHAPTER 3

FLOWERING HOUSE PLANTS

Flowers play an important role in the display of indoor plants. As the outdoor garden seems to come alive when the flower buds open in spring, so the indoor display takes on a new look when plants in bloom are added.

Flowering house plants are grown primarily for their floral effect, although a few·(Nertera, Duchesnea, Citrus etc.) are grown for their display of fruits. The choice seems almost limitless – for flower size you can grow a spectacular Bird of Paradise with 6 in. blooms or even a Stapelia gigantea with flowers the size of a dinner plate; at the other end of the scale you can pick Heliotrope,

with its tiny blossoms clustered together in order to be seen.

Take your choice of flowering season – Pink Jasmine and Kalanchoe in winter, Spathiphyllum and Anthurium in spring, Hibiscus and Campanula in summer or Heliotrope and Oleander in autumn. In some cases the flowering season is fleeting but with Busy Lizzie, African Violet, Brunfelsia and Beloperone it is possible with care to have flowers nearly all year round. You can even take your choice of fragrance, ranging from the strong, heady perfumes of Heliotrope, Oleander, Gardenia and Jasmine to the unpleasant stench of the Carrion Flower.

The flowering house plants come in many sizes, shapes and smells but with each of them there comes a time when it is no longer in flower. In most cases the plant is not particularly attractive at this stage, and is perhaps best grown in a Pot Group or Indoor Garden. Some varieties, however, have leaves which are so striking that they are worth growing for their foliage alone; good examples are Aphelandra, the Bromeliads, the Fancy-leaved Geraniums, Sanchezia and Sparmannia.

There are few general rules on cultivation – the plants range from the extremely difficult Acalypha to the cast-iron Beloperone, so look through the following A–Z guide for the specific needs of your plant. You will find that flowering house plants nearly always need more light than foliage ones.

ACACIA

Several Acacias are suitable for growing indoors but they have never been popular. The one most frequently seen is the Kangaroo Thorn, a shrubby plant reaching about 3 ft high which, in early spring, bears small yellow flower heads among the dark green, spiny 'leaves'. Cut back straggly or unwanted growth once flowering has finished. Kangaroo Thorn is a robust plant which is trouble-free provided you keep it in an unheated, well-lit spot in winter and take care not to overwater. If you can, place the pot outside once summer arrives and bring it back indoors in September.

A. armata
Kangaroo Thorn

SECRETS OF SUCCESS

Temperature: Average warmth; keep cool in winter (minimum temperature 40°F).

Light: Provide as much light as possible.

Water: Water moderately from spring to autumn; sparingly in winter.

Air Humidity: Misting not necessary.

Repotting: Repot every 2 – 3 years after flowering.

Propagation: Stem cuttings in summer. Use Bio Roota.

ACALYPHA

Red-hot Catstail is an apt name for the most popular Acalypha—the brightly-coloured flower spikes hang like long tassels from the stems during summer or autumn. Unfortunately this attractive plant is more suited to the greenhouse than to the living room as it requires constantly moist air. In a dry atmosphere leaf fall will occur and red spider mite will flourish. Prune old plants in the spring and remove dead tassels. Take cuttings each year; root them in a warm place and flowering can be expected when the plants are about one year old.

SECRETS OF SUCCESS

Temperature: Keep the shrub warm; 65° – 75°F during the day, minimum 60°F at night.

Light: Slight shade is best — avoid sun in spring and summer.

Water: Keep the compost moist at all times.

Air Humidity: Moist air is vital. Surround pot with damp peat and mist leaves frequently.

Repotting: Repot every year in spring.

Propagation: Stem cuttings in spring. Use Bio Roota and bottom heat.

A. hispida
**Red-hot Catstail
(Chenille Plant)**

AESCHYNANTHUS

The best way to display the trailing stems of Aeschynanthus is in a hanging basket or suspended pot. The most popular variety has a characteristic flower form and a descriptive common name — the Lipstick Vine. The stems bear glossy, pointed leaves which are soft and grey when young. At the tips of these stems scarlet flowers emerge from brown 'lipstick cases' between late spring and midsummer.

Lipstick Vine is not easy to grow under ordinary room conditions. Misting is essential in spring and summer, and in winter the plant must be allowed to rest with a temperature of about 60°F and infrequent watering. Keep it in a well-lit spot and cut back the stems immediately after flowering if pruning is necessary.

A. lobbianus
Lipstick Vine

SECRETS OF SUCCESS

Temperature: Average warmth; not less than 55°F.

Light: Bright light or slight shade; avoid direct sunshine.

Water: Water regularly from spring to autumn; sparingly in winter. Use tepid water.

Air Humidity: Moist air is necessary. Mist the leaves frequently, especially in hot weather.

Repotting: Repot every 2 – 3 years in spring.

Propagation: Stem cuttings in spring or summer. Use Bio Roota and bottom heat.

AGAPANTHUS

You will need space and a sunny position for the attractive Blue African Lily. Large round heads of blue tubular flowers are borne on tall stalks which appear in succession throughout the summer from the rosette of long strap-like leaves. There is no difficulty in growing this showy specimen plant as long as you can move it to a cold but frost-free room in winter. There it will need very little water until April, when it should be brought back to its well-lit spot and started into growth by watering and feeding. Frequent watering will be necessary during the flowering season.

Grow Agapanthus in a tub or large pot, and do not repot until the container is overcrowded as this plant blooms best when it is pot-bound.

A. africanus
Blue African Lily

SECRETS OF SUCCESS

Temperature: Average warmth; keep cool in winter (night temperature 40° – 45°F).

Light: Choose sunniest spot available.

Water: Keep compost moist at all times during the growing season; give very little water between November and early April.

Air Humidity: Misting is not necessary.

Repotting: Not required until division takes place.

Propagation: Divide plants in spring every 4 – 5 years.

ANTHURIUM

The exotic flowers of Anthurium have a distinct air of luxury — large waxy 'palettes' each with a coloured 'tail' at its centre. The flowering season extends over many months and each bloom lasts for many weeks. Unfortunately Anthuriums are not easy to grow, but A. scherzerianum (Flamingo Flower) is reasonably tolerant of ordinary room conditions. The leaves are spear-shaped, the tail is coiled and the flowers appear from February to July. The much larger Painter's Palette is more difficult to grow. Its leaves are heart-shaped and the tail is usually straight.

A. scherzerianum
Flamingo Flower

A. andreanum
Painter's Palette

SECRETS OF SUCCESS

Temperature: Average warmth; minimum temperature 60°F in winter.
Light: Bright in winter; protect from summer sun.
Water: Give a little water every few days to keep the compost moist at all times but never water-logged. Use soft, tepid water.
Air Humidity: Mist leaves very frequently.
Repotting: Repot when necessary in spring.
Propagation: Divide plants at repotting time.

SPECIAL PROBLEMS

BROWN LEAF TIPS, CURLED FOLIAGE, NO FLOWERS
Cause: Air humidity too low. Surround the pot with moist peat; mist leaves regularly.

YELLOW LEAF EDGES
Cause: Cold air is the usual cause, but this condition is also a symptom of dry air.

APHELANDRA

A well-grown Aphelandra makes a splendid double-purpose plant — for about six weeks it is a showy flowering plant with yellow cone-like blooms; for the rest of the year it is an attractive foliage plant with large white-veined leaves. A. squarrosa louisae is the most popular; A. squarrosa Dania is more compact and A. squarrosa Brockfeld has the most attractive foliage.

The fate of nearly all Zebra Plants is to become leggy and leafless. The way to avoid this is to feed regularly, never allow the compost to dry out, mist regularly and keep warm in winter. Remove dead blooms after flowering.

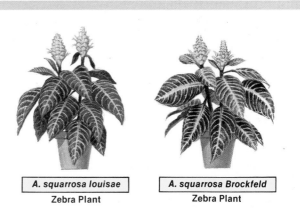

A. squarrosa louisae
Zebra Plant

A. squarrosa Brockfeld
Zebra Plant

SECRETS OF SUCCESS

Temperature: Average warmth; minimum temperature 55°F in winter.
Light: Brightly lit spot away from direct sun in summer.
Water: Keep compost moist at all times but never waterlogged. Reduce watering in winter. Use soft, tepid water.
Air Humidity: Mist leaves frequently.
Repotting: Repot every year in spring.
Propagation: Stem cuttings in spring. Bio Roota and warmth are necessary.

SPECIAL PROBLEMS

LOSS OF LEAVES
Cause: Most likely reason is dryness at the roots; even a short period of drying out can cause serious leaf loss. Cold air is another common cause of defoliation. Other possibilities are too much sun or draughts.

BROWN LEAF TIPS
Cause: Air humidity too low. Surround the pot with moist peat; mist leaves regularly.

ARDISIA

The glossy leathery leaves make this slow-growing shrub an attractive foliage plant, but its main feature is the presence of red berries at Christmas. These berries follow the tiny fragrant flowers which appear in summer and they stay on the plant for many months. The Coral Berry should be kept cool in winter and away from draughts at all times. Never let the compost dry out and prune back the shoots in early spring. Not many house plant suppliers offer Ardisia as it is so slow to grow.

SECRETS OF SUCCESS

Temperature: Average warmth; minimum temperature 45°F in winter.
Light: Brightly lit spot away from direct sun.
Water: Keep compost moist at all times but never waterlogged. Reduce watering in winter.
Air Humidity: Mist leaves frequently with tepid water.
Repotting: Repot when necessary in spring.
Propagation: Stem cuttings in spring or summer. Sow seeds in early spring.

A. crispa
Coral Berry

BEGONIA

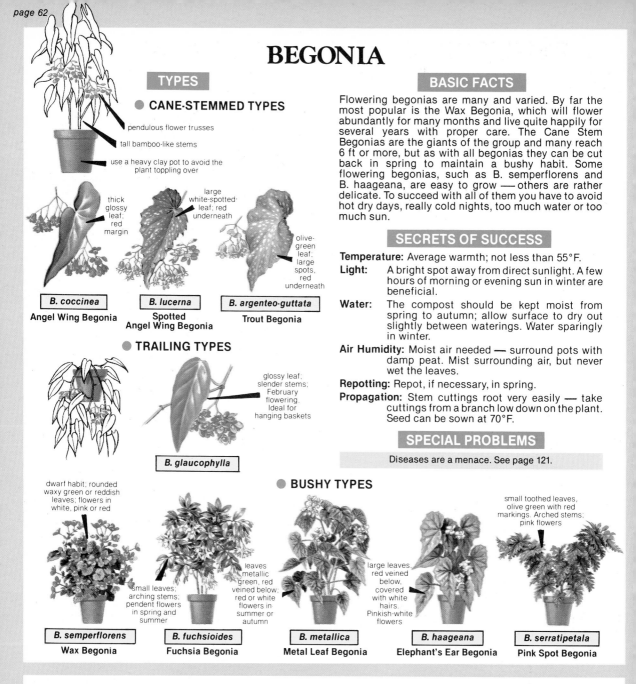

TYPES

● CANE-STEMMED TYPES

pendulous flower trusses

tall bamboo-like stems

use a heavy clay pot to avoid the plant toppling over

thick glossy leaf; red margin

large white-spotted leaf; red underneath

olive-green leaf; large spots, red underneath

B. coccinea
Angel Wing Begonia

B. lucerna
Spotted Angel Wing Begonia

B. argenteo-guttata
Trout Begonia

● TRAILING TYPES

glossy leaf; slender stems; February flowering. Ideal for hanging baskets

B. glaucophylla

● BUSHY TYPES

dwarf habit; rounded waxy green or reddish leaves; flowers in white, pink or red

small leaves; arching stems; pendent flowers in spring and summer

leaves metallic green, red veined below; red or white flowers in summer or autumn

large leaves, red veined below, covered with white hairs. Pinkish-white flowers

small toothed leaves, olive green with red markings. Arched stems; pink flowers

B. semperflorens
Wax Begonia

B. fuchsioides
Fuchsia Begonia

B. metallica
Metal Leaf Begonia

B. haageana
Elephant's Ear Begonia

B. serratipetala
Pink Spot Begonia

BASIC FACTS

Flowering begonias are many and varied. By far the most popular is the Wax Begonia, which will flower abundantly for many months and live quite happily for several years with proper care. The Cane Stem Begonias are the giants of the group and many reach 6 ft or more, but as with all begonias they can be cut back in spring to maintain a bushy habit. Some flowering begonias, such as B. semperflorens and B. haageana, are easy to grow — others are rather delicate. To succeed with all of them you have to avoid hot dry days, really cold nights, too much water or too much sun.

SECRETS OF SUCCESS

Temperature: Average warmth; not less than 55°F.

Light: A bright spot away from direct sunlight. A few hours of morning or evening sun in winter are beneficial.

Water: The compost should be kept moist from spring to autumn; allow surface to dry out slightly between waterings. Water sparingly in winter.

Air Humidity: Moist air needed — surround pots with damp peat. Mist surrounding air, but never wet the leaves.

Repotting: Repot, if necessary, in spring.

Propagation: Stem cuttings root very easily — take cuttings from a branch low down on the plant. Seed can be sown at 70°F.

SPECIAL PROBLEMS

Diseases are a menace. See page 121.

BRUNFELSIA

B. calycina
Yesterday, Today and Tomorrow

A slow-growing evergreen shrub with an unusual common name — Yesterday, Today and Tomorrow. It describes the changing flower colours — yesterday's purple, today's pale violet and tomorrow's white. The large fragrant flowers are borne nearly all year round, with just a short winter and early spring break. Brunfelsia can be easy to grow or very difficult, depending on whether you can put it in a room where there will be no sudden and drastic changes in temperature. With care the shrub will grow 2 ft tall, and can be kept compact by light pruning.

SECRETS OF SUCCESS

Temperature: Average warmth; not less than 50°F in winter.

Light: Semi-shade in summer; a well-lit spot in winter with a little direct sunlight.

Water: Water freely from spring to autumn. Water sparingly in winter.

Air Humidity: Mist leaves in summer.

Repotting: Repot, if necessary, in spring.

Propagation: Stem cuttings in summer. Bio Roota and bottom heat are necessary.

BELOPERONE

An easy to grow shrubby plant which bears salmon-coloured, prawn-shaped flower heads at the end of arching stems. The blooms appear nearly all year round, and the simple requirements are warm days, cool nights and a sunny windowsill.

When young, remove some of the first flowers to make sure that a vigorous bush is formed. Cut the plant back to half size each spring to maintain bushiness, and remember to feed regularly.

B. guttata

Shrimp Plant

SECRETS OF SUCCESS

Temperature: Minimum 45°F. Keep cool in winter.

Light: Some direct sun is essential.

Water: Water liberally from spring to late autumn. Water sparingly in winter.

Air Humidity: Mist occasionally.

Repotting: Repot, if necessary, in spring.

Propagation: Stem cuttings root easily.

BOUGAINVILLEA

An extremely showy climbing plant with brightly coloured, papery bracts. It is difficult to grow under ordinary room conditions, as it needs the bright light of a greenhouse. A well-grown plant brought indoors will bloom profusely in spring and summer on the windowsill, after which you have the challenge of trying to make it bloom next season.

Prune the stems in autumn and reduce watering. Keep the plant cool throughout the winter and then increase temperature and watering once spring arrives.

B. glabra

Paper Flower

SECRETS OF SUCCESS

Temperature: Warm in summer; cool (45° – 50°F) in winter.

Light: Choose sunniest spot available.

Water: Keep compost moist in spring and summer; almost dry in winter.

Air Humidity: Mist if room is heated.

Repotting: Repot, if essential, in spring.

Propagation: Stem cuttings in summer. Bio Roota and bottom heat are necessary.

BROMELIADS

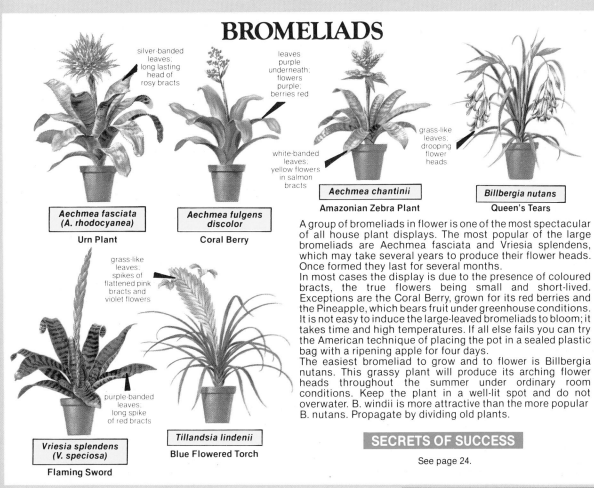

silver-banded leaves; long lasting head of rosy bracts

leaves purple underneath; flowers purple; berries red

white-banded leaves; yellow flowers in salmon bracts

grass-like leaves; drooping flower heads

Aechmea chantinii

Amazonian Zebra Plant

Billbergia nutans

Queen's Tears

Aechmea fasciata (A. rhodocyanea)

Urn Plant

Aechmea fulgens discolor

Coral Berry

grass-like leaves; spikes of flattened pink bracts and violet flowers

purple-banded leaves; long spike of red bracts

Vriesia splendens (V. speciosa)

Flaming Sword

Tillandsia lindenii

Blue Flowered Torch

A group of bromeliads in flower is one of the most spectacular of all house plant displays. The most popular of the large bromeliads are Aechmea fasciata and Vriesia splendens, which may take several years to produce their flower heads. Once formed they last for several months.

In most cases the display is due to the presence of coloured bracts, the true flowers being small and short-lived. Exceptions are the Coral Berry, grown for its red berries and the Pineapple, which bears fruit under greenhouse conditions. It is not easy to induce the large-leaved bromeliads to bloom; it takes time and high temperatures. If all else fails you can try the American technique of placing the pot in a sealed plastic bag with a ripening apple for four days.

The easiest bromeliad to grow and to flower is Billbergia nutans. This grassy plant will produce its arching flower heads throughout the summer under ordinary room conditions. Keep the plant in a well-lit spot and do not overwater. B. windii is more attractive than the more popular B. nutans. Propagate by dividing old plants.

SECRETS OF SUCCESS

See page 24.

FLOWERING HOUSE PLANTS

BOUVARDIA

Bouvardia is an uncommon plant which is well worth growing for the fragrant flowers that appear from midsummer to early winter. The white, pink or red tubular blooms are borne in large clusters above the pointed leaves. The main requirement is for a brightly-lit spot which is cool in winter. Pinch out the tips of young plants to promote bushy growth and cut back the stems once flowering is over. With proper care the shrub will grow about 2 ft high, but even in expert hands it will deteriorate after a few years.

SECRETS OF SUCCESS

Temperature: Average warmth; not less than 50°F in winter.

Light: As much light as possible, but shade from hot summer sun.

Water: Water liberally from spring until flowering stops, then keep the compost fairly dry until March.

Air Humidity: Mist leaves regularly.

Repotting: Repot when necessary in spring.

Propagation: Stem cuttings in spring. Use Bio Roota.

B. domestica
Jasmine Plant

CALLISTEMON

The flowering spikes of this vigorous shrub look like bottle brushes. It is an excellent choice if you want a 'novelty' flowering plant, and it is also a good choice if you want an easy-to-grow plant which blooms in summer. It does not mind dry air; all it needs is a sunny spot, cool conditions in winter and a good soaking in spring and summer whenever the compost begins to dry out. Prune the stems in early spring and if possible stand the pot outdoors in summer.

SECRETS OF SUCCESS

Temperature: Average warmth; not less than 45°F in winter.

Light: As much light as possible, but shade from hot summer sun.

Water: Water liberally from spring to late autumn. Water sparingly in winter.

Air Humidity: Misting is not necessary.

Repotting: Repot when necessary in spring.

Propagation: Stem cuttings in spring. Bio Roota and warmth are necessary.

C. citrinus
Bottlebrush Plant

CAMELLIA

C. japonica
Camellia

A Camellia bush can be a fine specimen plant for early spring — large waxy blooms in white, pink or red set among glossy, dark green leaves. It is a waste of time and money, however, to try to grow this temperamental shrub if the conditions are not right. The room must be cool and airy with an autumn to spring temperature of not more than 60°F. Buds appear in profusion in early spring, but they will rapidly drop if the plant is moved or if there is a sudden change in temperature or soil moisture. If you can, stand the pot outdoors in the garden once flowering has finished and bring it back indoors in autumn. May is the correct time for light pruning and repotting.

SECRETS OF SUCCESS

Temperature: Cool; room temperature should be in the 45°–60°F range.

Light: Bright light is necessary, but avoid direct sun in summer.

Water: Keep compost moist at all times but never waterlogged. Use soft water.

Air Humidity: Mist leaves frequently.

Repotting: Repot when necessary in spring. Do not repot until the plant obviously needs a larger container.

Propagation: Stem cuttings in summer. Bio Roota and warmth are necessary.

CAMPANULA

C. isophylla
**Italian Bellflower
(Star of Bethlehem)**

The Italian Bellflower is an old favourite, grown for generations before the house plant boom began. It remains one of the best of all summer-flowering trailing plants, its long grey-green stems bearing a profusion of star-shaped flowers throughout the summer. The white variety is the most popular and easiest to grow; blue and lilac varieties are also available. There are a few rules to remember — bright and cool conditions are necessary and after flowering the stems should be cut back. Keep the plant fairly dry and at about 45°–50°F during the winter rest period. New plants are easily raised from cuttings; remove stem tips from young plants to induce bushy growth.

SECRETS OF SUCCESS

Temperature: Cool or average warmth; not less than 45°F in winter.

Light: Brightly lit spot, but shade from direct sun in summer.

Water: Keep compost moist at all times; reduce watering in winter.

Air Humidity: Mist the leaves occasionally.

Repotting: Repot every year in spring.

Propagation: Stem cuttings in spring. Alternatively divide plants at repotting time or sow seeds in spring.

CARISSA

The Natal Plum is one of the few indoor shrubs to bear edible fruit. White, fragrant flowers open in early summer and these large blooms are followed by plum-like fruits. There are drawbacks — the stems bear spines and the sprawling nature of this tall bush makes it more suitable for the conservatory than the ordinary room. Apart from its need for winter warmth there are no difficulties. It requires fresh air on hot days and stem tips should be pruned to maintain bushy growth.

SECRETS OF SUCCESS

Temperature: Average warmth; not less than 55°F in winter.
Light: Brightly lit spot with some direct sunshine. Shade from summer noonday sun.
Water: Keep compost moist at all times; reduce watering in winter.
Air Humidity: Misting not necessary; wash leaves occasionally.
Repotting: Repot when necessary in spring.
Propagation: Stem cuttings in summer.

C. grandiflora
Natal Plum

CESTRUM

The Jessamines are more suited to the conservatory than to the living room as their tall, weak stems require support. Despite their size the Night Jessamines (C. nocturnum and C. parqui) are increasing in popularity as house plants in the U.S. as they can fill a room with the intense fragrance of their white tubular flowers. The most compact variety is C. aurantiacum which bears orange flowers in summer. Jessamines are rarities in British homes — the only one you are likely to find is C. elegans which bears pendent clusters of red flowers.

SECRETS OF SUCCESS

Temperature: Average warmth; not less than 45°F in winter.
Light: Brightly lit spot; protect from summer sun.
Water: Keep compost moist at all times; reduce watering in winter.
Air Humidity: Mist occasionally.
Repotting: Repot when necessary in spring.
Propagation: Stem cuttings in spring; Bio Roota and warmth are necessary.

C. nocturnum
Night Jessamine

CITRUS

There is an obvious fascination in having an orange or lemon tree at home. Pips will produce plants but if you want fruit on an attractive bush then you will have to pick a variety selected for indoor cultivation. Choose from C. sinensis, C. limon ponderosa or C. reticulata. In most cases the shrubs will not bear fruit until they are too large for an ordinary room, which explains the popularity of the Calamondin Orange. This small bush produces white fragrant flowers and small bitter oranges nearly all year round. The requirements are good drainage, careful watering, ample feeding, full sun, summer spent outdoors and cool conditions in winter.

SECRETS OF SUCCESS

Temperature: Average warmth; not less than 50°F in winter.
Light: Choose the sunniest spot available.
Water: Water moderately all year round; allow surface to become dry between waterings.
Air Humidity: Mist occasionally, especially when flower buds are opening.
Repotting: Repot when necessary in spring.
Propagation: Stem cuttings in spring; Bio Roota and warmth are necessary. Alternatively, sow pips in spring.

C. mitis
Calamondin Orange

CLERODENDRUM

The Glory Bower is usually regarded as a greenhouse plant, its tall climbing stems reaching 8 ft or more. By pruning back the stems in winter, however, it can be trained as a compact bush or hanging basket plant for home display. The clusters of red-tipped white flowers appear in summer among the dark green heart-shaped leaves. It is not an easy plant to grow — in summer it requires high air humidity, good light and warmth, but in winter it must be given a time of rest with infrequent watering and cool conditions (55°–60°F). Some of the leaves will fall during this winter rest period.

SECRETS OF SUCCESS

Temperature: Warm or average warmth; keep cool in winter. Minimum temperature 55°F.
Light: Brightly lit spot away from direct sunlight.
Water: Keep compost moist at all times throughout spring and summer; water very sparingly in winter.
Air Humidity: Mist leaves frequently.
Repotting: Repot every year in spring.
Propagation: Stem cuttings in spring; Bio Roota and warmth are necessary.

C. thomsonae
Glory Bower
(Bleeding Heart Vine)

CLIANTHUS

Lobster Claw is one of the common names given to Clianthus — an apt description of the large claw-like red flowers which are borne in clusters in late spring or summer. The foliage is feathery and cultivation is not difficult. Prune and train the stems once flowering is over and in summer provide adequate ventilation. Two types are available — the low-growing C. formosus (Glory Pea) is short-lived and is best treated as an annual; the tall-growing C. puniceus (Parrot Bill) can be kept as a room plant but is best grown in the conservatory.

SECRETS OF SUCCESS

Temperature: Average warmth; keep cool (50°-55°F) in winter.

Light: Keep in full sun.

Water: Water liberally from spring to autumn; let compost dry out slightly between waterings. Water sparingly in winter.

Air Humidity: Mist leaves occasionally on hot days.

Repotting: Repot when necessary in spring.

Propagation: Sow seeds in warm conditions in spring. Take Parrot Bill stem cuttings in summer.

C. formosus
Glory Pea

CLIVIA

The Kaffir Lily is an old favourite — ten to twenty red or orange flowers are borne in spring on top of a tall stalk arising from the rosette of long strap-like leaves. This plant has an undeserved reputation for being easy to grow; it will fail to bloom year after year if it is left in a heated room in winter or if the watering rules are not followed. In fact, it has special needs. It needs space. It needs winter rest — an unheated room, no fertilizer and just enough water to prevent wilting. And it needs to be undisturbed — don't move the pot when in bud or flower and don't repot unless the plant is pushing out of the container.

SECRETS OF SUCCESS

Temperature: Cool or average warmth; keep cool (40°-50°F) in winter.

Light: Bright light; avoid direct sun in summer.

Water: Water moderately from spring to autumn. Water sparingly from late autumn to early spring until flower stalk is 4-6 in. high.

Air Humidity: Sponge leaves occasionally.

Repotting: Repot after flowering only when necessary.

Propagation: Divide at repotting time.

C. miniata
Kaffir Lily

COLUMNEA

Columnea is one of the most colourful of all the hanging basket plants which bloom in winter or early spring. Success is not easy — it depends on maintaining sufficient moisture around the leaves; constant misting is usually the only answer. Another requirement is careful winter watering plus cool (less than 60°F) winter nights. Cut back stems as soon as flowering has finished. There are many varieties which with proper care will bear abundant yellow, orange or red tubular flowers year after year. One of the easiest to grow is C. banksii, which has waxy leaves. C. gloriosa has hairy leaves and red flowers with yellow throats.

C. banksii
Goldfish Plant

SECRETS OF SUCCESS

Temperature: Average warmth; not less than 50°F in winter.

Light: Bright light, away from direct sunlight.

Water: Keep compost moist at all times during growing season. Water sparingly in winter.

Air Humidity: Mist leaves frequently. If possible surround pot with damp peat.

Repotting: Repot every 2 years in late spring.

Propagation: Stem cuttings taken after flowering. Bio Roota and warmth are necessary.

C. gloriosa
Goldfish Plant

CROSSANDRA

C. undulifolia
Firecracker Flower

The Firecracker Flower is a small slow-growing plant with two special advantages. It starts to flower when seedlings are only a few months old and the flowering season lasts from spring to autumn. The tubular orange flowers are borne on top of green flowering spikes which are about 4 in. high. The glossy leaves make this an attractive plant all year round. The distinct disadvantage of the Firecracker Flower is its need for moist air — it will probably not survive unless it is frequently misted and surrounded by other plants. Alternatively it can be grown on a tray of wet pebbles (see page 15). Remove dead flowers to prolong the flowering season.

SECRETS OF SUCCESS

Temperature: Average warmth; not less than 55°F in winter.

Light: Bright light; avoid direct sun in summer.

Water: Keep compost moist at all times; reduce watering in winter.

Air Humidity: Mist leaves frequently. If possible surround pot with damp peat.

Repotting: Repot in spring before flowering. Only repot if it is necessary.

Propagation: Stem cuttings in summer; Bio Roota and warmth are necessary. Sow seeds in spring.

CUPHEA

A pretty plant, rather than a spectacular one. It can be used to add colour and variety to a mixed display, but the Cigar Plant is not bold enough to serve as a specimen plant. It grows quickly, reaching its adult height of 12 in. in a single season. Cigar-shaped flowers with ash-grey tips are borne in profusion among the narrow leaves in summer. Overwinter the plant in a cool room and water sparingly. Cut back the stems in early spring as growth tends to become straggly with age. For maximum display raise new plants each spring.

SECRETS OF SUCCESS

Temperature: Average warmth; not less than 45°F in winter.

Light: A well-lit spot; some direct sunlight is beneficial.

Water: Keep moist at all times; reduce watering in winter.

Air Humidity: Misting is not necessary.

Repotting: Repot in spring. Only repot if it is necessary.

Propagation: Stem cuttings in spring or summer. Sow seeds in spring.

C. ignea
Cigar Plant

DIPLADENIA

Dipladenia is grown for its large petunia-like flowers which appear during the summer months on the twining stems. It can be grown as a climber, reaching 10 ft or more, or it can be pruned back severely once flowering is finished in order to maintain it as a bush. The pink blossoms will appear on plants while they are still small, and the glossy leaves make it an attractive climber all year round. But Dipladenia has never become really popular because of its need for high air humidity and warm surroundings, especially in spring.

SECRETS OF SUCCESS

Temperature: Warm; not less than 55°F in winter.

Light: Bright light or semi-shade; not direct sun.

Water: Water regularly from spring to autumn; sparingly in winter.

Air Humidity: Mist regularly, especially when in bud or flower.

Repotting: Repot every year in spring.

Propagation: Stem cuttings in spring; Bio Roota and warmth are necessary.

**D. sanderi
(Mandevilla splendens)**
Pink Allamanda

DUCHESNEA

There has been a rapid increase in the popularity of hanging plants in recent years. Some excellent trailers, however, still remain rarities and the Indian Strawberry is a good example. It is a vigorous grower, quite hardy and easy to care for — it will quite happily spend the winter in an unheated room. Between June and October bright yellow flowers appear and these are followed by small strawberry-like fruits. These are edible, but unfortunately they are completely tasteless. True strawberries can be grown indoors, making up for their lack of year-round attractiveness by bearing edible fruit in summer or autumn.

SECRETS OF SUCCESS

Temperature: Cool or average warmth; keep cool but frost-free in winter.

Light: Bright light or semi-shade; not direct sun.

Water: Keep compost moist at all times; water sparingly in winter.

Air Humidity: Mist leaves occasionally.

Repotting: Repot every year in spring.

Propagation: Divide when repotting; Layer runners in spring.

**D. indica
(Fragaria indica)**
Indian Strawberry

EPISCIA

E. dianthiflora
Lace Flower

Episcia is an attractive trailing plant which has never enjoyed the popularity of its well-known relative, the African Violet. Because it requires high air humidity it is often difficult to grow as an isolated specimen plant or in a hanging basket, but it makes an excellent ground cover between taller plants. There are two types — the Flame Violet with orange flowers and silver-veined coppery leaves and the delicate Lace Flower with white frilled flowers and velvety leaves. Both bloom throughout the summer and the runners root in surrounding compost, forming plantlets for propagation. Shorten stems after flowering.

SECRETS OF SUCCESS

Temperature: Average warmth; not less than 55°F in winter.

Light: Bright light, away from direct sunlight in summer.

Water: Keep compost moist at all times during growing season. Reduce watering in winter.

Air Humidity: Mist leaves frequently. If possible surround pot with damp peat.

Repotting: Repot every year in spring.

Propagation: Layer runners in spring or summer (see page 114).

E. cupreata
Flame Violet

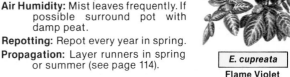

EUPHORBIA

E. fulgens
Scarlet Plume

The Crown of Thorns is an old favourite, but it still remains an excellent and undemanding choice for a sunny window. It does not need misting, will withstand some neglect and does not have to be moved to an unheated room in winter. The thick stems are armed with long spines and the upper part of this sprawling plant is studded with flowers from early spring until midsummer. Leaves may drop in winter but new leaf buds will appear within a month or two. Scarlet Plume is much less common and its growth habit is quite different. Long arching branches bear willow-like leaves, and in winter scarlet flowers appear. Keep cool and rather dry for a month or two after flowering.

SECRETS OF SUCCESS

Temperature: Average warmth; not less than 55°F in winter.

Light: As much light as possible, but shade from hot summer sun.

Water: Water moderately from spring to autumn; sparingly in winter. Let soil surface dry between waterings.

Air Humidity: Mist E. fulgens occasionally in spring and summer.

Repotting: Repot every 2 years in spring.

Propagation: Stem cuttings in spring or summer. Let milky sap dry before placing in compost. Note — E. milii splendens sap is poisonous.

E. milii splendens
Crown of Thorns

GARDENIA

G. jasminoides
Cape Jasmine

The Gardenia can be a delight indoors. In spring the large, waxy white flowers appear and the surrounding air is filled with fragrance. For the rest of the year the glossy, dark green leaves make the bush an attractive foliage plant. Sadly the Gardenia is more often a disappointment than a delight, because it is extremely temperamental. For flower buds to form a night temperature of 60°–65°F is required, and the day temperature should be about 10°F higher. An even temperature and careful watering are needed to prevent the buds dropping off, and soft water must be used to prevent the foliage turning yellow.

SECRETS OF SUCCESS

Temperature: Average warmth; not less than 60°F in winter.

Light: Bright light is essential, but avoid direct midday sun in summer.

Water: Keep moist at all times; reduce watering in winter. Use soft, tepid water.

Air Humidity: Mist leaves frequently.

Repotting: Repot every 2–3 years in spring.

Propagation: Stem cuttings in spring. Bio Roota and warmth are necessary.

HELIOTROPIUM

Heliotrope is a good choice if you are looking for an easy-to-grow flowering plant with a strong fragrance. The tiny flowers are borne in large heads in summer and autumn, and hybrid varieties are available in white and lavender as well as the familiar purple shades. The leaves are dull green and prominently veined, and the plant can be trained as a standard (see page 86 for instructions). Heliotrope can be kept for years as a house plant but the ability to produce attractive flower heads rapidly deteriorates with age, so raise new cuttings each year.

SECRETS OF SUCCESS

Temperature: Cool or average warmth; keep at 40°–50°F in winter.

Light: As much light as possible, but shade from hot summer sun.

Water: Keep moist at all times; reduce watering in winter.

Air Humidity: Mist occasionally.

Repotting: Repot every year in spring.

Propagation: Stem cuttings in summer; use Bio Roota. Sow seeds in spring.

H. hybrida
Heliotrope

HYPOESTES

H. sanguinolenta (Freckle Face) is grown for its pink-spotted foliage — see page 40. A close relative, H. taeniata, is grown for its floral display. In late autumn and early winter this shrubby species bears large clusters of purplish-pink tubular flowers, each cluster being carried on a tall stalk above the plain green foliage. H. taeniata is a rarity, and you will have to go to a specialist supplier of greenhouse plants for a specimen. It requires a warm, well-lit spot and the stem tips should be pinched out in spring to keep the plant bushy.

SECRETS OF SUCCESS

Temperature: Warm or average warmth; not less than 55°F in winter.

Light: Bright light; protect from hot summer sun.

Water: Keep soil evenly moist. Water liberally from spring to autumn; more sparingly in winter.

Air Humidity: Mist leaves frequently.

Repotting: Repot annually in spring.

Propagation: Stem cuttings in spring. Bio Roota and warmth are necessary.

H. taeniata

HIBISCUS

Hibiscus is becoming increasingly popular as a specimen plant for the sunny windowsill. Its large papery flowers last for only a day or two, but with proper care there will be a continuous succession of blooms from spring to autumn. White, yellow, orange, pink and red varieties are available and there are both single and double forms. A Hibiscus bush can live for 20 years or more, and may be kept small by regular pruning. In a large tub it will reach 5-6 ft and can also be trained as a standard (see page 86). It is not a difficult plant to grow — provide good light, plenty of water and food when in flower, mild conditions in winter (55°-60°F) and prune back stems in February to induce bushiness.

H. rosa-sinensis
Rose of China

H. rosa-sinensis Cooperi
Variegated Rose of China

SECRETS OF SUCCESS

Temperature: Average warmth; not less than 55°F in winter.
Light: As much light as possible, but shade from hot summer sun.
Water: Keep moist at all times; frequent watering will be necessary in summer. Reduce watering in winter.
Air Humidity: Mist leaves occasionally.
Repotting: Repot every year in spring.
Propagation: Stem cuttings in late spring.

SPECIAL PROBLEMS

BUD DROP
Cause: Dry compost is the usual reason. Other causes are underfeeding or a sudden change in temperature or location.

CURLING OF LEAVES
Cause: Air too dry. Mist leaves in spring and summer.

LOSS OF LEAVES
Cause: Dry compost is the usual reason. Other possibilities are draughts and overwatering.

INSECTS
Aphid and red spider mite can be a problem; see page 120.

HOYA

single flower

The Wax Plant (H. carnosa) is a popular and easy-to-grow flowering climber. Its vigorous twining stems can reach 15 ft or more, and they must be trained on wires, trellis work or on a moss stick. New stems are bare; the leaves which later appear are fleshy and green, or green-and-white on the Variegated Wax Plant. The main attraction is the umbrella-like head of waxy star-shaped flowers; these fragrant heads appear between late spring and early autumn. The Miniature Wax Plant (H. bella) is more difficult to grow, needing more heat and humidity but less light; it is best planted in a hanging basket. There are several 'do nots' for growing Hoyas — do not disturb the plant once buds appear, do not remove the dead flowers and do not repot until it is unavoidable.

H. bella
Miniature Wax Plant

SECRETS OF SUCCESS

Temperature: Average warmth; keep at 50°-55°F in winter.
Light: Bright light; some direct sun is beneficial but protect from midday summer sunlight.
Water: Water liberally from spring to autumn; sparingly in winter. Allow surface to dry out slightly between waterings.
Air Humidity: Mist regularly, but not when plant is in bloom.
Repotting: Repot, when necessary, in spring.
Propagation: Stem cuttings, using mature shoots, in spring.

single flower

H. carnosa
Wax Plant

HYPOCYRTA

The Clog Plant blooms in spring and summer, producing large numbers of orange flowers which look like tiny goldfish. When not in bloom it is an attractive foliage plant with shiny, dark green succulent leaves. It is often used for planting in mixed arrangements or bottle gardens, and its arching stems make it a good subject for a hanging basket. In the growing season the main needs of the Clog Plant are careful watering and frequent misting; in winter place the plant in a cool, sunlit spot and cut the stems back to encourage flowering growth next spring.

SECRETS OF SUCCESS

Temperature: Average warmth; not less than 50°F in winter.
Light: Bright or light shade; some direct sun in winter.
Water: Water moderately from spring to autumn; sparingly in winter.
Air Humidity: Mist leaves regularly.
Repotting: Repot every 2 years in spring.
Propagation: Stem cuttings in spring or summer.

H. glabra
Clog Plant

IMPATIENS

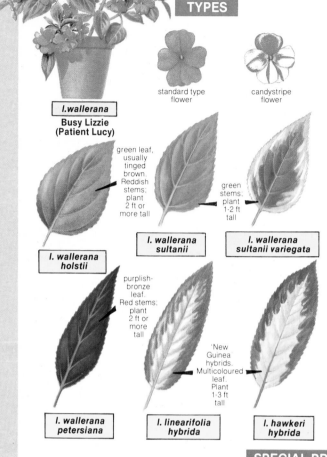

TYPES

standard type flower

candystripe flower

I.wallerana
Busy Lizzie
(Patient Lucy)

green leaf, usually tinged brown. Reddish stems; plant 2 ft or more tall

green stems; plant 1-2 ft tall

I. wallerana holstii

I. wallerana sultanii

I. wallerana sultanii variegata

purplish-bronze leaf. Red stems; plant 2 ft or more tall

'New Guinea hybrids. Multicoloured leaf. Plant 1-3 ft tall

I. wallerana petersiana

I. linearifolia hybrida

I. hawkeri hybrida

There is a Busy Lizzie in about one quarter of Britain's households. Some of these plants have been bought, but many more have been raised at home from cuttings which root very easily at any time of the year. The basic type, I. wallerana, has been extremely popular for generations because, with proper care, it will bear its 1–2 in. flowers almost all year round.

Breeders and plant hunters have introduced many new varieties in recent years. Most of the Busy Lizzies sold today are small, compact hybrids with flowers in white, orange, pink, purple or red. Even more exciting are the 'New Guinea' varieties with multicoloured leaves.

Busy Lizzies are not difficult to grow but they do need regular care. Pinch out the tips of young plants several times to ensure bushy plants; prune mature plants each spring. The stems are succulent and brittle; tall plants may require staking. Feed regularly during the growing season and provide ventilation on hot days. Above all, remember to water frequently in summer.

SECRETS OF SUCCESS

Temperature: Average warmth; not less than 55°F in winter. Keep at 60°F or more to ensure flowering during winter.

Light: Bright light is necessary, but avoid direct sunlight in summer. A few hours of sun are necessary in winter if the plant is to continue flowering.

Water: Keep the compost moist at all times — daily watering may be necessary in summer. Reduce water in winter.

Air Humidity: Mist leaves occasionally, but avoid open blooms.

Repotting: Pot must be filled with roots before the plant will flower freely. Repot, only when necessary, in spring.

Propagation: Sow seeds in spring. Stem cuttings root readily at any time of the year.

SPECIAL PROBLEMS

LOSS OF LEAVES
Cause: Usual reason for sudden leaf fall is prolonged exposure to low temperatures. Irregular watering and severe insect attack are other common causes.

LEAVES WILTED
Cause: Underwatering. Wilting can occur the day after watering in summer. Frequent watering is the only answer — do not keep the plant standing in a saucer of water.

POOR FLOWERING
Cause: Many possibilities — the five most common causes are too little light, too little food, too much food, too cold or repotting too early.

INSECTS
Red spider mite is a menace in hot, dry weather; leaves become bronzed and mottled. Both aphid and whitefly can be a serious nuisance, disfiguring and weakening the plant. See Chapter 9 for methods of insect control.

SPINDLY GROWTH
Cause: Too much warmth coupled with too little light will certainly produce this condition, but some older varieties soon become lanky with age even when well grown. Choose a modern compact hybrid; take cuttings and discard old plants.

NO FLOWERS
Cause: Repotting is the usual reason why a mature plant fails to flower. Busy Lizzie must be kept somewhat pot-bound.

ROTTING STEMS
Cause: This is always caused by overwatering, especially in cool, shady conditions. Always reduce watering in winter; water very sparingly if plant is kept below 60°F.

LOSS OF FLOWERS
Cause: Too little light is the usual reason. Other possibilities are dry air, dry compost or red spider mite attack.

IXORA

Flame of the Woods (I. coccinea) is a handsome shrub, 2-3 ft tall, with glossy leathery leaves. From late spring to autumn it bears large clusters of red tubular flowers. There are many named hybrids with white, yellow, pink and red flowers. This is definitely not a plant for the novice — leaves drop if it is exposed to cool air for even a short time; flower buds drop if it is moved from one spot to another. Humid air is essential. After flowering in early summer keep rather dry for a month, then resume normal watering to bring back into flower.

SECRETS OF SUCCESS

Temperature: Warm or average warmth; not less than 60°F in winter.

Light: Bright light; avoid direct sun in summer.

Water: Keep compost moist at all times; reduce watering in winter. Use soft water.

Air Humidity: Mist leaves regularly.

Repotting: Repot, when necessary, in spring.

Propagation: Difficult. Stem cuttings in spring; Bio Roota and warmth are needed.

I. coccinea
Flame of the Woods

JACOBINIA

When seen in bloom the King's Crown seems a most desirable house plant; the large flowering heads look like fluffy pink pompons borne on stalks above the soft downy foliage. Unfortunately the flowering period in late summer is short. This bushy plant can reach 4 ft or more, but attractiveness suffers with age and so 1- or 2-year-old plants are grown for display. Cut plants back after flowering; during winter keep the pot in a well lit, fairly warm spot. In summer both air and compost must be kept constantly moist.

SECRETS OF SUCCESS

Temperature: Average warmth; not less than 55°F in winter.

Light: Bright indirect light in summer; some direct sun in winter.

Water: Keep compost moist at all times; reduce watering in winter.

Air Humidity: Mist leaves frequently in summer.

Repotting: Repot every 2-3 years in spring.

Propagation: Stem cuttings in spring; Bio Roota and warmth are needed.

J. carnea
King's Crown

JASMINUM

The most popular and one of the easiest to grow is the Pink Jasmine, so called because of the pinkish colour of its flower buds. In January these buds open into clusters of starry white flowers with a delightful fragrance. This plant is a vigorous climber which must be cut back after flowering; when young it can be trained around a wire hoop in the pot. Not all Jasmines are white and fragrant — the Primrose Jasmine produces yellow, semi-double flowers in spring which have no fragrance. The basic rules for success with Jasmines are to keep the plant cool in winter, stand it outdoors in summer, give it plenty of light and never let it dry out.

J. primulinum
Primrose Jasmine

SECRETS OF SUCCESS

Temperature: Cool or average warmth; not less than 45°F in winter.

Light: Bright light with some direct sun; protect from hot summer sunshine.

Water: Keep compost moist at all times.

Air Humidity: Mist leaves frequently.

Repotting: Repot, when necessary, in spring.

Propagation: Stem cuttings in spring; use Bio Roota.

J. polyanthum
Pink Jasmine

KALANCHOE

Several types of Kalanchoe are grown as foliage house plants; one species (K. blossfeldiana) is a popular Christmas flowering gift plant. Under natural conditions this easy-to-grow succulent blooms in early spring, but by reducing its light supply each day growers are able to induce it to bloom in midwinter. The flowers are usually red, but yellow and orange hybrids are available. The green fleshy leaves turn reddish in sunlight and the large flower heads last for many weeks. After flowering prune the tops and place the pot on a shady windowsill. Keep the compost nearly dry for a month then put the plant in a well-lit spot and water normally.

SECRETS OF SUCCESS

Temperature: Average warmth; not less than 50°F in winter.

Light: East- or west-facing windowsill from spring to autumn; a south-facing windowsill in winter.

Water: Water thoroughly, then leave until compost is moderately dry.

Air Humidity: No need to mist the leaves.

Repotting: Repot each year after spring rest period.

Propagation: See Propagation of Succulents, page 54.

K. blossfeldiana
Flaming Katy

LANTANA

When not in bloom this shrub is an unimpressive plant with coarse wrinkled leaves and prickly stem. However, the globular flower heads which are borne throughout the summer have the unusual property of changing colour from pale yellow to red as the tiny flowers mature. Both leaves and flowers are pungently fragrant. The main requirements are for full sun and adequate water in summer. Keep watch for whitefly, which find Lantana particularly attractive. Cut back the stems after flowering and raise new plants from cuttings every 2 or 3 years as old plants become unattractive.

SECRETS OF SUCCESS

Temperature: Average warmth; not less than 55°F in winter.

Light: Give as much light as possible, but shade from summer noonday sun.

Water: Water regularly from spring to autumn; sparingly in winter. Let surface dry between waterings.

Air Humidity: Mist leaves occasionally.

Repotting: Repot when necessary in spring.

Propagation: Sow seeds in spring; stem cuttings at any time of the year.

L. camara
Shrub Verbena

MANETTIA

The colourful Firecracker Plant should be more popular. The thin twining stems will quickly cover a wire support or trelliswork, or they can be left to trail from a hanging basket. From spring to autumn the tubular yellow-tipped flowers appear in profusion, sometimes almost covering the dark green, pointed leaves. Pinch out the tips occasionally to stop the plant becoming straggly. In winter this vine needs a period of rest — keep it at 55°-60°F. In summer it needs some sunshine to make it flower for months on end.

SECRETS OF SUCCESS

Temperature: Warm or average warmth; not less than 50°F in winter.

Light: Bright light; some direct sun is essential.

Water: Keep compost moist at all times; reduce watering in winter.

Air Humidity: Mist leaves regularly.

Repotting: Repot every year in spring.

Propagation: Stem cuttings in summer; use Bio Roota.

M. inflata
Firecracker Plant

MYRTUS

M. communis
Myrtle

Myrtle has been grown as a decorative plant for thousands of years and yet it is still a rarity in Britain. This surprising situation is not due to difficulty of cultivation nor to lack of beauty. It is easy to care for in a well-lit unheated room and it is attractive all year round. The small oval leaves are shiny and aromatic; the white flowers, fluffy with stamens, appear in large numbers between June and September. In autumn the purple berries appear. The foliage can be cut and trained at any time of the year, making it an ideal specimen for indoor topiary. The shrub will grow about 2 ft tall if left untrimmed and can be stood outdoors during the summer months.

SECRETS OF SUCCESS

Temperature: Cool or average warmth; not less than 40°F in winter.

Light: Bright with some direct sunlight, but protect from midday summer sun.

Water: Water regularly from spring to autumn; sparingly in winter. Use soft water.

Air Humidity: Mist leaves frequently.

Repotting: Repot when necessary in spring.

Propagation: Stem cuttings in summer; use Bio Roota.

NERIUM

N. oleander
Oleander

Oleander grows into a tall, spreading bush and needs a large room or conservatory. The fragrant blooms appear from June to October and are borne in clusters above the willow-like foliage. The usual flower colour is pink, but white and red varieties are available. The wood and sap are poisonous. Oleander is not an easy plant to care for when it is large — the pot or tub must be moved to an unheated room in winter and it benefits from a summer vacation in the garden. In autumn cut back the stems which have flowered and keep watch for scale and mealy bug.

SECRETS OF SUCCESS

Temperature: Average warmth; not less than 45°F in winter.

Light: Choose sunniest spot available.

Water: Water liberally in spring and summer; sparingly in winter. Use tepid water.

Air Humidity: Do not mist leaves.

Repotting: Repot when necessary in spring.

Propagation: Stem cuttings in spring or summer.

ORCHIDS

It is possible to grow orchids in your living room, but only a tiny fraction of the 100,000 known types are suitable. Choose from the 'house plant' group illustrated here and buy a well-grown plant in late summer. Each type has its own special needs, but there are a number of general rules for orchids.

You can't just place the plant anywhere. Miniature varieties can be grown in a terrarium (see page 19) but the usual home for a potted orchid is on a Pebble Tray (see page 15). Place this tray on a windowsill which is close to a radiator. The window may need a blind or screen to provide protection from strong direct sunlight. Turn the pot occasionally and move the tray away from the window on frosty nights.

House plant orchids cannot tolerate hot, stuffy conditions so good ventilation is required even in winter — don't be afraid to stand the pot outdoors on warm, sunny days. Indoors, however, you must avoid cold draughts which can be fatal.

Feed during the summer months. Orchids appreciate being pot-bound but after a few years repotting and division may be necessary. You will require a special orchid compost.

SECRETS OF SUCCESS

Temperature: Individual types vary, but the general rule is a day temperature of about 70°F in summer, 60°F in winter and a drop at night of 10°F. Cool nights are important.

Light: Good light, shaded from hot sun. Orchids need 10 – 15 hours of light each day — in winter supplement daylight with artificial light.

Water: Keep the compost moist, reduce watering in winter. With Cattleya, Miltonia and Oncidium let surface dry between waterings. Use tepid, soft water.

Air Humidity: Moist atmosphere essential. Mist leaves occasionally.

Repotting: Do not worry if a few roots grow outside the pot. Repot only when growth begins to suffer.

Propagation: Divide plants at repotting time. Leave at least 3 shoots on each division. Stake each newly potted plant.

SUITABLE TYPES

Cattleya
Corsage Orchid
Large classical orchids; good for beginners

Cypripedium
Slipper Orchid
Choose C. insigne; good for beginners

Coelogyne
Choose C. cristata; good for beginners

Miltonia
Pansy Orchid
Flat-faced orchids; many colours available

Oncidium
Butterfly Orchid
Many small flowers on long arching stems

Odontoglossum
Tiger Orchid
Choose O. grande; good for beginners

SPECIAL PROBLEMS

BROWN SPOTS ON LEAVES
Cause: If the spots are hard and dry, the plant has been scorched by the sun. Provide shade; there is no need to remove the spots. If the spots are soft, then a fungus disease is present and the affected parts should be removed immediately.

HORIZONTAL OR DROOPING GROWTH
Cause: Lack of light is the common reason; orchids need good illumination. If the growth is limp and the light is good then incorrect watering may be the cause of loss of vigour.

MOULD ON LEAVES
Cause: Mildew may develop if the leaves are thoroughly misted under cool conditions and the water does not quickly evaporate.

NO FLOWERS
Cause: When growth is unhealthy any incorrect cultural condition can be the reason. If growth appears healthy then insufficient light is the probable cause.

PACHYSTACHYS

The Lollipop Plant was relatively unknown a few years ago but it is now often seen on display, with its cone-shaped yellow flower heads above the oval leaves. The main appeal of the Lollipop Plant is its long flowering season — from late spring until autumn if the plant is liberally watered and fed regularly. Leaf fall is a sign of dryness at the roots. This shrubby plant can get out of hand if it is not pruned in the spring. The stem tips which are removed can be used as cuttings; nip out the growing points of young plants to induce bushy growth.

SECRETS OF SUCCESS

Temperature: Average warmth; not less than 55°F in winter.

Light: Brightly lit spot away from direct sun in summer.

Water: Water liberally from spring to late autumn; sparingly in winter.

Air Humidity: Mist leaves in summer.

Repotting: Repot every year in spring.

Propagation: Stem cuttings in spring or summer.

P. lutea
Lollipop Plant

PASSIFLORA

P. caerulea
Passion Flower

The Passiflora flower has an intricate structure — the early Spanish missionaries believed that its symbols of Christ's Passion had been put there to convert the S. American Indian. Despite the delicacy of the flower there is nothing delicate about the plant. It is a rampant climber which will soon outgrow its welcome if it is not cut back hard each spring. This pruning induces branching, and the stems produced bear deeply-lobed leaves, tendrils and short-lived flowers from July to September. The Passion Flower is hardy enough to be grown outdoors in sheltered districts and so it requires cool conditions indoors in winter. In summer it can be stood outdoors.

SECRETS OF SUCCESS

Temperature: Average warmth; keep at 40°–50°F in winter.
Light: Choose sunniest spot available.
Water: Keep compost moist at all times; may need daily watering in summer. Reduce watering in winter.
Air Humidity: Mist leaves occasionally.
Repotting: Repot every year in spring.
Propagation: Stem cuttings in summer. Sow seeds in spring.

PENTAS

The Egyptian Star Cluster is not a plant you are likely to find in your local garden shop, but it is well worth growing in a sunny window if you can obtain a rooted cutting. The leaves are rather hairy and the growth becomes straggly if you fail to pinch out the stem tips regularly. Keep the plant about 18 in. high. The long terminal clusters of white, pink, red or lavender tubular flowers may appear at any time of the year. Pentas is easy to grow; keep the plant at about 60°F in winter and prune the stems in March before repotting.

SECRETS OF SUCCESS

Temperature: Average warmth; not less than 50°F in winter.
Light: Bright light with some direct sun.
Water: Keep compost moist at all times; reduce watering in winter.
Air Humidity: Mist leaves occasionally.
Repotting: Repot every year in spring.
Propagation: Stem cuttings in spring; use Bio Roota.

P. lanceolata
Egyptian Star Cluster

PLUMBAGO

Clusters of beautiful sky blue flowers appearing throughout the summer and autumn make the Cape Leadwort an outstanding house plant when trained around a window. This vigorous and rambling climber can be kept as a specimen plant on a sunny windowsill by regular pruning. The secret of successful Plumbago culture is to keep it cool throughout the winter and early spring. If it gets too cool the leaves may fall but new foliage will appear when growth starts again. Cut back old shoots in February; stand pots outdoors in warm weather.

SECRETS OF SUCCESS

Temperature: Cool or average warmth; not less than 45°F in winter.
Light: Bright light with some direct sun.
Water: Keep compost moist at all times; water sparingly in winter.
Air Humidity: Mist occasionally.
Repotting: Repot when necessary in spring.
Propagation: Stem cuttings in autumn. Sow seeds in spring.

P. capensis
Cape Leadwort

ROCHEA

R. coccinea
Crassula

The proper name of the flowering succulent sold as 'Crassula' is Rochea coccinea. The plants in the shops have usually been forced into bloom in early spring, but 'the natural flowering time is June–July. R. coccinea is a neat plant with erect stems which grow about 12–18 in. high. These stems are clothed with ranks of leathery triangular leaves and at their tips the showy clusters of flowers appear. The scarlet blooms are tubular and fragrant. Rochea needs standard succulent treatment — plenty of light and water in summer and a period outdoors in sunny weather. Good ventilation is important and let it rest with cool conditions and drier compost in winter. Cut back stems after they have flowered.

SECRETS OF SUCCESS

Temperature: Cool or average warmth; not less than 45°F in winter.
Light: Brightly lit spot with some direct sunshine. Shade from summer noonday sun.
Water: Water thoroughly when the compost begins to dry out. Water sparingly in winter.
Air Humidity: Misting is not necessary.
Repotting: Repot when necessary in spring.
Propagation: Stem cuttings in spring or summer. Allow cuttings to dry for 2–3 days before inserting in compost.

PELARGONIUM (GERANIUM)

TYPES

● GERANIUMS

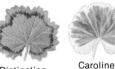

flowers ½ – 1 in. across. White, pink, salmon, red, purple

rounded leaves; nearly all varieties have a horseshoe marking or 'zone'

SINGLE

DOUBLE

STELLAR

CACTUS

P. hortorum hybrid

Geranium (Zonal Pelargonium)

Marechal MacMahon

Distinction

Caroline Schmidt

Verona

Black Cox

Mrs Henry Cox

Happy Thought

Mrs Pollock

● REGAL PELARGONIUMS

flowers 1½ – 2 in. across. Frilled – white, pink, salmon, red, purple usually marked with darker colour

serrated leaves

P.domesticum hybrid

Regal Pelargonium (Martha Washington Pelargonium)

Elsie Hickman

● IVY-LEAVED GERANIUMS

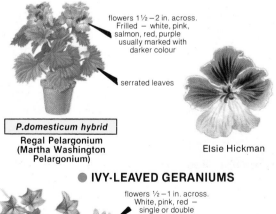

flowers ½ – 1 in. across. White, pink, red – single or double

ivy-shaped leaves

L'Elégante

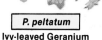

P. peltatum

Ivy-leaved Geranium

It is not surprising that the Pelargonium is one of the world's favourite house plants. It is easy to grow and propagate, it has a long flowering period and the clusters of blooms are large and colourful.

By far the most popular type is the ordinary Geranium. It will bloom almost all year round if kept on a sunny windowsill at 55°F or more. Keep the compost rather dry — overwatering is the main enemy of Geraniums.

The Regal Pelargonium is the glamorous relation. Unfortunately it has a shorter flowering season and it is not as easy to grow. Overwinter at 45°–50°F.

The Ivy-leaved Geranium is becoming increasingly popular. Its long pliable stems bear long-stalked flower clusters almost all year round if the plant is kept in a sunny spot.

There are a few general rules for all Pelargoniums. Pinch back young plants to induce bushiness. Do not repot until it is essential. Provide plenty of fresh air and not much humidity. Remove dead flowers and prune in early spring (Regal Pelargonium in autumn).

SECRETS OF SUCCESS

Temperature: Average warmth with cool nights; not less than 45°F in winter (50°F for Ivy-leaved Geranium).

Light: Provide as much light as possible. Direct sunlight is essential.

Water: Water thoroughly, then leave until compost is moderately dry. Avoid overwatering. Reduce watering frequency in winter, compost should be barely moist if plant is not in bloom.

Air Humidity: Do not mist the leaves.

Repotting: Repot, when necessary, in spring.

Propagation: Stem cuttings in summer. Do not use a rooting hormone and do not cover.

SPECIAL PROBLEMS

YELLOWING OF LOWER LEAVES
Cause: If the leaves remain firm or are crisp with scorched edges then underwatering is the reason. If the leaves wilt or rot then overwatering is the cause. In both cases leaf fall may occur.

REDDENING OF LEAF EDGES
Cause: Temperature too low. Move pot away from window on frosty nights.

BLACKENING OF STEM BASE
Cause: Black leg disease. Destroy infected plant; in future use sterile compost and avoid overwatering.

SPINDLY GROWTH: LOSS OF LOWER LEAVES
Cause: Too little light; Pelargoniums will not grow in shade.

WATER-SOAKED CORKY PATCHES ON LEAVES
Cause: Oedema disease, associated with over-moist conditions. Non-infectious – reduce watering.

GREY MOULD ON LEAVES
Cause: Botrytis disease, associated with over-wet conditions. Infectious – remove diseased leaves, spray with Benlate, improve ventilation and reduce watering.

NO FLOWERS ON REGAL PELARGONIUM
Cause: If the plant is healthy the likely reason is too much heat in winter.

INSECTS
Whitefly, aphid and vine weevil can be troublesome; see page 120.

SAINTPAULIA

violet-like flowers. White, pink, blue, purple, red; bicolours available. Prominent yellow stamens at centre of flower

rosette of fleshy velvety leaves

S. ionantha
African Violet

It is only 50 years since the first African Violet was grown as a house plant, but in that time it has become a world-wide favourite. Its main attraction is the ability to flower at almost any time of the year and its compact size means it can fit on a narrow windowsill.

The original African Violet was notoriously difficult to grow, but modern varieties are much more robust and freer flowering. A beginner cannot expect to match the expert in keeping the plant in bloom continually for 10 months or more, but there should be no difficulty in producing several flushes of flowers each year.

There are five basic needs — steady warmth, careful watering, good light, high air humidity and regular feeding. Read the Secrets of Success carefully and note these few extra tips from the experts: Keep the leaves off the windowpane. Remove dead flowers and damaged leaves immediately — do not leave a stalk. Remove side shoots on older plants as they develop. Keep the plant moderately root-bound; when repotting is essential, use a plastic pot.

TYPES

● LEAF TYPES

  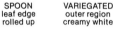

BOY	GIRL	SPOON	VARIEGATED
standard plain green leaf	small white area at base	leaf edge rolled up	outer region creamy white

● FLOWER TYPES

SINGLE	STAR	FRINGED	CRESTED
standard flower shape	5 equal sized petals	frilly edged petals	small petals obscure stamens

DOUBLE	BICOLOUR	GENEVA
additional full sized petals	two distinct colours	white edge to petals

SECRETS OF SUCCESS

Temperature: Average warmth; not less than 60°F in winter. Avoid cold draughts and sudden changes in temperature.

Light: Bright light —— ideally an east or south window in winter, and a west window in summer. Always protect from strong sunlight. For winter blooming provide some artificial light at night. To grow entirely by artificial light use two 40W fluorescent tubes about 12 in. above the plants for 14 hours each day.

Water: Keep compost moist; wait until the surface is dry before watering. Use tepid water. Push the spout below the foliage to keep water off the leaves and crown. Occasionally water by the immersion method.

Air Humidity: High humidity is essential. Surround the pot with damp peat or place on a Pebble Tray (see page 15). Mist with care — tepid water, very fine spray and keep misted plant away from sunshine.

Repotting: Repot when necessary in spring.

Propagation: Leaf cuttings in spring or sow seeds in spring.

SPECIAL PROBLEMS

STRAW-COLOURED PATCHES ON LEAVES
Cause: Too much direct sun in summer. Leaf edges may turn yellow and holes may develop.

BROWN SPOTS ON LEAVES
Cause: Cold water has been used for watering. Always use tepid water.

YELLOWING LEAVES
Cause: There are several possible reasons. Dry air is a frequent cause, so is too much sun and incorrect watering. Overfeeding can result in yellowing; make sure you follow the instructions.

PALE GREEN LEAVES WITH LONG STALKS; LEAF EDGES CURLED
Cause: The plant has been chilled. The minimum temperature should be 60°F, although it will survive short periods at 50°–60°F if the compost is fairly dry. Move pots away from the window on frosty nights.

LIMP LEAVES; CENTRE CROWN ROTTEN
Cause: Crown rot disease, caused by overwatering and wide fluctuations in temperature. This is a difficult disease to control and it is infectious; the best plan is to remove and destroy the plant as soon as possible.

NO FLOWERS
Cause: There are many possible reasons. The most likely cause is insufficient light, especially in winter. Other possibilities are dry air, cold air, too frequent repotting and failure to remove side shoots. Moving the pot to a new location can cause the plant to cease blooming for some time.

MOULDY LEAVES & FLOWERS
Cause: Botrytis or powdery mildew disease. Stop misting the leaves. Pick off and destroy diseased parts. Spray the plant with Benlate; use tepid water and keep out of sun until the spray deposit has dried.

INSECTS
Whitefly, mealy bug and cyclamen mite can be troublesome. See page 120.

SANCHEZIA

This striking greenhouse shrub can be grown as a house plant if its requirement for high air humidity is met; stand the pot on a Pebble Tray (page 15) and mist the leaves frequently. The yellow tubular flowers, 2 in. long, are borne in upright clusters above the foliage. These autumn flowers are attractive, but the large leaves, up to 12 in. long, provide the main display with their yellow or ivory veins. Unlike its smaller relative, the Zebra Plant (see page 61), this shrub will grow about 3 ft high under room conditions. Prune each spring.

SECRETS OF SUCCESS

Temperature: Average warmth; not less than 55°F in winter.
Light: Brightly lit spot away from direct sun in summer.
Water: Keep compost moist at all times; reduce watering in winter.
Air Humidity: Use Pebble Tray; mist leaves frequently.
Repotting: Repot every year in spring.
Propagation: Stem cuttings in summer; Bio Roota and warmth are necessary.

S. nobilis

SPARMANNIA

The House Lime is a useful plant for the larger room, where its pale downy leaves make a pleasant contrast to the dark leathery foliage of Philodendron or Ficus. The tree-like growth of Sparmannia can reach 3 ft or more, and its broad leaves may be 8 in. across. It grows quickly and may need repotting more than once a year. Keep growth in check by pinching out the stem tips of young plants and by cutting back the stems after flowering. Sparmannia blooms in early spring if it has been kept in direct sunlight during winter, and it may bloom again in early summer if kept in a cool room. The yellow-stamened white flowers are attractive.

SECRETS OF SUCCESS

Temperature: Cool or average warmth; not less than 45°F in winter.
Light: Brightly lit spot away from direct sun in summer.
Water: Keep compost moist at all times; may require daily watering in summer. Water more sparingly in winter.
Air Humidity: Mist leaves occasionally in summer.
Repotting: Repot every year in spring.
Propagation: Stem cuttings root easily in spring or summer; use Bio Roota.

S. africana
House Lime

SPATHIPHYLLUM

The Peace Lily is a good choice if it can be kept out of direct sunlight in a room which is reasonably warm in winter. There must be no cold draughts and the pot should be surrounded by moist peat or stood on a Pebble Tray (page 15). The glossy leaves grow directly out of the compost; in spring and sometimes again in autumn the flowers appear. These arum lily-like blooms, borne on long stalks, are long lasting although they fade from white to pale green after the first few days. Wash the leaves occasionally and feed regularly. There are two types to choose from — the popular S. wallisii which is about 12 in. high and free flowering, and the less hardy but much larger S. Mauna Loa.

SECRETS OF SUCCESS

Temperature: Warm or average warmth; not less than 55°F in winter.
Light: Semi-shade in summer; bright light in winter. Strong sunlight will damage the leaves.
Water: Keep the compost moist at all times; reduce watering in winter.
Air Humidity: Mist leaves very frequently.
Repotting: Repot every year in spring.
Propagation: Divide plants at repotting time.

S. wallisii
Peace Lily

STAPELIA

The smell of the blooms of the Carrion Flower has been described as 'disagreeable', 'offensive', and 'disgusting'. It is therefore not surprising that these flowering succulents have never been popular, although some varieties produce flowers which have little or no smell. All Stapelias have spectacular flowers — the almost odourless S. gigantea has blooms which are 12 in. across. By far the most popular type is S. variegata, which bears 2–3 in. blooms in summer at the base of the fleshy, erect stems. Unfortunately it is one of the strong-smelling species and it may be necessary to stand the pot outdoors when in flower.

SECRETS OF SUCCESS

Temperature: Average warmth; not less than 50°F in winter.
Light: As much light as possible, but shade from hot summer sun.
Water: Water moderately, then leave until the compost surface is dry. Water sparingly in winter.
Air Humidity: No need to mist leaves.
Repotting: Repot when necessary in spring.
Propagation: See Propagation of Succulents, page 54.

S. variegata
Carrion Flower

STEPHANOTIS

Stephanotis is usually associated with bridal bouquets, in which it provides heavily scented, waxy white flowers and glossy, oval leaves. It can also be grown as a free-flowering house plant, producing clusters of tubular blooms from May to October. Its vigorous climbing stems must be trained on a support and should be cut back once flowering has finished. The Madagascar Jasmine is a beautiful but difficult plant — it hates sudden changes in temperature, needs constant cool conditions in winter and is particularly attractive to scale and mealy bug. Do not turn or move the pot when the plant is in flower.

SECRETS OF SUCCESS

Temperature: Average warmth; keep at 55° – 60°F in winter.

Light: Brightly lit spot, away from direct sun in summer.

Water: Keep compost moist at all times; water sparingly in winter.

Air Humidity: Mist leaves occasionally.

Repotting: Repot every 2 years in spring.

Propagation: Stem cuttings in summer; Bio Roota and warmth are necessary.

S. floribunda
Madagascar Jasmine

STRELITZIA

Surely the most spectacular of all the flowers which can be grown in the home is the Bird of Paradise. The vivid red, orange and blue flowers, 6 in. across, last for several weeks on top of tall stalks, surrounded by large, paddle-shaped leaves. As a house plant it needs patience (new plants take 3 – 4 years before flowering starts) and space (mature plants in a 10 in. pot grow 3 – 4 ft high). But it is surprisingly easy to grow if it can be kept well-lit and cool in winter. Do not repot mature plants — root restriction is vital for annual blooming.

SECRETS OF SUCCESS

Temperature: Average warmth; keep at 55° – 60°F in winter.

Light: As much light as possible, but shade from hot summer sun.

Water: Water thoroughly, then leave until surface is dry. Water sparingly in winter.

Air Humidity: Mist occasionally.

Repotting: Repot young plants every year in spring.

Propagation: Divide overcrowded plants in spring.

S. reginae
Bird of Paradise

STREPTOCARPUS

Many colourful hybrids have appeared in recent years, and the large trumpet-shaped flowers of the Cape Primrose are now available in white, blue, purple, pink and red. The throat of the flower of these modern hybrids is often veined in a contrasting colour, but the old favourite Constant Nymph still remains the most popular Streptocarpus. When growing conditions are satisfactory a succession of blooms appear above the rosette of coarse, stemless leaves from May until October, but the Cape Primrose can be temperamental. It needs a shallow pot, moist air, bright light and freedom from draughts and cold air in winter. Remove flowers as they fade.

S. hybridus
Cape Primrose

SECRETS OF SUCCESS

Temperature: Average warmth; not less than 55°F in winter.

Light: Brightly lit spot away from direct sun in summer.

Water: Water freely, then leave until the compost surface is dry. Reduce watering in winter.

Air Humidity: Mist occasionally, but do not wet the leaves.

Repotting: Repot every year in spring.

Propagation: Divide plants at repotting time or take leaf cuttings in summer. Seeds may be sown in spring.

VALLOTA

The Scarborough Lily is an excellent plant for a sunny windowsill. The long strap-like leaves are evergreen, and in late summer clusters of large trumpet-shaped flowers appear on top of 1 – 2 ft stalks. Bright scarlet is the usual flower colour, but white and pink varieties are available. In spring plant the bulb firmly in a 5 in. pot; leave the top half of the bulb uncovered. Vallota is an easy plant to care for — keep it cool during the winter resting period, remove dead flowers and leaves, and let the compost dry out slightly between waterings. Don't repot until the clump of bulbs becomes overcrowded. Pot up each large bulb separately; flowering size bulbs are 1½ in. across.

V. speciosa
Scarborough Lily

SECRETS OF SUCCESS

Temperature: Average warmth; keep at 50° – 55°F in winter.

Light: Bright light with some direct sun.

Water: Water thoroughly when the compost begins to dry out. Water sparingly in winter.

Air Humidity: Sponge leaves occasionally.

Repotting: Repot every 3 – 4 years in spring.

Propagation: Divide plants at repotting time, or detach offsets from mature plants and pot up in summer.

CHAPTER 4
FLOWERING POT PLANTS

Don't choose a flowering pot plant if you want something which will permanently adorn your living room. Unlike the flowering house plants members of this group can only be temporary residents, and once the flowers fade their display days are over. This lack of permanence is, of course, a disadvantage but it has its own attraction. Like the days of a short and exciting holiday, they must be enjoyed *now*.

An important group of flowering pot plants, sometimes known as 'florist' or 'gift' plants, have an essential part to play in the indoor plant scene. During the dark winter months they provide a welcome splash of colour when garden flowers are absent and cut flowers are expensive. The Azalea, Poinsettia, Cyclamen, Solanum and Chrysanthemum, bought in bud or full flower, are found in countless homes as the first flowers to welcome in the New Year.

The second important group are the Garden Bulbs, providing an ever-popular spring display. The remaining flowering pot plants are a mixed bag — quick-growing climbers such as Gloriosa and Thunbergia, shrubs like Cytisus and Punica, and scores of pretty annuals like Browallia, Exacum and many garden favourites.

With practically all of them, after a few weeks or perhaps months, the flowers will fade and the leaves will fall. This is not your fault, because it is a basic feature of the group. Of course, flower fading and leaf fall should not take place in a matter of days — this would indicate that you were doing something wrong. As a general rule flowering pot plants need bright, cool conditions and moist compost — warm air is the biggest enemy of all.

However skilful you are, flowering will come to an end and the A-Z guide will tell you what to do with each plant. Many have to be thrown away, but some can be made to provide another display next season. As the following pages reveal, millions of flowering pot plants are needlessly thrown away every year.

ACHIMENES

A. hybrida
Cupid's Bower

The modern varieties of Achimenes bear masses of large flowers amid glistening hairy leaves. White, blue, purple, pink and yellow varieties are available. Each bloom is short-lived, but the flowering season extends from June until October. The stems are weak and wiry, making this plant an excellent subject for a hanging basket in a well-lit spot. If you want to grow it as a bushy plant then pinch out the tips of young shoots and provide support for tall stems. Proper care is quite easy — just keep the plant reasonably warm and make sure that the compost does not dry out for even a single day.

SECRETS OF SUCCESS

Temperature: Average warmth; not less than 55°F during the growing season.

Light: Brightly lit spot away from direct sun in summer.

Water: Keep the compost moist at all times during the growing season with tepid water. Take care not to overwater.

Air Humidity: Mist occasionally around the plant with tepid water. Do not wet leaves.

Care After Flowering: Stop watering once flowering has finished in autumn. Cut off stems and store rhizomes in dry peat or sand in a frost-free room. Plant in compost (½ – 1 in. deep) in early spring.

Propagation: Separate rhizomes at planting time, or take stem cuttings in May.

ASTILBE

A. japonica
Spiraea

This popular garden plant is sometimes offered for sale in spring as a flowering pot plant. The foliage is fern-like and the large feathery clusters of white, pink or red flowers make the Astilbe a decorative specimen plant or an attractive centrepiece for a group of low-growing plants. It needs a cool, well-lit spot. Its most important requirement is for abundant moisture — thorough and frequent watering is essential and the leaves should be misted in warm weather. Despite the attractiveness of Astilbe indoors its real home is the garden, and it should be planted outside once the flowers have faded.

SECRETS OF SUCCESS

Temperature: Cool or average warmth; not less than 50°F.

Light: Brightly lit spot, but shade from hot summer sun.

Water: Keep the compost moist at all times. Water freely in summer.

Air Humidity: Mist leaves occasionally.

Care After Flowering: Place the pot in a cool, well-ventilated room for a few days, then plant outdoors in a moist, shady site.

Propagation: Divide plants in spring.

AZALEA

Countless Azaleas are bought every year at Christmas time to provide decoration during the holiday season and into the New Year. By far the more usual type is the Indian Azalea, with red, pink, orange or white flowers almost covering the whole of the dwarf bush. The Japanese or Kurume Azalea is less frequently seen and has the drawback of fewer and smaller flowers, but it can be planted outdoors when its stay indoors is over.

When buying a plant pick one with a few open flowers and a mass of buds. Without correct care the flowers wilt and the leaves drop in a week or two. The secret of keeping a plant in bloom for many weeks and capable of coming back into flower the following year is to keep it wet (not just moist), distinctly cool and brightly lit. Remove faded flowers promptly.

Azalea indica hybrid (Rhododendron simsii)
Indian Azalea

Rhododendron obtusum hybrid
Japanese Azalea

SECRETS OF SUCCESS

Temperature: Cool; 50° – 60°F is ideal.

Light: Brightly lit spot away from direct sunlight.

Water: Keep the compost wet at all times, using rainwater in hard water areas. Water by the immersion method (see page 105).

Air Humidity: Mist leaves daily during flowering season.

Care After Flowering: Move pot to a cool but frost-free room; continue watering and repot if necessary, using lime-free compost. Place pot in a shady spot in the garden once the danger of frost is past — keep fed, watered and sprayed until September. Bring into a cool room; when flowers open move into display area.

SPECIAL PROBLEMS

SHRIVELLED LEAVES
Cause: The most likely reason for leaf shrivelling and leaf loss is underwatering. A thorough soaking may be needed several times each week. Other common causes are too little moisture in the air (surround pot with damp peat), too much heat or too much sun.

SHORT FLOWERING PERIOD
Cause: Hot dry air is the usual culprit. Keep the pot well away from radiators and mist the foliage daily. Too much sun and too little water can also bring flowering to a premature end.

YELLOWING LEAVES
Cause: Lime in the compost or lime in the water. Treat with Sequestrene; water with soft water.

BEGONIA

TYPES

● TUBEROUS TYPES

plants 6 in. high; free-flowering and compact habit

large blooms 3-5 in. across, available in many colours. Plants 1 ft high

slender, drooping stems; pendent flowers

B. tuberhybrida

B. multiflora

B. pendula
Basic Begonia

● LORRAINE HYBRIDS   ● HIEMALIS HYBRIDS

B. Gloire de Lorraine

B. Fireglow

BASIC FACTS

There are many begonias which can be used as part of the permanent collection of plants in the home — see pages 26 and 62. There are also begonias which are used as temporary residents to provide a splash of winter colour or summer display, and the three groups of pot plant types are shown here.

The most popular are the Tuberous Begonias, which bloom in summer and autumn. All of them can be raised by planting tubers in March in boxes of moist peat. Keep at 60° – 70°F and when shoots are a couple of inches high transplant into 5 in. pots. Repot later into 8 in. pots. At the end of the flowering season withhold water, cut off shoots, lift tubers and store in peat.

The second group are the Lorraine or Cheimantha Hybrids, which are old favourites as they bloom around Christmas. The third group, the Hiemalis Hybrids, have been greatly improved in recent years by the introduction of the Elatior Rieger strain of which B. Fireglow is an example. They can be bought in flower at any season and will last for months with proper care.

SECRETS OF SUCCESS

Temperature: Average warmth; not less than 55°F in winter. Avoid temperatures above 70°F.

Light: A bright spot away from direct sunlight. A few hours of winter sun are beneficial.

Water: Water freely when plant is in flower, but do not keep compost constantly soggy.

Air Humidity: Moist air needed — surround pots with damp peat. Mist air around plant.

Care After Flowering: Tuberous Begonias — see above. Other types are usually discarded; otherwise cut back and keep cool with little water. Increase water in April. New shoots can be used as cuttings.

SPECIAL PROBLEMS

BROWN BLOTCHES, TURNING GREY & MOULDY
Cause: Botrytis disease. Move away from other begonia plants, cut off diseased parts and spray with Benlate. Avoid low light and over-damp conditions. Improve ventilation.

INSECTS
Keep watch for aphid and red spider mite.

YELLOWING LEAVES
Cause: Too little light; too little or too much water. Look for other symptoms.

LOSS OF LEAVES
Cause: There are a number of possible causes and you must look for other symptoms. There is not enough light if the stems are thin and leggy; too much heat if leaves are dry and curled; and too much water if leaves are wilted and rotten.

LEAVES WITH BROWN TIPS
Cause: Air humidity too low. Follow rules in Secrets of Success.

PALE, ROTTING LEAVES
Cause: Overwatering. Follow rules in Secrets of Success.

WHITE POWDERY SPOTS
Cause: Powdery mildew disease. Move away from other begonia plants, cut off diseased leaves and spray with Benlate. Avoid over-damp conditions and low temperatures. Improve ventilation.

FLOWER BUDS DROP
Cause: Dry air or underwatering.

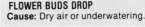

PLANT COLLAPSE
Cause: Several possible reasons — stem rot disease due to overwatering, root knot eelworm (look for swollen bumps on roots) or vine weevil (look for tunnels in tubers). Read Chapter 9.

B. speciosa
Bush Violet

BROWALLIA

The Bush Violet is usually bought in flower, but it can be easily raised at home from seed. Sow in early spring for summer flowers or delay sowing until summer for winter flowering. The blooms, vivid blue with white throats, are borne in profusion on the weak, branching stems. Pinch out the growing tips occasionally to promote bushiness. With proper care the flowering period will last for many weeks — keep the pot in a cool room where it will receive some direct sunlight. Feed regularly and pick off the flowers as they fade.

SECRETS OF SUCCESS

Temperature: Cool; 50°–60°F is ideal during the flowering season.

Light: Bright light with some direct sun.

Water: Keep the compost moist at all times.

Air Humidity: Mist leaves occasionally.

Care After Flowering: Plant should be discarded.

Propagation: Sow seeds in spring or summer.

C. herbeohybrida
Slipper Flower

CALCEOLARIA

The Slipper Flower is a springtime favourite. The soft leaves are large and hairy and the flowers are curious and colourful. They are pouch-shaped in yellow, orange, red or white with dark-coloured spots or blotches. The plant is bought in flower (propagation is a skilled job best left to the nurseryman) and should last about a month if kept in a cool spot which is brightly lit. Provide moist conditions — stand the pot on a Pebble Tray or surround with moist peat. Keep away from draughts, keep water off the leaves and flowers when watering and keep careful watch for aphids.

SECRETS OF SUCCESS

Temperature: Cool; 50°–60°F is ideal.

Light: Bright light away from direct sunlight.

Water: Keep compost moist at all times.

Air Humidity: Mist occasionally around the plant — take care not to wet leaves or flowers.

Care After Flowering: Plant should be discarded.

Propagation: Difficult; sow seeds in summer in a cool greenhouse for flowering next year.

C. annuum
Christmas Pepper

CAPSICUM

One of the popular names of this plant is Christmas Pepper, as large quantities are sold in December to provide traditional colour during the festive season. The cone-shaped miniature peppers change colour as they ripen, and yellow, red and purple 1 in. fruits are sometimes found on one plant. The fruits are edible — but very hot! Plants are available from September onwards, and the peppers should remain attractive for 2 or 3 months with care. Some direct sunlight is essential, and the compost must never be allowed to dry out. Hot dry air will cause the fruit to fall, and attacks of aphid and red spider mite are likely.

SECRETS OF SUCCESS

Temperature: Cool or average warmth; not less than 55°F.

Light: Brightly lit spot with morning or afternoon sun.

Water: Keep the compost moist at all times. Water occasionally by the immersion method (see page 105).

Air Humidity: Mist the leaves frequently.

Care After Flowering: Plant should be discarded.

Propagation: Difficult; sow seeds in early spring.

C. plumosa
Plume Flower

CELOSIA

There are two distinct types of this showy summer-flowering pot plant. Celosia plumosa has red or yellow feathery plumes; C. cristata has a curious velvety 'cockscomb' which may be yellow, orange or red. Celosia is sometimes sold for bedding outdoors, but it can be kept in full flower for many weeks indoors. Some direct sunlight during the day is essential, and regular feeding is necessary. It needs cool, airy conditions to prolong the flowering season. The usual height is 1–2 ft, but dwarf forms are available. Celosia can be raised from seed, but it is usually more satisfactory to buy nursery-grown plants.

SECRETS OF SUCCESS

Temperature: Cool; 50°–60°F is ideal.

Light: As much light as possible, but shade from hot summer sun.

Water: Keep compost moist at all times.

Air Humidity: Mist leaves occasionally.

Care After Flowering: Plant should be discarded.

Propagation: Sow seeds in March at 60°–65°F.

C. cristata
Cockscomb

CHRYSANTHEMUM

The Pot Chrysanthemum has become one of the most popular of all pot plants. The nurseryman uses chemicals to dwarf its growth and keeps it in the dark for part of the day to make it bloom on a set date. By this means Pot Chrysanthemums, less than 1 ft high but large-flowered in every colour but blue, are offered for sale in bloom throughout the year. If you choose your plant carefully and look after it properly then it should stay in bloom for 6–8 weeks. In the shop there should be a few open blooms and a mass of buds which are showing colour. At home place the pot in a cool room on a windowsill where it will get some early morning or evening sunlight.

By comparison the other Chrysanthemums are rarities. The Marguerites, with daisy-like flowers and fern-like foliage, are summer-flowering. The Cascade Chrysanthemums are charming, their pendent stems covered with hundreds of tiny blooms. Unlike other Chrysanthemums the Cascade varieties can be raised at home from seed.

SECRETS OF SUCCESS

Temperature: Cool; 50°–60°F is ideal.

Light: Bright light is essential, but Pot Chrysanthemums must be shaded from midday sun.

Water: Keep the compost moist at all times. It may be necessary to water several times each week.

Air Humidity: Mist the leaves occasionally.

Care After Flowering: Most plants are discarded, but Pot Chrysanthemums can be planted out in the garden where, if they survive, they will revert to their natural growth habit.

Propagation: Raising Pot Chrysanthemums is for the professional. Marguerites —— take stem cuttings in early summer. Cascade Chrysanthemums — sow seeds in spring.

SPECIAL PROBLEMS

WILTED LEAVES
Cause: Underwatering is the most likely reason. Even a short period of dryness will lead to wilting and this generally causes the lower leaves to fall.

SHORT FLOWERING PERIOD
Cause: The plant is too warm. Temperatures of 70°–75°F result in the flowers rapidly opening and then wilting.

FLOWER BUDS FAIL TO OPEN
Cause: Two major reasons cause buds not to open. The buds may have been all-green when the plant was purchased or the plant was not placed in a bright enough spot.

INSECTS
Aphid and red spider mite can be a problem; see Chapter 9.

● MARGUERITE VARIETIES

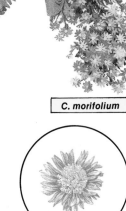

C. frutescens

● POT CHRYSANTHEMUM VARIETIES

C. morifolium

● CASCADE VARIETIES

C. morifolium

SINGLE-FLOWERED

ANEMONE-FLOWERED

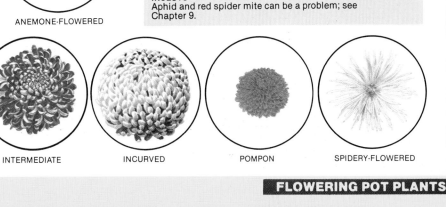

REFLEXED

INTERMEDIATE

INCURVED

POMPON

SPIDERY-FLOWERED

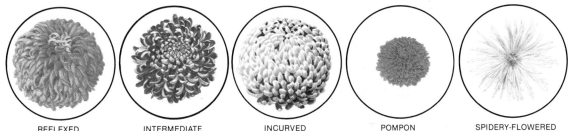

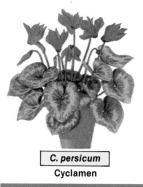

GRANDIFLORA strain

NANA strain   STELLATA strain

Senecio cruentus
Cineraria

CINERARIA

A well-grown Cineraria (proper name Senecio cruentus) is always a welcome gift. Masses of daisy-like flowers cover the soft, heart-shaped leaves and the colour range is impressive — white, blue, purple, pink and red varieties are available. The most popular strain is the Grandiflora group — large-flowered plants about 12–18 in. high. The tallest Cinerarias are varieties belonging to the Stellata group, reaching a height of 2–3 ft with small, star-shaped flowers. At the other end of the scale is the Nana group, small and compact, with masses of brightly-coloured flowers.

Flowering plants can be bought between Christmas and May, and should last for 4–6 weeks. Unfortunately Cineraria can be a disappointing plant and will collapse in a week or two in a hot room or if it is not watered properly.

SPECIAL PROBLEMS

YELLOWING, WILTED FOLIAGE
Cause: Cold draughts are the usual culprit, although wilting is the first sign of underwatering. A wilted plant may recover if watered and moved to a draught-free spot, but the flowering period is bound to be shortened.

SHORT FLOWERING PERIOD
Cause: Too much warmth; temperature above 60°F speeds up flower death. Too much sun and too little water can also bring flowering to a premature end.

SUDDEN PLANT COLLAPSE
Cause: Waterlogging due to overwatering or poor drainage.

INSECTS
Both aphid and whitefly can be a nuisance. See Chapter 9.

SECRETS OF SUCCESS

Temperature: Cool; 45°–55°F is ideal.
Light: Bright light away from direct sunlight.
Water: Keep the compost moist at all times with tepid water. Take care not to overwater.
Air Humidity: Stand pot on a Pebble Tray (see page 15) or surround with damp peat. Occasionally mist air around the plant.
Care After Flowering: Plant should be discarded.
Propagation: Not easy; sow seeds in May–July in a cool greenhouse.

CYCLAMEN

C. persicum
Cyclamen

Cyclamens are available from September until Christmas. Their charm is obvious — compact growth, beautiful swept-back flowers on long stalks and decorative foliage which is patterned in silver and green. The blooms are white, pink, red or purple; large and sometimes frilled in the standard types, small and perfumed in the miniature varieties.

Most Cyclamens are unfortunately consigned to the dustbin after a few weeks. With care they will bloom indoors for several months and then can be kept to provide another display next winter. First of all, try to buy a plant in autumn and not midwinter, and choose one with plenty of unopened buds. Then put it in a suitable home; a north-facing windowsill is ideal. The spot must be cool and away from direct sunlight; a warm room means a short life for a Cyclamen.

SPECIAL PROBLEMS

YELLOWING FOLIAGE, CROWN FIRM & HEALTHY
Cause: Hot, dry air is the usual reason; Cyclamen dislikes temperatures above 60°F. Other possible causes are underwatering and direct sunlight.

PLANT COLLAPSE, CROWN SOFT & ROTTEN
Cause: Overwatering, especially from above. Never let water stand on the fleshy crown.

SHORT FLOWERING PERIOD
Cause: There are many possible reasons—too much warmth, incorrect watering and dry air are common causes. Feed regularly during the growing and flowering season.

TWISTED, STUNTED LEAVES
Cause: Cyclamen mite; see page 120 for more details.

GREY MOULD ON LEAVES & CROWN
Cause: Botrytis desease; spray with Benlate. Always remove dead flowers and leaves promptly. Twist and pull; do not cut.

SECRETS OF SUCCESS

Temperature: Cool; 50°–60°F is ideal.
Light: Bright light away from direct sunlight.
Water: Keep the compost moist at all times. Employ the immersion method (see page 105), using soft, tepid water.
Air Humidity: Stand pot on a Pebble Tray (see page 15) or surround with damp peat. Occasionally mist air around the plant.
Care After Flowering: Reduce watering and stop feeding. Place pot on its side in a cool spot and keep it dry until July. Then repot using fresh compost, burying the tuber to half its depth. Stand the pot in a cool, well-lit spot; water to keep the compost moist.
Propagation: Sow seeds in late summer at 60°–70°F. It will take 15–18 months to flower.

CONVALLARIA

The dainty white bells of Lily of the Valley appear at Christmas or in early spring. Their fragrance makes them especially welcome, but the flowering season is short. Try to buy crowns ('pips') which have been forced for indoor use — the period between planting and flowering is only 3 or 4 weeks. Plant about a dozen in a 6 in. pot, just covering the points, in Seed and Cutting Compost. Keep warm and dark for 7 days and then move to a sunny windowsill in a cool room. Crowns from the garden or sold for outdoor cultivation will be less satisfactory. Plant in October, keep cold but frost-free until January then move into a warm room until flower spikes appear. Place in a light, cool spot for display.

SECRETS OF SUCCESS

Temperature: Cool; keep at 50°–60°F when in flower.
Light: Bright light with some direct sun.
Water: Water freely to keep the compost moist at all times during the flowering season.
Air Humidity: Misting is not necessary.
Care After Flowering: Plants should be discarded; planting the crowns outdoors will give disappointing results.

C. majalis
Lily of the Valley

CYTISUS

Two types of Cytisus are commonly called Genista and are sold for indoor cultivation — C. canariensis and the more attractive form C. racemosus. These small-flowered shrubs will produce long sprays of yellow fragrant flowers each spring but they are still included in this section because, unlike true house plants, they must spend their summers outdoors in the garden. They are stood out after the shoots which have borne flowers are cut back. In September the plants are brought back indoors and kept in a cool but frost-free room. In January they are moved to a bright, warmer spot and watered more freely to promote growth and flowering.

SECRETS OF SUCCESS

Temperature: Cool; not less than 40°F in winter.
Light: Well-lit during flowering season; light shade in winter.
Water: Water liberally during flowering season; sparingly in winter.
Air Humidity: Mist leaves frequently during flowering season.
Repotting: Repot, when necessary, after flowering.
Propagation: Stem cuttings in summer; use Bio Roota.

C. racemosus
Genista

ERICA

The Cape Heaths are small shrubby plants which are bought in flower between late autumn and Christmas. Their tiny leaves and masses of bell-shaped flowers are attractive, but these plants will give disappointing results in a centrally heated room. In hot, dry air the leaves drop very rapidly, so only choose an Erica for winter decoration if you can provide a cool and well-lit spot. Pay careful attention to watering — never use hard water and make sure that the compost is never allowed to dry out. There are two popular varieties to choose from — E. gracilis bears tiny globular pink or pale purple flowers, E. hyemalis bears larger tubular flowers which are pink with white tips.

SECRETS OF SUCCESS

Temperature: Cool; must be kept at 40°–55°F when in flower.
Light: Bright light; some direct sun is beneficial.
Water: Keep the compost moist at all times; frequent watering may be necessary. Use soft water.
Air Humidity: Mist leaves frequently.
Care After Flowering: Plant is usually discarded. To keep for a second year, trim back shoots after flowering and stand pot outdoors from May to September.
Propagation: Not easy. Stem cuttings in late summer; use Bio Roota.

E. gracilis
Cape Heath (Christmas Heather)

E. hyemalis
Cape Heath

EXACUM

Exacum is a small plant, a few inches high when offered for sale. Its flowers, pale purple with a yellow centre, are also small, but this plant still has several points in its favour. The blooms are abundant and fragrant, and the flowering season extends from midsummer to late autumn. It is easy to care for and new plants can be easily raised from seed. Keep the plants reasonably cool and in good light. To ensure the maximum flowering period pick a plant which is mainly in bud and not in full flower when buying Exacum, and remove faded flowers before they set seed.

SECRETS OF SUCCESS

Temperature: Cool or average warmth; keep at 50°–70°F.
Light: Bright light; protect from hot summer sun.
Water: Keep compost moist at all times.
Air Humidity: Mist leaves frequently.
Care After Flowering: Plant should be discarded.
Propagation: Sow seeds in late summer.

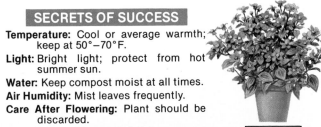
E. affine
Persian Violet

FUCHSIA

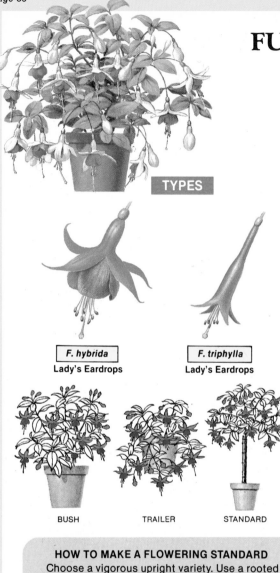

TYPES

F. hybrida
Lady's Eardrops

F. triphylla
Lady's Eardrops

BUSH   TRAILER   STANDARD

BASIC FACTS

Fuchsias occur in a wide range of colours, shapes and sizes. There are hundreds of named varieties of F. hybrida, with the familiar bell-shaped flowers hanging from the stems. These blooms may be single or double, with colour combinations of white, pink, red or purple. A collection of these hybrids can provide blooms from March to October, and some experts regard the Fuchsia as the most satisfactory of all flowering house plants.

Unfortunately nearly all of the plants bought for home decoration or as gifts are consigned to the dustbin once flowering stops and the leaves begin to fall. It is, however, quite easy to overwinter the plant in a cool room. The leaves will fall but growth begins again in the spring and with proper care the plant can be kept for many years. Flowers are borne on new growth, so cut back the stems in early spring just before growth begins.

Regular training and pruning are necessary to keep the plant free-flowering and shapely. With young plants pinch out the stem tips to promote bushy growth, and with flowering plants remove dead blooms to induce bud formation.

SECRETS OF SUCCESS

Temperature: Cool or average warmth; plant may suffer if temperature exceeds 70°F. Keep at 50°–60°F in winter.

Light: Bright light, away from direct sunshine.

Water: Keep compost moist at all times from spring to autumn. Water sparingly in winter.

Air Humidity: Mist leaves occasionally during the growing season.

Repotting: Repot every year in spring.

Propagation: Stem cuttings in spring or summer. Use Bio Roota.

SPECIAL PROBLEMS

LOSS OF LEAVES
Cause: Hot dry atmosphere is the usual reason for general leaf fall; mist leaves occasionally and stand the plant outdoors in hot weather. The common causes of the progressive loss of lower leaves are underwatering and lack of light.

FLOWER BUDS DROP
Cause: Poor watering (too much or too little) is the common cause. Other possibilities are too little light, too much heat and moving or turning the pot.

POOR FLOWERING
Cause: Many factors can shorten the flowering period. Keeping the plant moist and warm in winter will certainly have this effect; so will too little food or water and too little light.

BROWN SPOTS WITH YELLOW MARGINS ON LEAVES
Cause: Leaf spot disease, encouraged by over-watering in cold weather.

INSECTS
Both red spider mite and whitefly can be serious in hot and dry conditions.

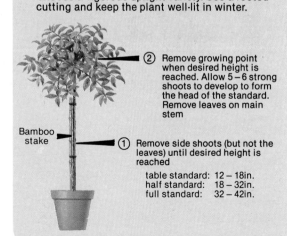

HOW TO MAKE A FLOWERING STANDARD
Choose a vigorous upright variety. Use a rooted cutting and keep the plant well-lit in winter.

Bamboo stake

② Remove growing point when desired height is reached. Allow 5 – 6 strong shoots to develop to form the head of the standard. Remove leaves on main stem

① Remove side shoots (but not the leaves) until desired height is reached

table standard: 12 – 18in.
half standard: 18 – 32in.
full standard: 32 – 42in.

GARDEN ANNUALS

BASIC FACTS

Many flowering pot plants can be raised at home from seed. Exacum and Browallia are examples of indoor plants which are grown from seed as annuals. A number of popular flowering pot plants, such as Celosia, Salpiglossis, Schizanthus and Thunbergia, are sometimes found in the garden as well as in the greenhouse, conservatory and living room.

Outside this limited list there is a large number of garden annuals which can be grown indoors as flowering pot plants. Some of the most successful examples are illustrated on this page. The technique of propagating from seed is described on page 116, and a vital requirement is to ensure that the seedlings receive maximum light by keeping them in a greenhouse or on a sunny windowsill. Failure to provide ample light will result in spindly growth with few flowers. If you don't wish to raise plants at home then buy bedding plants in spring. The best plan is to buy them in small pots and repot them at home. If you wish to create an indoor bedding scheme (see page 18) then buy the young plants in seed trays. Tagetes are extremely useful for this purpose. Feed regularly when the plants are established. When in flower, pots of annuals should be given as much light as possible, but temperatures should be below average.

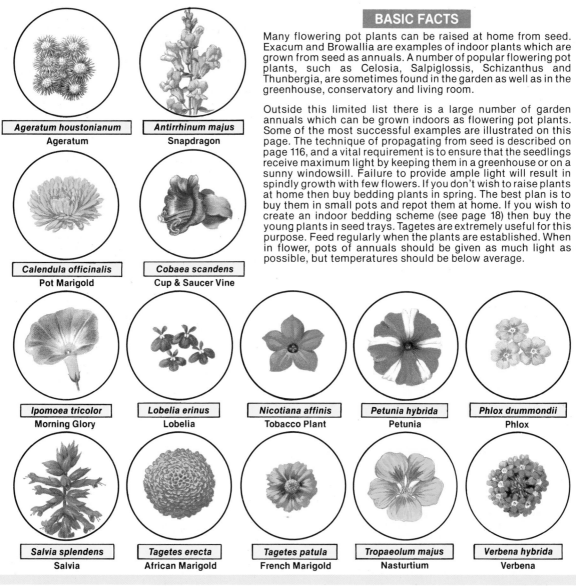

Ageratum houstonianum
Ageratum

Antirrhinum majus
Snapdragon

Calendula officinalis
Pot Marigold

Cobaea scandens
Cup & Saucer Vine

Ipomoea tricolor
Morning Glory

Lobelia erinus
Lobelia

Nicotiana affinis
Tobacco Plant

Petunia hybrida
Petunia

Phlox drummondii
Phlox

Salvia splendens
Salvia

Tagetes erecta
African Marigold

Tagetes patula
French Marigold

Tropaeolum majus
Nasturtium

Verbena hybrida
Verbena

GLORIOSA

The Glory Lily is a quick-growing climber which bears large lily-like flowers. The spear-shaped leaves bear tendrils at their tips, and some form of support must be provided. The spectacular red and yellow blooms appear from June to August and at this time a warm and well-lit environment is required. Gloriosa is either bought in flower or raised at home from a tuber. Plant the tuber vertically in a 6 in. pot in March, with the tip about 1 in. below the surface. Water sparingly at first, then more freely as the stems start to grow. Watch for aphid, which can be troublesome.

SECRETS OF SUCCESS

Temperature: Warm or average warmth; not less than 60°F in the growing season.

Light: Brightly lit spot, but shade from hot summer sun.

Water: Water liberally during the growing season.

Air Humidity: Mist leaves occasionally.

Care After Flowering: Reduce and then stop watering. Store tuber in its pot at 50°–55°F. Repot in spring.

Propagation: Remove and plant offsets at repotting time.

G. rothschildiana
Glory Lily

GARDEN BULBS

BASIC FACTS

Many of the popular bulbs which flower in the garden during the spring months can be grown indoors. There are two basic growing techniques — the large bulbs are nearly always 'forced' so that they will bloom well ahead of their garden counterparts. This forcing technique involves keeping them cold and dark to make the roots grow and then providing more light and warmth for leaf and flower development. Hyacinths are the most reliable — Tulips the least satisfactory. The second growing technique is used for small bulbs and is simpler than forcing. The pots are placed outdoors after planting and then simply brought indoors when the flower buds have formed and are ready to open. In this case flowering will only be a few days ahead of similar bulbs in the garden.

TYPES

● FORCED BULBS

Tulip

Early Single	Early Double	Darwin	Lily-flowered

The most satisfactory types for growing indoors are the Early Single and Early Double varieties. Darwin tulips will need support.

plant: Sept – Oct
in flower: Jan – April

Narcissus

Daffodil	Narcissus	Jonquil	Early Narcissus
Large-cupped. King Alfred will bloom in Jan	Short-cupped. Many white and yellow varieties	Small flowers. Tiny-cupped and fragrant	Several blooms on stem. Paperwhite will bloom before Christmas

plant: Aug – Oct
in flower: Jan – April

plant: Aug – Sept
in flower: Dec – Jan

Hyacinth

Roman Hyacinth
Dainty blooms; slender stems. White, blue and pink varieties available.
plant: Aug – Sept
in flower: Dec – Jan

Dutch Hyacinth
Large compact heads; strongly fragrant. Wide range of colours available.
plant: Sept – Oct
in flower: Jan – March

● GARDEN-GROWN BULBS

Crocus
plant: Sept – Oct
in flower: Feb – March

Iris reticulata
plant: Sept
in flower: Jan

Scilla
plant: Sept – Oct
in flower: Jan – March

Snowdrop
plant: Sept – Oct
in flower: Jan

Chionodoxa
plant: Sept – Oct
in flower: Feb – March

Grape Hyacinth
plant: Sept – Oct
in flower: Jan – March

HOW TO MAKE BULBS BLOOM AT CHRISTMAS

It is quite simple to raise Hyacinths, Narcissi and Tulips which will be in bloom on Christmas Day, but it is not a matter of planting the bulbs earlier than the recommended time. The essential step is to buy bulbs which have been specially prepared for early flowering. These bulbs are more expensive than ordinary garden types and they must be planted as soon as possible after purchase. September is the usual time for planting, and the technique described on the next page for Forced Bulbs should be followed. Bring the pots indoors when the shoots are 1 in. high; this should not be later than the first day of December. After flowering the bulbs can be stored for planting outdoors in autumn.

SECRETS OF SUCCESS

● FORCED BULBS

Planting: Choose varieties which are recommended for indoor cultivation and make sure that the bulbs are good-sized, disease-free and firm. Bulb fibre is sometimes used as the growing medium, but if you intend to save the bulbs for garden use after blooming then choose Bio Seed and Cutting Compost. Place a layer of moist compost in the bottom of the bowl and set the bulbs on it. They should be close together but must not touch each other nor the sides of the bowl. Never force bulbs downwards into compost. Fill up with more compost, pressing it firmly but not too tightly around the bulbs. When finished the tips should be above the surface and there should be about ½ in. between the top of the compost and the rim of the bowl.

Care After Planting: The bulbs need a 'plunging' period of complete darkness and a temperature of about 40°F. The best spot is in the garden covering the bowl with about 4 in. of peat. Failing this, place the container in a black polythene bag and stand it in a shed, cellar or garage. Any warmth at this stage will lead to failure. The plunging period lasts for about 6 – 10 weeks. Check occasionally to make sure that the compost is still moist.

Care During Growth: When the shoots are about 1 – 2 in. high move the bowl into a cool room indoors— 50°F is the ideal temperature. Place in a shady spot at first, then move near to the window after a few days. The leaves will now develop and in a few weeks the flower buds will appear. Now is the time to move the bowl to the chosen site for flowering. This spot should be bright but not sunny, free from draughts, away from a radiator or heater and fairly cool — 60° – 70°F is the ideal. Keep the compost moist at all times. Turn the bowl occasionally so that growth will be even and provide some support for tall-flowering types. Feed with Baby Bio.

Care After Flowering: Cut off flowers, not flower stalks. Continue watering and feeding until leaves have withered. Remove bulbs and allow to dry, then remove dead foliage and store in a cool dry place. These bulbs will not provide a second display indoors; plant in the garden in autumn.

● GARDEN-GROWN BULBS

Planting: It is essential to choose a container with adequate drainage holes. Place a layer of crocks at the bottom and add a layer of Seed and Cutting Compost. Plant the bulbs closely together and add more compost. The tips of the bulbs should be completely covered.

Care After Planting: Place the pot in the garden.

Care During Growth: When the plants are fully grown and flower buds are present bring the pot indoors to the site chosen for flowering. Treat in the same way as Forced Bulbs.

Care After Flowering: Treat in the same way as Forced Bulbs.

SPECIAL PROBLEMS

YELLOW LEAVES
Cause: Draughts are the usual reason. Other possible causes are incorrect watering and keeping the bowl in a spot with insufficient light.

BUDS FAIL TO OPEN
Cause: Water is the problem here. Erratic watering can cause buds to die without opening; so can wetting the buds by watering carelessly.

ERRATIC FLOWERING
Cause: The most likely reason is that the bulbs were either different in size or vigour. If the bulbs were evenly matched then the probable cause was failure to turn the bowl occasionally.

LONG, LIMP LEAVES
Cause: A clear sign of keeping the bowl in the dark for too long. Another possibility is too little light at flowering time.

STUNTED GROWTH
Cause: The usual reason is that the bowl has not been kept in the dark for the required period— the shoots should be an inch or two high before being exposed to light. Another cause is dry compost.

NO FLOWERS AT ALL
Cause: There are several possible reasons. The trouble may start at planting time by using undersized bulbs. Keeping the bowl too warm or bringing it too quickly into bright sunlight will have this effect. Dry compost will also inhibit flowering.

DEFORMED FLOWERS
Cause: A clear symptom of keeping the bowl too warm during the plunging period. At this first stage the temperature should be about 40°F – do not keep the pot in a stuffy cupboard or sunny room even if unheated.

ROTTING FLOWERS
Cause: Overwatering is the problem. A bowl without drainage holes kept under cool conditions can easily become waterlogged—take care. Remove excess water by carefully tipping the bowl.

GLOXINIA

Sinningia speciosa
Gloxinia

Gloxinias (proper name Sinningia speciosa) are usually bought in flower during summer. Choose a plant with plenty of unopened buds and with proper care it should continue to bloom for 2 months or more. Tubers for potting up are available in spring; for details of planting see Secrets of Success. The bell-shaped velvety blooms are 3 in. or more in diameter; white, pink, red and purple varieties can be purchased. Gloxinia, unlike so many gift plants, can be kept for growing again next season but it is not a particularly easy plant for the novice. It needs moist air, freedom from draughts, regular feeding and careful watering.

SPECIAL PROBLEMS

CURLED LEAVES WITH BROWN TIPS
Cause: Hot, dry air is the usual reason. During flowering it is essential to increase the humidity around the plant.

PLANT COLLAPSE, TUBER SOFT & ROTTEN
Cause: Waterlogging due to overwatering or poor drainage. Another possible cause is the use of cold instead of tepid water.

PALE ELONGATED LEAVES WITH BROWN EDGES
Cause: Not enough light. Gloxinia needs protection from hot summer sun but it will not tolerate dark places.

FLOWER BUDS FAIL TO OPEN
Cause: Several possibilities – most usual reasons are dry air and cold draughts.

SECRETS OF SUCCESS

Temperature: Average warmth; not less than 60°F.
Light: Bright light away from direct sunlight.
Water: Keep the compost moist at all times. Use tepid water; keep off leaves and flowers.
Air Humidity: Stand pot on a Pebble Tray (see page 15) or surround with damp peat. Occasionally mist the air around the plant.
Care After Flowering: Reduce watering and stop feeding. Allow to dry out completely when leaves turn yellow; store pot at about 50°F. Repot tuber in fresh compost in spring; plant hollow side up with top of tuber level with compost surface. Keep warm and rather dry until leaves appear, then treat as above.
Propagation: Sow seeds in spring or take leaf cuttings in early summer.

HIPPEASTRUM

H. hybrida
Amaryllis

Hippeastrum, usually sold as Amaryllis, is a truly spectacular plant. The giant trumpet-shaped flowers are borne on top of a stout flower stalk; white, pink, orange and red varieties are available. The strap-like leaves emerge after the flowers appear. This plant is usually bought as a large dry bulb in autumn; the normal flowering season is spring but specially prepared bulbs for Christmas flowering can be purchased. Plant each bulb in a 6 in. pot, leaving about half the bulb exposed. Keep it warm and fairly dry until growth appears, then treat as described in Secrets of Success. Remove the stalk after flowering is finished and with care a Hippeastrum will last for many years.

SECRETS OF SUCCESS

Temperature: Average warmth; keep at about 65°F when in flower.
Light: Bright light with some direct sun.
Water: Start watering when growth begins. Allow surface to dry between thorough soakings; use tepid water.
Air Humidity: Mist occasionally.
Care After Flowering: Continue watering and feeding until early autumn, then allow compost to dry out. Foliage will wither. Keep frost-free. Move to a reasonably warm spot and resume watering when new growth appears in early spring. Repot every 3–5 years.
Propagation: Plant up offsets at repotting time.

HYDRANGEA

H. macrophylla
Hydrangea
(Hortensia)

Hydrangeas are usually bought in flower during spring or summer. With care the blooms will last for about 6 weeks and the plants can be kept to provide Easter displays in future years. The heads of white, purple, blue, pink or red flowers are so large that they may need staking. Pink varieties can be 'blued' by adding alum (½ teaspoonful per pot) or a proprietary blueing compound before the flowers open. The two vital needs at the flowering stage are cool conditions (temperatures over 70°F will bring the blooming period to a rapid end) and compost which is never allowed to dry out — this may mean watering every day. After flowering cut back the stems to half their height.

SECRETS OF SUCCESS

Temperature: Cool; not less than 45°F in winter.
Light: Bright light away from direct sunlight.
Water: Keep the compost moist at all times from spring to autumn. Use rainwater if tap water is hard.
Air Humidity: Mist leaves occasionally.
Care After Flowering: Repot and continue to water and feed; stand pot outdoors during summer if possible. Overwinter in a cold but frost-free room. Water sparingly. In January move to warmer, brighter room and increase watering.
Propagation: Not practical in the home.

LACHENALIA

Cape Cowslip is an attractive plant, providing a host of pendent, tubular flowers between December and March. The blooms are yellow tinged with green or red, and both the flower stalks and the strap-like leaves bear brown or purple blotches. Despite its novel appearance, Lachenalia has never been popular, which is probably due to its inability to live in a heated room. In August or September plant 6 – 8 bulbs in a 6 in. pot with the tips of the bulbs just below the surface. Keep in a cool bright room, water once and then leave until shoots appear. At this stage start to water and feed regularly.

SECRETS OF SUCCESS

Temperature: Cool; not less than 40°F in winter.

Light: Bright light with some direct sun.

Water: Keep compost moist at all times during the flowering season.

Air Humidity: Mist leaves occasionally.

Care After Flowering: Continue watering for several weeks, then reduce and stop. Keep dry; repot in September.

Propagation: Remove and plant offsets at re-potting time.

L. aloides
Cape Cowslip

LILIUM

The most popular Lilium species for growing indoors is the Easter Lily. The tall stems grow 3 ft high and the white 6 in. long trumpet-shaped blooms are heavily scented. The main requirements are space and cold nights. In the U.S. millions are forced by nurserymen for sale in bloom at Easter; in Britain it is an unusual summer-flowering plant grown at home from a bulb. Make sure that the bulb is plump and not shrivelled. In autumn plant it in a 6 in. pot immediately after purchase, covering the tip with 1½ – 2 in. of compost. Keep cold, dark and moist. When shoots appear move to a brightly lit spot.

SECRETS OF SUCCESS

Temperature: Cool, not less than 35°F. Night temperature should not exceed 50°F during the growing season.

Light: Bright light away from direct sunlight.

Water: Keep compost moist at all times during the growing season.

Air Humidity: Mist leaves occasionally.

Care After Flowering: Reduce watering as leaves turn yellow and stems die down. Keep the compost just moist and repot bulb in autumn. Unfortunately growth will be less vigorous and the flowers smaller than on plants raised from newly-purchased bulbs.

L. longiflorum
Easter Lily

NERINE

This plant is a rarity, but well worth growing if you can obtain a bulb. Set it in potting compost in a 4 in. pot in August, leaving the tip exposed. Start to water and feed when the flower buds appear. In late autumn and early winter the 1 – 2 ft stalks bear beautiful white, pink or red flowers which look like miniature lilies. The narrow, strap-like leaves appear after the flowers and provided the plant is kept dry and warm during its resting period from May to September it should live for many years. Repot every 3 – 4 years.

SECRETS OF SUCCESS

Temperature: Average warmth; not less than 50°F in winter.

Light: Choose sunniest spot available.

Water: Keep compost moist during the growing season. Water sparingly in winter.

Air Humidity: Misting not necessary.

Care After Flowering: Stop watering and feeding when leaves turn yellow in May. Do not water again until new growth appears in autumn.

Propagation: In August remove and plant offsets taken from base of bulb.

N. flexuosa

NERTERA

The distinctive feature of the Bead Plant is the multitude of glassy orange berries which cover the creeping stems during autumn. These berries follow the tiny flowers which appear in early summer among the small leaves. It should be provided with plenty of water, fresh air and strong light during the growing season. The Bead Plant is classed as a temporary pot plant because nearly all of them are discarded once the display of berries is finished. With care, however, this plant can be kept for several years. It needs a resting period in winter and a spell outdoors in summer.

SECRETS OF SUCCESS

Temperature: Cool; not less than 40°F in winter.

Light: Bright light with some direct sun.

Water: Keep compost moist at all times; water sparingly in winter.

Air Humidity: Mist occasionally.

Care After Flowering: Keep cool and rather dry during winter; increase watering when new growth appears. Place outdoors from late spring until the berries have appeared. Bring indoors for display.

Propagation: Divide plants in spring before placing outdoors.

N. depressa
Bead Plant

OXALIS

O. deppei
Lucky Clover

Several varieties of Oxalis (Wood Sorrel) can be grown as pot plants, and are useful for hanging baskets and windowsill decoration. The most popular type is O. deppei, popularly known as Lucky Clover because of its leaf shape. Each of the four leaflets bears brown zig-zag markings and the yellow-throated pink flowers appear in early summer. Both leaves and flowers close at night and in dull weather, and this plant needs direct sun, cool growing conditions and careful watering. To raise Oxalis from tubers plant them just below the compost surface in late autumn or early spring. Keep at 50°F or below until flower buds form.

SECRETS OF SUCCESS

Temperature: Cool or average warmth; avoid temperatures above 70°F.

Light: Direct sunlight, but shade from hot summer sun.

Water: Water moderately during the growing season.

Air Humidity: Mist leaves occasionally.

Care After Flowering: Stop watering when foliage withers. Keep pot in a cool, shady spot. Repot in early spring and resume watering.

Propagation: Remove and plant offsets at repotting time.

POINSETTIA

Euphorbia pulcherrima
Poinsettia

The symbol of Christmas outdoors is the Holly with its bright red berries. Indoors it is now the Poinsettia (proper name Euphorbia pulcherrima) with its large, scarlet flower heads. This was not always so — in the early 1960's it was a tall-growing shrub which was distinctly difficult to keep in leaf or flower in the average home. Two things have changed — modern varieties are bushier, more attractive and much less delicate; in addition modern chemicals are used to keep the plants small. The result is that the Poinsettia of today is compact (1–1½ ft high) and the flowers (which are really coloured bracts) should last for 2–6 months. Red remains the favourite colour, but white and pink varieties are available. When buying a plant look at the true flowers (yellow and tiny in the centre of the flower head); they should be unopened for maximum flower life. Also the plant should not have been stood outdoors or in an icy shop. Once in your living room put it in a well-lit spot away from draughts and keep it reasonably warm. Surround the pot with moist peat if you can and avoid overwatering.

HOW TO MAKE A POINSETTIA BLOOM AGAIN NEXT CHRISTMAS

When the leaves have fallen cut back the stems to leave stumps 4 in. high. The compost should be kept almost dry and the pot placed in a mild, shady position. In early May water and repot the plant, removing some of the old compost. Continue watering and shoots will soon appear. Feed regularly and remove some of the new growth to leave 4–5 strong new stems. The prunings can be used as cuttings.

From the end of September careful light control is essential. Cover with a black polythene bag from early evening and remove next morning so that the plant is kept in total darkness for 14 hours. Continue daily for 8 weeks, then treat normally. Your Poinsettia will again be in bloom at Christmastime, but it will be taller than the plant you bought.

SECRETS OF SUCCESS

Temperature: Average warmth; not less than 55°–60°F during the flowering season.

Light: Maximum light during winter; protect from hot summer sun if plant is to be kept for next Christmas.

Water: Water thoroughly; wait until the compost is moderately dry before watering again. Water immediately if leaves begin to wilt. Water more liberally in summer.

Air Humidity: Mist leaves frequently during the flowering season.

Care After Flowering: Plant should be discarded, but if you like a challenge it can be kept and will bloom again next Christmas. The lighting will have to be very carefully controlled in autumn — see detailed instructions on this page.

Propagation: Stem cuttings in early summer. Use Bio Roota.

SPECIAL PROBLEMS

LOSS OF FLOWER HEADS; LEAF MARGINS YELLOW OR BROWN
Cause: The usual reason is dry air in a warm room. Poinsettia needs moist air—mist leaves frequently.

INSECTS
Red spider mite and mealy bug are the main pests; see Chapter 9.

LOSS OF LEAVES FOLLOWING WILTING
Cause: Overwatering is the likely culprit; the surface of the compost must be dry before water is applied. Of course, failure to water when the compost around the roots is dry will also cause leaves to wilt and fall.

LOSS OF LEAVES WITHOUT WILTING
Cause: If the temperature is too low or if the plant has been subjected to hot or freezing draughts then the leaves will suddenly fall. Another cause of leaf fall is poor light.

PRIMULA

The Primula group contains some of the best of all winter- and spring-flowering pot plants. From December to April these plants bear large numbers of flowers, clustered in the centre of the leaf rosette (the stalkless varieties) or on long, erect flower stems (the stalked varieties).

The ordinary Primrose has large flowers in white, yellow, red or blue; the blooms of the Fairy Primrose are star-like and much smaller, but they are scented and arranged in tiers on slender stalks. The Poison Primrose (so called because it can cause a rash on sensitive skins) has large flowers in white, pink, mauve or blue with a distinct green eye at the centre. Another large-flowering Primula is the Chinese Primrose, with yellow-eyed frilled blooms in pink or purple. The only yellow-flowering stalked Primula is P. kewensis.

Keep your plant well-lit, free from draughts, away from heat and protected from direct sun. Remove dead flowers and feed regularly.

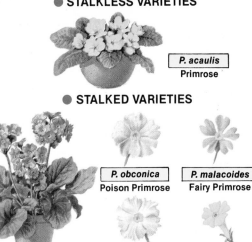

● **STALKLESS VARIETIES**

P. acaulis
Primrose

● **STALKED VARIETIES**

P. obconica
Poison Primrose

P. malacoides
Fairy Primrose

P. sinensis
Chinese Primrose

P. kewensis

SECRETS OF SUCCESS

Temperature: Cool; keep at 55°–60°F during the flowering season.

Light: Maximum light, but protect from direct sunlight.

Water: Keep compost moist at all times during flowering season.

Air Humidity: Mist leaves occasionally. Place on a Pebble Tray (see page 15) if conditions are rather warm.

Care After Flowering: Plant P. acaulis in the garden; other types are generally discarded. P. obconica and P. sinensis can be kept — repot and provide cool airy conditions in light shade throughout summer. Water very sparingly; in autumn remove yellowed leaves and resume normal watering.

Propagation: Sow seeds in June or July.

SPECIAL PROBLEMS

SHORT FLOWERING PERIOD
Cause: There are many possible reasons but the usual cause is too much heat—Primulas suffer at over 60°F. Failure to remove dead flowers will also bring blooming to an end.

YELLOWING FOLIAGE
Cause: Hot, dry air is the most likely reason.

CROWN SOFT & ROTTEN
Cause: Planting too deeply; the crown should be slightly above the compost surface.

PUNICA

The ordinary Pomegranate is not suitable for the average-sized living room but the Dwarf Pomegranate makes an excellent pot plant for a sunny window. Scarlet bell-shaped flowers appear in summer and they may be followed by bright orange fruit. Unfortunately, these miniature pomegranates will not ripen. In spring cut back any unwanted growth but do not heavily prune the bush. In summer the pot can be stood outdoors and in winter a cool but frost-free spot is required. During this winter dormant period the leaves will drop and the compost must be kept barely moist. Water more liberally when new growth starts in spring.

SECRETS OF SUCCESS

Temperature: Average warmth; not less than 40°F in winter.

Light: Bright light; some direct sun is essential.

Water: Water liberally from spring to autumn; very sparingly in winter.

Air Humidity: Mist leaves occasionally in summer.

Repotting: Repot when necessary in spring.

Propagation: Stem cuttings in summer; Bio Roota and warmth are necessary.

P. granatum nana
Dwarf Pomegranate

RECHSTEINERIA

The Cardinal Flower is closely related to Gloxinia, and the treatment required by both plants is very similar. The shape of the flowers, however, is completely different — R. cardinalis bears 2 in. tubular blooms quite unlike the large open bells of Gloxinia. The bright red blooms of R. cardinalis appear from June to September; removing stems which bear faded blooms will prolong the flowering season. Plants are usually bought in flower in May but you can raise them by planting tubers in February. Like Gloxinia the plant needs warm moist air, no draughts and careful watering.

SECRETS OF SUCCESS

Temperature: Average warmth; not less than 60°F.

Light: Bright light; protect from summer sun.

Water: Keep the compost moist at all times. Use tepid water and keep it off the leaves and flowers.

Air Humidity: Mist around plants frequently.

Care After Flowering: Water sparingly; stop when leaves turn yellow. Keep at 50°–60°F. Repot tuber in February.

Propagation: Sow seeds in spring or take stem cuttings in early summer.

R. cardinalis
Cardinal Flower

ROSA

**R. chinensis
minima hybrid**

Miniature Rose

It may seem surprising that roses are found in nearly all gardens but very few homes possess an indoor rose. This cannot be due to a lack of appeal — Miniature Roses bear lovely ½ – 1½ in. blooms which are similar to their larger outdoor relatives. There is fragrance, a wide array of colours and a variety of shapes including bushes (9 – 12 in. high), climbers and standards. The reason for the lack of popularity is their inability to flourish in the average room, but with care they can be grown successfully, providing blooms from early spring to late summer. The secret is to treat it as an outdoor plant which is brought indoors for flowering. Outdoors it needs little care — keep pests and diseases at bay and remove flower buds. Indoors it needs abundant light, cool airy conditions, high humidity and plenty of water. Remove faded blooms to prolong the flowering season.

SECRETS OF SUCCESS

Temperature: Average warmth; keep at 50°–70°F during the growing season.

Light: Maximum light; a sunny windowsill is ideal. In the short-day months extra light will be needed; place the pot near a fluorescent lamp at night.

Water: Water liberally when indoors. Allow to dry out slightly between waterings.

Air Humidity: Stand pot on a Pebble Tray (see page 15) if the room is warm. Mist leaves frequently.

Care After Flowering: Repot in autumn and transfer outdoors; bury the pot in soil if you can. Bring indoors in January and remove top half of stems — move into an unheated spot for a week or two before placing it in a heated room.

Propagation: Take stem cuttings in early spring; use Bio Roota.

SALPIGLOSSIS

S. sinuata

Painted Tongue

You will not find Salpiglossis mentioned in many house plant books, but it is an outstanding pot plant. When grown as a garden annual the beauty of the individual flowers is often lost; indoors the yellow, orange, red or lilac flowers with their dark network of veins provide a colourful display. Plants are raised from seed — sow in early spring for summer flowering or sow in late summer for an early spring display. Transfer each seedling to a 5 in. pot. Provide cool, well lit and airy conditions; stake the 2 ft tall stems.

SECRETS OF SUCCESS

Temperature: Cool or average warmth; keep at 50°–65°F.

Light: Bright light with some direct sun.

Water: Keep compost moist at all times.

Air Humidity: Mist leaves occasionally.

Care After Flowering: Plant should be discarded.

Propagation: Sow seeds in spring or autumn.

SCHIZANTHUS

S. hybrida

**Poor Man's Orchid
(Butterfly Flower)**

Poor Man's Orchid is an apt name for this plant; exotic multicoloured blooms can be obtained for the price of a packet of seed. Sowings are made in spring for late summer flowering or in autumn for blooming in spring. Pinch out the tips of young plants to induce bushiness. Move seedlings into larger pots as required; final pot size should be 5 in. for dwarf varieties, 7 in. for taller types. The smaller compact varieties, such as Hit Parade, are the best choice for indoor cultivation. Keep the plants cool, well lit and provide fresh air on warm days.

SECRETS OF SUCCESS

Temperature: Cool or average warmth; keep at 50°–65°F.

Light: Bright light with some direct sun.

Water: Keep compost moist at all times.

Air Humidity: Mist leaves occasionally.

Care After Flowering: Plant should be discarded.

Propagation: Sow seeds in spring or autumn.

SMITHIANTHA

S. hybrida

Temple Bells

Temple Bells, the popular name given to Smithiantha hybrids, describes the pendent bell-like flowers which appear on long stalks in autumn above the mottled velvety leaves. The 2 in. long flowers are usually scarlet with yellow throats but new hybrids in yellow, orange and pink are now available. Smithiantha is not an easy plant to grow in the average room; it needs the warm humid conditions associated with the greenhouse or conservatory. It is raised from rhizomes planted on their sides in potting compost in February; they should be ½ in. below the surface and you will need about three rhizomes for a 4 in. pot.

SECRETS OF SUCCESS

Temperature: Warm or average warmth; not less than 60°F.

Light: Brightly lit spot away from direct sun.

Water: Keep the compost moist at all times.

Air Humidity: Mist frequently around the plant but do not wet the leaves.

Care After Flowering: Stop watering and leave rhizome to overwinter in the pot. Repot in February.

Propagation. Divide rhizomes at repotting time.

SOLANUM

The Winter Cherry (S. capsicastrum) is a familiar sight at Christmas. The orange or red berries among the dark green leaves provide a festive touch, and if this small shrubby plant is placed on a sunny windowsill in a cool room then the berries will last for months. A closely related species, Jerusalem Cherry (S. pseudocapsicum) bears larger berries and is popular in the U.S. Solanum plants bear tiny flowers in summer and these are followed in autumn by green berries which change colour as winter approaches. A word of warning — these fruits can be poisonous. The Winter Cherry should last till February — early leaf fall usually means overwatering; dropping berries indicate too little light or hot, dry air.

SECRETS OF SUCCESS

Temperature: Cool; keep at 50°–60°F during winter.
Light: Bright light with some direct sun.
Water: Keep the compost moist at all times.
Air Humidity: Mist leaves frequently.
Care After Flowering: Prune back stems to half their length in February. Keep the compost almost dry until March, then repot. Stand the pot outdoors during the summer months; spray the plants when in flower. Bring back indoors in September.
Propagation: Sow seeds or take stem cuttings in spring.

S. capsicastrum
Winter Cherry

THUNBERGIA

Black-eyed Susan is one of the best pot plants to choose for covering a large area quickly and for providing summer colour. A few seeds sown in early spring will produce enough plants to clothe a screen or trellis with twining stems several feet long which bear a profusion of yellow or orange flowers with chocolate brown centres. When grown as a climber some form of support is essential; it can also be grown as a trailing plant in a hanging basket. Pinch out tips of young plants; remove faded flowers before they produce seed. Plants can be overwintered, but they are nearly always discarded in autumn.

SECRETS OF SUCCESS

Temperature: Average warmth; not less than 50°F in winter.
Light: Bright light with some direct sun.
Water: Keep the compost moist at all times.
Air Humidity: Mist leaves occasionally, especially in hot weather.
Care After Flowering: Plant should be discarded.
Propagation: Sow seeds in early spring.

T. alata
Black-eyed Susan

VELTHEIMIA

The Forest Lily is a striking plant which deserves to be better known. In midwinter or early spring the 1–2 ft spotted flower stalk appears, bearing about sixty tubular pendent flowers which last for a month or more. When not in flower the rosette of wavy-edged leaves forms an attractive display. Plant the bulb in autumn in a 6 in. pot, leaving about half the bulb exposed. Water sparingly until leaves appear, and then move to a sunny windowsill and water more liberally. Flowers should appear about 3 months after planting. The major difficulty is the need for cool conditions in winter.

SECRETS OF SUCCESS

Temperature: Average warmth; keep at 50°–60°F in winter.
Light: Bright light; out of direct sunlight during the flowering season.
Water: Keep the compost moist at all times during the growing and flowering season.
Air Humidity: Mist leaves occasionally.
Care After Flowering: Remove flower stalk and reduce watering. When foliage dies down store bulb in its pot. Do not water again until growth starts in autumn. Repot every 3–5 years.
Propagation: Plant up offsets at repotting time.

V. capensis
Forest Lily

ZANTEDESCHIA

The large trumpet-like blooms on yard-long flower stalks standing above fleshy, arrow-shaped leaves make the Calla Lily a spectacular plant. Despite its appeal it should not be grown unless you can provide adequate space, adequate light and a daily soaking when the plant is in full leaf. The most popular variety is the White Calla or Arum Lily (Z. aethiopica) which will bloom in winter or early spring if kept dry in summer. Plant the rhizome in autumn about 1 in. below the surface in a 6 or 8 in. pot. Keep the compost just moist until growth starts and then water more liberally.

SECRETS OF SUCCESS

Temperature: Average warmth; not less than 50°F in winter.
Light: Bright light with some direct sun.
Water: Keep the compost wet at all times during the growing season.
Air Humidity: Mist leaves occasionally.
Care After Flowering: Gradually reduce watering; stop watering altogether when foliage turns yellow. Repot in autumn.
Propagation: Divide rhizomes or plant up offsets at repotting time.

Z. aethiopica
White Calla Lily
(Arum Lily)

CHAPTER 5

CACTI

Cacti are perhaps the most popular and least understood of all house plants. Their popularity is easy to appreciate when you remember that hardly any other indoor living thing can be expected to put up with so much neglect and yet outlive its owner.

There are scores of millions of cactus plants in the homes of this country, yet in most cases they are kept as semi-alive, green ornaments which hardly alter throughout their stay. This lack of active growth is due to a misunderstanding of their needs. After all, in the popular view they enjoy neglect, only flower once every seven years and come from deserts where they exist on a staple diet of sand, drought and year-round heat.

The truth is that too much fine sand may actually kill them and summer drought will put them to sleep. For proper development and regular flowering they need winter temperatures which will make you shiver, and in summer many prefer fresh air outdoors to overheated stuffy rooms. Given proper treatment, as outlined in the Secrets of Success on the next page, your dusty desert cactus will come alive and, depending on the variety, may flower as regularly as the daffodils in the spring.

The cacti are a vast and varied family of plants, but every variety has a few features in common. All cacti (except Pereskia and young Opuntia) are leafless. On the stems you will find a number of areoles (woolly or bristly cushions). In most cases you will find outgrowths from these areoles — there may be spines, needles, long hairs or short hooks.

The cactus family is divided into two groups — the desert cacti and the forest cacti. The original home and the cultural needs of these two groups are different, as outlined below:

DESERT CACTI	FOREST CACTI 
Natural home is the warm semi-desert regions of America. Despite the name of the group very few can exist in sand alone.	Natural home is the forest regions of tropical America, where they grow as epiphytes on trees.
Nearly all cacti belong to this group and there are hundreds to choose from. Most types are easily propagated from cuttings.	Only a few varieties are commercially available, and most of them can be recognised by their trailing habit and their flattened leaf-like stems.
Need very little or no water between mid October and late March.	May need some water and feeding during winter months.
Require as much sunshine as possible, especially for flowering. Suitable for south-facing windowsills.	Require some shade during hottest months of the year. Suitable for north- and east-facing windowsills.

DESERT CACTI

HOW TO MAKE A DESERT CACTUS BLOOM

Although some cacti, especially the ones illustrated, will bloom when the plant is still quite young, there are others, such as Opuntia and Cereus, which will not bloom under ordinary conditions.

About half the cactus varieties can be expected to bloom indoors by the time they are three or four years old. They will continue to bloom each year, and although spring is the usual flowering season even a modest collection can be selected to provide a few blooms all year round.

The secret lies in the fact that most cacti will only flower on new growth. This calls for summer care and winter 'neglect' as described in Secrets of Success. Another point to remember is that flowering is stimulated when the plant is slightly pot-bound.

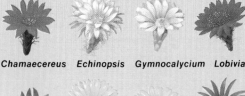

Chamaecereus   Echinopsis   Gymnocalycium   Lobivia

Mammillaria   Notocactus   Parodia   Rebutia

Temperature: Average warmth from spring to autumn. Keep cool in winter; 50°—55°F is ideal but no harm will occur at 40°F. Windowsill plants should be brought into the room at night if the weather is very cold and there is no artificial heat. The hairy cacti (Cephalocereus senilis and Espostoa lanata) need a minimum of 60°F in winter.

Light: Choose the sunniest spot available, especially in winter. In the greenhouse some shading may be necessary in the hottest months.

Water: Increase watering in April, and in the May-August period treat as an ordinary house plant by watering thoroughly when the compost begins to dry out. Use tepid water. In late summer give less water and after mid October keep almost dry — just enough water to prevent shrivelling.

Air Humidity: Do not mist in summer (exception — Cleistocactus). The main requirement is for fresh air; open windows on hot summer days.

Repotting: Repot annually when young; after that only repot when essential. Transfer in spring into a pot which is only slightly larger than the previous one.

Propagation: Cuttings of most varieties root easily. Take stem cuttings or offsets in spring or summer. It is vital to let the cuttings dry for a few days (large cuttings for 1 — 2 weeks) before inserting in peat-based compost. Another propagation method is seed sowing — germination temperature 70°—80°F.

SPECIAL PROBLEMS

STEM TIP SHRIVELLED, SOFT ROT BELOW
Cause: Overwatering, especially in winter. Carry out standard remedial treatment (see page 122).

NO GROWTH
Cause: Underwatering in summer or overwatering in winter. See Secrets of Success.

BRONZY MOTTLING ON SURFACE
Cause: Red spider mite (see page 120).

CORKY PATCHES ON SURFACE
Cause: Localised damage due to insects, physical injury or sudden chilling. Another possible reason is underwatering in summer.

BROWN SOFT PATCHES
Cause: Stem rot disease—well-grown plants are rarely attacked. Cut out infected tissue and water compost with Benlate. Improve growing conditions.

STEM ELONGATED & MISSHAPEN
Cause: Too much warmth in winter or too little light in summer. Refer to Secrets of Success; turn pots occasionally to ensure even growth.

PATCHES OF WHITE WOOL ON SURFACE
Cause: Mealy bug (see page 120).

BROWN HARD SHELLS ON SURFACE
Cause: Scale insect (see page 120).

ROT AT BASE FOLLOWED BY STEM COLLAPSE
Cause: Basal rot disease, due to overwet conditions in winter. Use upper stem for propagation. Next time avoid overwatering in winter, and cover compost surface with a layer of stone chippings.

TYPES

Astrophytum

globular white-flaked stem; prominent ribs; curved spines

globular white-coated stem; prominent spineless ribs

A. capricorne
Goat's Horn Cactus

A. myriostigma
Bishop's Cap

Chamaecereus

finger-like stems; white spines

C. silvestrii
Peanut Cactus

Cephalocereus

grey-green columnar stem covered with long silvery hairs

C. senilis
Old Man Cactus

Cleistocactus

slender many-ribbed columnar stem covered with fine white bristles

C. straussii
Silver Torch Cactus

Cereus

columnar stem; prominent ribs; brown spines

distorted branched stems; irregular ribs

C. peruvianus
Column Cactus

C. peruvianus monstrosus

Echinocactus

globular ribbed stem; sharp yellow spines

E. grusonii
Golden Barrel

Echinocereus

small globular dark green stem; small spines

columnar stem; numerous ribs; small comb-like spines

E. pectinatus

E. knippelianus

Echinofossulocactus

globular pleated stem; long spines

E. zacatecasensis
Brain Cactus

Echinopsis

globular or columnar stem; long spines

globular or short columnar stem; brown spines

E. eyriesii

E. rhodotricha

Espostoa

columnar stem covered with silky white hairs

E. lanata
Peruvian Old Man

Ferocactus

grey-green globular stem; prominent ribs; large red hooked spines

F. latispinus
Fish Hook Cactus

Gymnocalycium

brightly coloured offset, grafted on to another cactus stock

G. mihanovichii Hibotan

Haageocereus

columnar stem; dense cover of yellow spines

H. chosicensis

Hamatocactus

globular or short columnar stem; curved ribs; large spines

H. setispinus

Lobivia

globular stem; many low ribs; pale brown spines

columnar stem; many low ribs; yellow spreading spines

L. aurea
Golden Lily Cactus

L. famatimensis
Sunset Cactus

TYPES

Lemaireocereus

columnar stem; prominent ribs; closely packed areoles form white line

L. marginatus

Mammillaria

globular stem; hooked spines; dense white hairs

globular stem, becoming columnar; hooked spines; white hairs

short columnar stem; prominent tubercles; hooked spines

M. bocasana
Pincushion Cactus

M. bombycina

M. wildii

Myrtillocactus

branched columnar stem; prominent ribs; long spines

M. geometrizans

Opuntia

angular pads; tree-like growth

oval pads; long yellow spines

oval pads; tufts of golden bristles

oval pads; tufts of brown bristles

columnar stem; white areoles and spines; small leaves at top

O. brasiliensis
Tree Opuntia

O. bergeriana

O. microdasys
Bunny Ears

O. rufida
Cinnamon Cactus

O. cylindrica

Notocactus

columnar stem; yellow spines; flat top slopes towards sun

globular stem; spreading red spines

N. leninghausii
Goldfinger Cactus

N. ottonis

Oreocereus

columnar stem; yellow spines; long white hairs

O. celsianus
Old Man of the Andes

Parodia

globular stem; yellow bristly spines

globular stem; red hooked spines

P. chrysacanthion

P. sanguiniflora
Tom Thumb Cactus

Pereskia

evergreen shrub; spiny stem; green leaves

evergreen shrub; spiny stem; leaves red on underside

P. aculeata
Leaf Cactus

P. godseffiana
Leaf Cactus

Rebutia

globular stem; short white spines

finger-like stems; tiny spines

R. miniscula
Mexican Sunball

R. pygmaea

Trichocereus

columnar stem; large areoles with long yellow spines

T. candicans

CACTI

FOREST CACTI

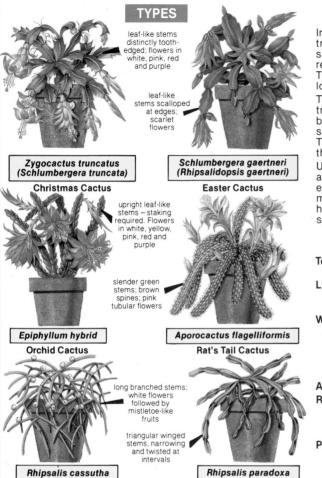

leaf-like stems distinctly tooth-edged; flowers in white, pink, red and purple

leaf-like stems scalloped at edges; scarlet flowers

Zygocactus truncatus (Schlumbergera truncata)
Christmas Cactus

Schlumbergera gaertneri (Rhipsalidopsis gaertneri)
Easter Cactus

upright leaf-like stems – staking required. Flowers in white, yellow, pink, red and purple

slender green stems; brown spines; pink tubular flowers

Epiphyllum hybrid
Orchid Cactus

Aporocactus flagelliformis
Rat's Tail Cactus

long branched stems; white flowers followed by mistletoe-like fruits

triangular winged stems, narrowing and twisted at intervals

Rhipsalis cassutha
Mistletoe Cactus

Rhipsalis paradoxa
Chain Cactus

BASIC FACTS

In their natural home the forest cacti are attached to trees in woodlands and jungles, and so it is not surprising that they are so different in form and requirements from the spine-covered desert cacti. There is an exception — the Rat's Tail Cactus, which looks like and should be treated like a desert cactus.

The typical forest cactus has leaf-like stems and a trailing growth habit, making it suitable for hanging baskets. A few, such as Rhipsalis, are grown for their stem form but their main attraction is their flowers. The most spectacular group are the Epiphyllums, with their fragrant saucer-size blooms.

Unfortunately the forest cacti can be shy bloomers, and there are rules to follow if you want a good display every year. Provide a cool and dry resting period, never move a·plant once buds appear and allow stems to harden outdoors during summer. There are also specific needs for each type, as illustrated below.

SECRETS OF SUCCESS

Temperature: Ideal temperature range is 55°–70°F. During resting periods keep at 55°–60°F.

Light: Choose a well-lit spot, shaded from direct sunlight for most varieties. Epiphyllum thrives on an east-facing windowsill.

Water: Increase watering when resting period is over and buds begin to form. Treat as an ordinary house plant when flowers appear and during active growth — water liberally when compost begins to dry out. Use rain water if tap water is very hard.

Air Humidity: Mist the leaves frequently.

Repotting: Repot annually shortly after flowering has finished. Epiphyllum is an exception — flowering is encouraged by pot-bound conditions so do not repot annually.

Propagation: Cuttings of most varieties root easily. Take stem cuttings in summer, using a terminal 'leaf' pad or stem tip. Allow cutting to dry for a few days before inserting in peat-based compost.

HOW TO MAKE A FOREST CACTUS BLOOM

	Christmas Cactus	Easter Cactus	Epiphyllum
JAN	FLOWERING PERIOD	RESTING PERIOD	RESTING PERIOD Keep cool (maximum temperature 50°F). Water infrequently
FEB	RESTING PERIOD Keep cool. Water infrequently	PRE-FLOWERING PERIOD Keep dryish and cool until flower buds form. Then increase water and temperature	
MAR			PRE-FLOWERING PERIOD Keep dryish and cool until flower buds form. Then increase water and temperature
APR	Treat normally; water thoroughly when compost begins to dry out	FLOWERING PERIOD Water normally. Maintain a minimum temperature of 60°F	
MAY			FLOWERING PERIOD Water normally. Maintain a minimum temperature of 60°F
JUN			
JULY	OUTDOORS Place in a shady spot; protect from slugs	OUTDOORS Place in a shady spot; protect from slugs	OUTDOORS Place in a shady spot; protect from slugs
AUG			
SEPT			
OCT	PRE-FLOWERING PERIOD Keep dryish and cool until flower buds form. Then increase water and temperature	RESTING PERIOD Keep cool (55°F). The soil ball should be moist, but do not overwater	Treat normally; water thoroughly when compost starts to dry out
NOV	FLOWERING PERIOD Water normally. Maintain a minimum temperature of 55°F		
DEC			RESTING PERIOD

CHAPTER 6

PLANT CARE

Plants growing in the garden rely to a large extent on the natural elements for their needs. All house plants, however, must depend entirely on you to provide them with their essential requirements. Leave them in deep shade or forget to water them and they will die. Without food they will steadily deteriorate. Virtually all varieties must be kept frost-free and the tender types require a minimum temperature of 60°F. Many plants find the air too dry in heated rooms, and you will have to increase the humidity around them to prevent browning and withering of the foliage. The least important requirement is fresh air, but some varieties demand adequate ventilation.

Light, water, food, warmth, humidity, fresh air . . . a long list of needs but success calls for neither hard work nor great skill. It is simply a matter of satisfying the particular basic requirements of each plant and not trying to treat all plants in the same way. Remember that excesses can be fatal — too much sun and too much water are common mistakes, and feeding more than the fertilizer manufacturer recommends is foolhardy. Also remember that there is a resting period, usually in winter, when much less water, food and heat are required.

Talk to your plants if you wish, but there is no scientific evidence that it will have any effect at all. What your plants do need is for you to spend a few minutes looking carefully at the leaves, stems and compost. This should be done daily, if possible, during the growing season. You will soon learn to tell when things are wrong. The appearance and feel of the compost will tell you when water is required. The appearance of the foliage will tell you when the water, temperature, light, food or humidity level is wrong. Pick off withered leaves and dead flowers; look for pests and diseases. Some people grow indoor plants for years without ever really looking at them or bothering to learn what the leaves have to tell.

Give them the FRESH AIR they need

Plants, unlike pets, do not have to be provided with air to enable them to breathe. Green leaves manufacture oxygen, and some plants will grow quite happily in sealed glass containers. Despite this unique property of plants, fresh air is still an important need of some varieties.

A change of air:
- Lowers the temperature in hot weather.
- Lowers the humidity where overcrowded, moist conditions encourage Botrytis.
- Strengthens the stems and increases disease resistance.
- Removes traces of toxic vapours.

Vapours arising from a number of sources commonly found in rooms have been reported as damaging to house plants or their flowers. These include coke and anthracite fires, coke stoves, dirty oil heaters, fresh paint and ripe apples. Plants with thick, leathery leaves are the ones most likely to withstand the effect of these fumes. One menace has disappeared — plant-damaging coal gas has been replaced by natural gas. Tobacco smoke is never present in sufficient amount to be harmful.

Fresh air is provided by *ventilation* — which is the opening of either a door *or* a window in the room in which the plant is growing. Provide summer ventilation for the following plants:

Araucaria, Cacti, Fatsia, Impatiens, Pelargonium, Schizanthus, Succulents, Tolmiea

Guard against *draughts*, which are air currents moving rapidly and directly across the plants. Do not ventilate when the temperature outside is appreciably less than that of the room.

Ventilation is not enough for some plants — they need to be stood outdoors during the summer months. Examples are:

Acacia, Citrus, Cytisus, Euonymus, Forest Cacti, Jasminum, Laurus, Passiflora, Punica, Yucca

Give them the LIGHT they need

HOUSE PLANT LIGHT GUIDE

◄ FULL SUN
Area with as much light as possible, within 2 ft of a south-facing window
Very few house plants can withstand scorching conditions—only the Desert Cacti, Succulents and Pelargonium can be expected to flourish in unshaded continuous sunshine during the summer months. By providing light shade at midday during hot weather a much larger list can be grown—see page 8.

◄ SOME DIRECT SUN
Brightly-lit area, with some sunlight falling on the leaves during the day
Examples are a west-facing or an east-facing windowsill, a spot close to but more than 2 ft away from a south-facing windowsill or on a south-facing windowsill which is partly obstructed. This is the ideal site for many flowering and some foliage house plants—see page 8 for a list of examples.

◄ BRIGHT BUT SUNLESS
Area close to but not in the zone lit by direct sunlight
Many plants grow best when placed in this region which extends for about 5 ft around a window which is sunlit for part of the day. A large sunless windowsill may provide similar conditions. See page 8 for a list of suitable varieties.

◄ SEMI-SHADE
Moderately-lit area, within 5–8 ft of a sunlit window or close to a sunless window
Very few flowering plants will flourish in this part of the room, but many foliage house plants will grow quite happily here—see page 8 for a list of examples. Most of the Bright but Sunless foliage plants will adapt to these conditions.

◄ SHADE
Poorly-lit area, but bright enough to allow you to read a newspaper during several hours of the day
Few foliage plants will actually flourish here—Aglaonema, Aspidistra and Asplenium are exceptions. Many Semi-Shade plants, however, will adapt and are capable of surviving in the darker conditions. No flowering plants are suitable.

◄ DEEP SHADE
•Unsuitable for all indoor plants.

Correct lighting is more than just a matter of giving a plant the brightness it needs; there are two distinct aspects which control growth. The *duration* a plant requires is fairly constant for nearly all types— there must be 12–16 hours of natural light or sufficiently strong artificial illumination in order to maintain active growth. Less light will induce a slowing down in food production, which is why the resting period of foliage plants is not broken by bright days in winter.

The light *intensity* requirement is not constant—it varies enormously from plant to plant. Some types will flourish on a sunny windowsill but quickly deteriorate in a shady corner; others will grow in light shade but cannot survive exposure to sunlight.

The human eye is an extremely poor instrument for measuring light intensity. As you move from a sunny window towards a corner of the room you will pass from Full Sun to Shade in about 8 ft. Walking with your back to the window you may notice little change, yet the light intensity will have dropped by more than 95% over a distance of a few feet.

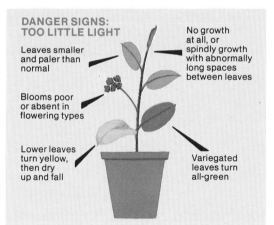

DANGER SIGNS: TOO LITTLE LIGHT
No growth at all, or spindly growth with abnormally long spaces between leaves
Leaves smaller and paler than normal
Blooms poor or absent in flowering types
Lower leaves turn yellow, then dry up and fall
Variegated leaves turn all-green

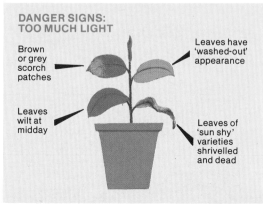

DANGER SIGNS: TOO MUCH LIGHT
Leaves have 'washed-out' appearance
Brown or grey scorch patches
Leaves wilt at midday
Leaves of 'sun shy' varieties shrivelled and dead

Natural light

- White or cream-coloured walls and ceiling improve plant growth by reflecting light in a poorly-lit room. A white background for a plant grown within the room will reduce the tendency for its stem to bend towards the window.

- The leaves and stems of a windowsill plant will bend towards the glass. To prevent lop-sided growth it is necessary to turn the pot occasionally; only make a slight turn each time. Do not turn the pot of a flowering plant when it is in bud.

- A flowering plant will suffer if it is moved from the recommended lighting to a shadier spot. The number and quality of the blooms is strictly controlled by both the duration and intensity of the light. Without adequate lighting the foliage may grow perfectly happily but the floral display is bound to disappoint.

- If possible move plants closer to the window when winter arrives. This will increase both the duration and intensity of the light falling on the leaves.

- Keep the windows clean in winter–removing dust can increase light intensity by up to 10%.

- A plant should not be suddenly moved from a shady spot to a sunny windowsill or the open garden. It should be acclimatised for a few days by moving it to a brighter spot each day.

- A foliage house plant can be suddenly moved from its ideal location to a shadier spot with no ill-effect. It will survive but not flourish— try to move it back to a brighter area for about a week every 1–2 months to allow it to recuperate.

- Practically all plants must be screened from summer sun at midday. New unfolding leaves will suffer most of all if some form of shade is not provided.

> **LIGHT RULE**
> Foliage house plants require bright light without direct sunlight; most of them will adapt to semi-shade. Plants with variegated leaves need more light than all-green ones, and flowering plants generally need some direct sunlight. Cacti and Succulents have the highest light requirement of all. There are many exceptions to these rules so consult the A-Z guide for details of specific needs.

Artificial light

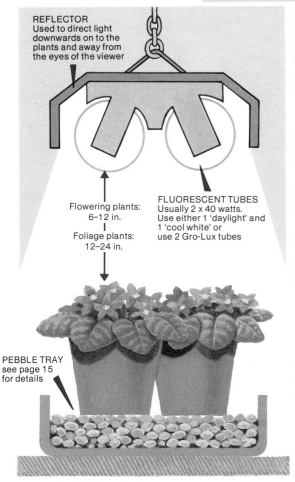

REFLECTOR
Used to direct light downwards on to the plants and away from the eyes of the viewer

Flowering plants:
6–12 in.

Foliage plants:
12–24 in.

FLUORESCENT TUBES
Usually 2 x 40 watts.
Use either 1 'daylight' and 1 'cool white' or use 2 Gro-Lux tubes

PEBBLE TRAY
see page 15
for details

Indoor gardening under lights adds two new dimensions. It means that you can grow flowering and foliage house plants in gloomy or even windowless rooms. It also means that you can supplement the duration and intensity of natural light in winter so that the plants remain in active growth—African Violets can be kept in bloom almost all year round.

Ordinary electric bulbs are not suitable for this purpose — the heat generated would scorch the leaves. Fluorescent lighting is used, usually in the form of long tubes. Many types of suitable units can be bought in countries where artificial-light gardening is popular. In Britain it is more usual to make an installation at home.

The basis of the unit is a tube or series of tubes mounted under a reflector. This arrangement may be permanently fixed above the growing surface or it may be suspended so that it can be raised or lowered as required. The plants should be kept in a Pebble Tray (see page 15). You will need to provide about 20 watts per sq. ft of growing area–if you use a light meter the reading should be the same as for a shady spot outdoors in summer. Look for danger signs – scorched leaves indicate that the lights are too close; spindly growth and pale leaves indicate that they are not close enough. Change the tubes once a year–do not change all of them at the same time.

The most popular varieties chosen for artificial-light gardening are usually colourful and compact. Examples are Begonia, Bromeliads, Cineraria, Gloxinia, Orchids, Peperomia and Saintpaulia.

Give them the WATER they need

HOUSE PLANT WATERING GUIDE

◀ **DRY IN WINTER Plants**
Desert Cacti and Succulents should be treated as Moist/Dry Plants during the active growth season from spring to autumn. During the winter the compost should be allowed to dry out almost completely.

◀ **MOIST/DRY Plants**
Most foliage house plants belong in this group. The standard recommendation is to water thoroughly and frequently between spring and autumn, and to water sparingly in winter, letting the top ½ in. of compost dry out each time between waterings. This drying out of the surface between waterings is especially important during the resting period from late October to March.

◀ **MOIST AT ALL TIMES Plants**
Most flowering plants belong in this group. The compost is kept moist, *but not wet,* at all times. The standard recommendation is to water carefully each time the surface becomes dry, but never frequently enough to keep the compost permanently saturated. There is no rule to tell you which plant belongs in this group—look up individual needs in the A-Z guide.

◀ **WET AT ALL TIMES Plants**
Very few plants belong in this group. Water thoroughly and frequently enough to keep the compost wet, not merely moist. Examples are Acorus, Azalea and Cyperus.

Without water a house plant must die. This may take place in a single day in the case of a seedling in sandy soil, or it may take months if the plant has fleshy leaves. But in the end the result is always the same.

Because of this obvious fact many beginners give daily dribbles of water, they fail to reduce the frequency of watering once winter arrives and they immediately assume that the plant is thirsty whenever leaves wilt or turn yellow. This produces a soggy mass in which practically no house plant can survive. Waterlogging kills by preventing vital air getting to the roots and by encouraging root-rotting diseases. More plants die through overwatering than any other single cause—they are killed by kindness.

Each plant has its own basic need for water – see the chart on the left. Unfortunately the proper frequency of watering is not a constant feature; it depends on the size of plant, the size of pot, the environment and especially the time of year. Because of this your best guide is observation rather than a moisture meter.

Self-watering pots and devices have a role to play in caring for the Moist At All Times group and for plants when you are on holiday, but they have the distinct disadvantage of not reducing the water supply in winter.

Watering troubles

Water runs straight through

Cause: Shrinkage of compost away from the side of the pot

Cure: Immerse the pot to compost level in a bucket or bath of water

Water not absorbed

Cause: Surface caking

Cure: Prick over the surface with a fork or miniature trowel. Then immerse the pot to compost level in a bucket or bath of water

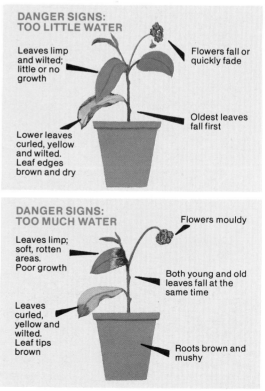

DANGER SIGNS: TOO LITTLE WATER

Leaves limp and wilted; little or no growth

Flowers fall or quickly fade

Oldest leaves fall first

Lower leaves curled, yellow and wilted. Leaf edges brown and dry

DANGER SIGNS: TOO MUCH WATER

Flowers mouldy

Leaves limp; soft, rotten areas. Poor growth

Both young and old leaves fall at the same time

Leaves curled, yellow and wilted. Leaf tips brown

Roots brown and mushy

The water to use

Tap water is suitable for nearly all plants. Ideally the water should be stood overnight in a bowl to allow it to lose some of its chlorine and to reach room temperature. This standing period is not essential for hardy plants but it is necessary for delicate varieties.

If you live in a hard water area a white crust may develop in time on the surface of the compost. This crust is harmless, but hard water can be harmful to lime-hating plants which are permanent residents indoors. For lime-haters which last for only a comparatively short time in our rooms (e.g. Azalea, Erica) the use of hard water will not really pose a problem.

The standard source of soft water is rainwater. Collect it by standing a large, clean bowl outdoors; never use rainwater from a stagnant water-butt.

When to water

Tapping the pot is useless; measuring water loss by estimating its weight calls for great skill. The simplest way of discovering when to water remains the best. Look at the surface – weekly in winter, daily if possible in midsummer. If the surface is dry and powdery all over, water if the A-Z guide states that the plant should be moist at all times. With the remaining plants insert your forefinger in the compost to the full depth of your fingernail. If your fingertip remains dry then the pot needs watering. The most important exceptions are the Cacti and Succulents in winter – if the room is cool leave them alone unless there are signs of shrivelling.

WATERING RULE
Roots need air as well as water, which means that the compost should be moist but not saturated. Some plants need a partial drying-out period between waterings, others do not. All will need less water during the resting period. Don't guess your plant's watering requirement – look it up in the A-Z guide.

The way to water

Both the watering can and the immersion methods have their devotees, and both have advantages. The best technique for most plants is to use the quick and easy watering can method as the standard routine and to occasionally water by the immersion method where it is practical.

THE WATERING CAN METHOD

Use a watering can with a long, thin spout. Insert the end of the spout under the leaves and pour the water steadily and gently. During the growing season fill up the space between the surface of the compost and the rim of the pot. In the winter stop as soon as water begins to drain from the bottom of the pot. In either case empty the drip tray after about 30 minutes. Never water in full sun as splashed leaves may be scorched. In winter, water in the morning if the room is unheated. Take great care when watering containers without drainage holes – add a little at a time and pour off any free-standing water immediately.

Although an occasional droop of the leaves will do no serious harm to most plants, do not make them beg for water in this way, for when this stage is reached the compost is definitely too dry. The leaves of woody plants, such as Azalea, should never be allowed to wilt.

THE IMMERSION METHOD

Plants such as Saintpaulia, Gloxinia and Cyclamen which do not like water on their leaves or crowns can be watered from below. Immerse the pots in water to just below the level of the compost and leave them to soak until the surface glistens. Allow them to drain and then return the pots to their growing quarters.

How often to water

You must never allow watering to become a regular routine whereby the pots are filled up every Sunday. The correct interval will vary greatly – Busy Lizzie may need watering daily in summer, Bishop's Cap may not need watering all winter. The interval between watering for an individual plant also varies with the season and changes in growing conditions.

THE PLANT	THE TIME OF THE YEAR	THE ENVIRONMENT

Fleshy-leaved plants can tolerate much drier conditions than thin-leaved varieties and a rooted cutting will take up much less water than a mature plant. With any plant, the larger the leaf surface and the more rapidly it is growing, the greater will be its need for frequent watering.

In winter, growth slows down and may stop; overwatering must be avoided during this resting season. Until new growth starts in the spring, watering one to three times a month is usually sufficient. During the spring and summer, watering will be necessary one to three times a week.

As the temperature and light intensity increase, so does the need for water. Plants in small pots and those which have not been repotted for some time need more frequent watering than those in large containers or ones which have been recently potted on. Plants in clay pots will need watering more often than those in plastic containers; double potted plants (see page 107) will need watering less frequently.

Give them the WARMTH they need

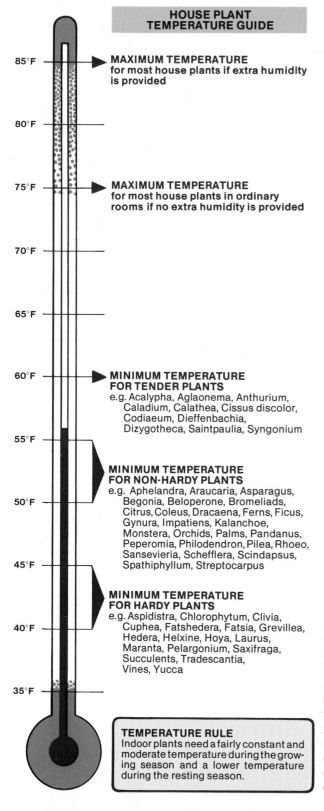

HOUSE PLANT TEMPERATURE GUIDE

85°F — **MAXIMUM TEMPERATURE**
for most house plants if extra humidity is provided

80°F

75°F — **MAXIMUM TEMPERATURE**
for most house plants in ordinary rooms if no extra humidity is provided

70°F

65°F

60°F — **MINIMUM TEMPERATURE FOR TENDER PLANTS**
e.g. Acalypha, Aglaonema, Anthurium, Caladium, Calathea, Cissus discolor, Codiaeum, Dieffenbachia, Dizygotheca, Saintpaulia, Syngonium

55°F

MINIMUM TEMPERATURE FOR NON-HARDY PLANTS
e.g. Aphelandra, Araucaria, Asparagus, Begonia, Beloperone, Bromeliads, Citrus, Coleus, Dracaena, Ferns, Ficus, Gynura, Impatiens, Kalanchoe, Monstera, Orchids, Palms, Pandanus, Peperomia, Philodendron, Pilea, Rhoeo, Sansevieria, Schefflera, Scindapsus, Spathiphyllum, Streptocarpus

50°F

45°F

MINIMUM TEMPERATURE FOR HARDY PLANTS
e.g. Aspidistra, Chlorophytum, Clivia, Cuphea, Fatshedera, Fatsia, Grevillea, Hedera, Helxine, Hoya, Laurus, Maranta, Pelargonium, Saxifraga, Succulents, Tradescantia, Vines, Yucca

40°F

35°F

TEMPERATURE RULE
Indoor plants need a fairly constant and moderate temperature during the growing season and a lower temperature during the resting season.

The natural home of most indoor plants lies in the Tropics. In this country they are raised commercially in glasshouses. These two simple facts have given rise to the widespread belief that high temperatures are essential for the proper cultivation of house plants.

The truth is that very few types will grow satisfactorily at temperatures above 75°F under ordinary room conditions. The reason is that the amount of light falling on the leaves and the amount of moisture in the air are far less in a room than outdoors in the Tropics or under glass in Britain, so the need for heat is correspondingly less.

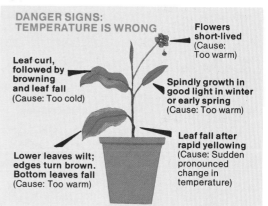

DANGER SIGNS: TEMPERATURE IS WRONG

Flowers short-lived (Cause: Too warm)

Leaf curl, followed by browning and leaf fall (Cause: Too cold)

Spindly growth in good light in winter or early spring (Cause: Too warm)

Leaf fall after rapid yellowing (Cause: Sudden pronounced change in temperature)

Lower leaves wilt; edges turn brown. Bottom leaves fall (Cause: Too warm)

Nearly all indoor plants will flourish if the temperature is kept within the 55°–75°F range – most types will grow quite happily in rooms which are a little too cool for human comfort. There are exceptions to this general rule – many popular flowering pot plants and some foliage house plants need much cooler conditions with a maximum temperature of 60°F in winter. At the other end of the scale the tender varieties require a minimum of 60°F; with warmth- and moisture-loving plants the pots can be stood in a Pebble Tray (see page 15) on a wide shelf above a radiator.

Most plants are remarkably tolerant and will survive temperatures slightly above or below the preferred range for short periods. The real enemy is temperature fluctuation. As a rule plants appreciate a drop of 5°–10°F at night but a sudden cooling down by 20°F can be damaging or fatal. Try to minimise the winter night drop in temperature by sealing window cracks and moving pots off windowsills in frosty weather. Cacti and Succulents are an exception—in their desert home they are adapted to hot days and cold nights, and so find the fluctuations in the centrally-heated home no problem at all.

Give them the HUMIDITY they need

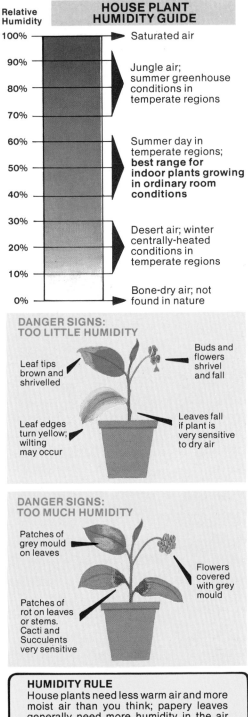

Relative Humidity

HOUSE PLANT HUMIDITY GUIDE

- 100% — Saturated air
- 90%
- 80% — Jungle air; summer greenhouse conditions in temperate regions
- 70%
- 60% — Summer day in temperate regions; **best range for indoor plants growing in ordinary room conditions**
- 50%
- 40%
- 30%
- 20% — Desert air; winter centrally-heated conditions in temperate regions
- 10%
- 0% — Bone-dry air; not found in nature

DANGER SIGNS: TOO LITTLE HUMIDITY

- Leaf tips brown and shrivelled
- Buds and flowers shrivel and fall
- Leaf edges turn yellow; wilting may occur
- Leaves fall if plant is very sensitive to dry air

DANGER SIGNS: TOO MUCH HUMIDITY

- Patches of grey mould on leaves
- Flowers covered with grey mould
- Patches of rot on leaves or stems. Cacti and Succulents very sensitive

HUMIDITY RULE

House plants need less warm air and more moist air than you think; papery leaves generally need more humidity in the air than thick, leathery ones. If your room is centrally heated and you wish to grow more than the dry-air plants listed on page 8, then group the pots together, double-pot specimen plants and mist the foliage as frequently as recommended.

Cold air requires only a small amount of water vapour before it becomes saturated, and so on an average winter day the air is moist. When you turn on a radiator to warm up this cold air, its capacity to hold water vapour is greatly increased. As the room becomes comfortable the amount of water vapour in the air is no longer enough to keep it moist. The air becomes "dry"; in technical terms the Relative Humidity has fallen.

Central heating in the depths of winter can produce air with the Relative Humidity of the Sahara Desert. Very few plants actually like such conditions; many foliage plants and most flowering plants will suffer if you don't do something to increase the humidity around the leaves. You can, of course, avoid the problem by finding a moist home for your plants — the kitchen, bathroom or a terrarium, but the living room atmosphere will be dry. You can use a humidifier to increase the moisture content of the whole room, but it is much more usual to use one or more of the techniques below to produce a moist microclimate around the plant whilst the atmosphere in the rest of the room remains as dry as ever.

Misting

Use a mister to deposit a coating of small droplets over the leaves. It is best to use tepid water and under cool conditions do this job in the morning so that the foliage will be dry before nightfall. Cover all the plant, not just one side, and do not mist when the foliage is exposed to bright sunlight. Misting does more than provide a temporary increase in humidity; it has a cooling effect on hot sunny days, it discourages red spider mite and it reduces the dust deposit on leaves.

Grouping

Plants grown in Pot Groups and Indoor Gardens have the benefit of increased moisture arising from damp compost and the foliage of surrounding plants. The air trapped between them will have an appreciably higher Relative Humidity than the atmosphere around an isolated plant. The best method of raising the humidity is to use a Pebble Tray — see page 15. There is a danger of too much humidity when grouping plants together — make sure that there is enough space between them to avoid the onset of Botrytis — see page 121.

Double Potting

Use an outer waterproof container and fill the space between the pot and the container with moist peat. Keep this packing material thoroughly and continually moist so that there will always be a surface layer of moisture to evaporate and raise the Relative Humidity. Double potting does more than raise the humidity; it provides a moisture reservoir below the pot and it insulates the compost inside the pot from sudden changes in temperature.

Give them the FOOD they need

What fertilizers contain

NITROGEN (N)	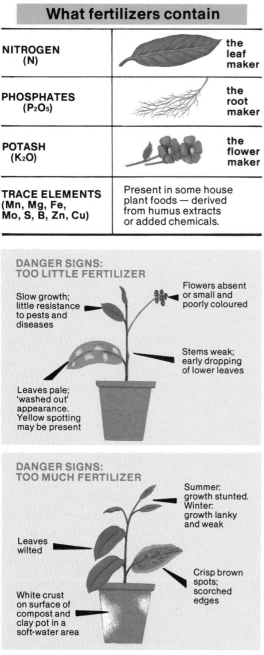	the leaf maker
PHOSPHATES (P₂O₅)		the root maker
POTASH (K₂O)		the flower maker
TRACE ELEMENTS (Mn, Mg, Fe, Mo, S, B, Zn, Cu)	Present in some house plant foods — derived from humus extracts or added chemicals.	

All plants, indoors and out, need an adequate supply of nitrogen, phosphates and potash together with small amounts of trace elements. Only then will they be capable of producing healthy growth with full-sized flowers and leaves.

In the garden it is usual to apply fertilizers to top up the soil's natural resources, but even in their absence the plant can continue to draw on the soil's supply of nutrients by sending out new roots. Indoors the position is quite different. The soil or compost in the pot contains a strictly limited amount of food, and this is continually depleted by the roots of the plant and by leaching through the drainage holes. Once the nutrient supply is exhausted regular feeding when the plant is actively growing must take place. Cacti can survive for a long time without any feeding, but vigorous foliage plants and flowering plants coming into bloom are seriously affected if not fed regularly.

DANGER SIGNS: TOO LITTLE FERTILIZER

Slow growth; little resistance to pests and diseases

Flowers absent or small and poorly coloured

Stems weak; early dropping of lower leaves

Leaves pale; 'washed out' appearance. Yellow spotting may be present

DANGER SIGNS: TOO MUCH FERTILIZER

Summer: growth stunted. Winter: growth lanky and weak

Leaves wilted

Crisp brown spots; scorched edges

White crust on surface of compost and clay pot in a soft-water area

FEEDING RULE

If the plant is growing in soil or compost it is advisable not to use a method of feeding which relies on a reservoir of nutrients. There are times when the plant may not need feeding, and when it is necessary, the amount of nutrients needed will depend on the size of the plant and the size of the pot. The most popular method is to feed each time you water when the plant is growing or flowering. Reduce or stop feeding when the plant is resting.

What to feed

House plant foods are nearly always compound fertilizers containing nitrogen, phosphates and potash. By law the label must state the content of each of these elements; if there is no statement for one of them then you can be sure it is missing. Other plant-feeding ingredients, such as humus extracts, trace elements, etc., may be present.

INSOLUBLE POWDERS AND GRANULES

Powder and granular fertilizers are widely used in the garden, but they are of limited use indoors. The plant food is deposited on the surface of the compost and it is not readily taken down to the roots where it is required. Furthermore you cannot cut off the supply when the resting period arrives.

PILLS AND STICKS

Pushing a pill or feeding stick into the pot is certainly labour-saving, but there are important disadvantages. The nutrients are concentrated in one spot which does not promote even root development, and you cannot easily cut off the nutrient supply when the resting period arrives.

LIQUID FEEDS

It is generally agreed that the most effective way to feed plants in pots is to use a liquid fertilizer. With Baby Bio, watering and feeding are carried out as a single operation, thus saving an extra job and avoiding the danger of overfeeding. Five drops are added to a pint of water, and this is used instead of plain water when watering.

When to feed

Potting composts contain enough plant food for about 2 months after repotting. After this time feeding will be necessary, provided the plant is not dormant. The time to feed regularly is during the growing and flowering seasons — March to October for foliage and most flowering plants, and during winter for winter-flowering types. Feeding should be reduced or stopped during the resting period.

Give them the REST they need

Articles on house plant care always trot out the same list of essential needs — light, water, warmth, humidity, fertilizer but one requirement is often omitted — a period of rest.

Nearly all indoor plants need a dormant or resting period during the year, and this generally takes place in winter. Some plants give unmistakeable signs that they are at the end of their growing period and even an absolute beginner can tell that the usual maintenance routine will have to change. The top growth of bulbous and tuberous plants (Hyacinth, Cyclamen, Gloxinia, etc.) dies down; the leaves of deciduous woody plants (Punica, Poinsettia, etc.) drop off. Watering is greatly reduced or stopped altogether as recommended in the A-Z guide. The *dormant period* has arrived.

Evergreen house plants unfortunately give little or no indication that a period of rest is needed. But as midwinter approaches the duration of natural light is too short to support active growth. The *resting period* has arrived. It is essential to reduce the frequency of watering and feeding; cooler conditions may be required. If the plant is kept warmer than recommended and watered as frequently as in spring then it will certainly suffer.

The appearance of new growth in the spring is a sure sign that the resting period is over. Slowly resume normal watering and feeding and repot the plant if necessary. Some plants, such as African Violet and Busy Lizzie seem to have little need of a resting period, but they do benefit from a period of about a month when watering and feeding are reduced below normal.

There is an important exception to the need for a winter rest period. Winter-flowering pot plants must be fed and watered regularly for as long as they are on display indoors.

HOLIDAY CARE

Your time for rest and relaxation away from home is a period of strain for the indoor plants which remain behind, but a little preparation before you leave will ensure that they will be unaffected by your absence.

WINTER HOLIDAYS

Leaving plants for a week or two during the winter months should be a minor problem if you can provide them with the minimum temperature they require. On no account should the plants be left on windowsills; if possible put the pots on a table in the centre of the room and water so that the compost is moist.

SUMMER HOLIDAYS

Leaving plants during the summer months is much more of a problem because the plants will be actively growing and their water requirement will be much greater than during the winter months. If your holiday is for more than a week, the most satisfactory solution is to persuade a friend to call in occasionally and look after them. If your friend has little experience make sure that the perils of overwatering are explained.

When a plant babysitter is not available trim off buds and flowers, move the pots out of the sun and water them thoroughly. If you can, surround the pots with damp peat. This procedure will not be enough for a long holiday in midsummer. A number of automatic watering devices are available; capillary matting soaked by a dripping tap in the kitchen sink is an excellent answer to the problem. Individual pots can be stood on wick waterers or they can be slipped into polythene bags, after which the tops are twisted and sealed with self-adhesive tape.

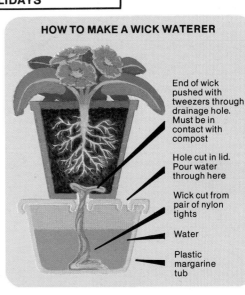

HOW TO MAKE A WICK WATERER

End of wick pushed with tweezers through drainage hole. Must be in contact with compost

Hole cut in lid. Pour water through here

Wick cut from pair of nylon tights

Water

Plastic margarine tub

CLEANING AND POLISHING

Dust is an enemy in several ways:
- It spoils the appearance of the foliage.
- It blocks the leaf pores so that the plant can no longer breathe properly.
- It forms a light-blocking screen so that the full effect of daylight is lost.
- It may contain plant-damaging chemicals. This is more likely to be a problem in industrial areas than in country districts.

It is therefore necessary to remove dust when it becomes obvious on the foliage. Small plants can be immersed in a bucket of water, but it is more usual to syringe or sponge the leaves with clean water. Wash plants early in the day so that they will be dry before nightfall. When the foliage is very dirty it should be lightly dusted with a soft cloth before washing — failure to do this may result in a strongly adhesive mud when it dries. Cacti, Succulents and plants with hairy leaves should not be sprayed or washed; use a soft brush to remove dust.

Foliage, even when clean, tends to become dull and tired-looking as it ages; the glossy sheen of the new leaf is soon lost. Many plant-polishing materials are available, and you should choose with care. Dilute vinegar, milk and beer are sometimes recommended, but they have virtually no shine-producing properties: Olive oil will certainly produce a shine, but it collects dust and can cause damage. Buy a product which is specially made for plants — both wipe-on liquids and aerosol sprays are available. Aerosols are simple to apply, but are not suitable for repeat treatments at regular intervals. Bio Leafshine, can be safely used on a wide range of smooth-leaved house plants; it is applied by gently wiping the foliage with a piece of cotton wool impregnated with the liquid.

There are a few rules when cleaning and polishing. Support the leaf in your hand. Do not wash or polish young leaves. Never press down on the leaf surface.

PRUNING AND TRAINING

Stopping, Pinching out — removal of the growing point of a stem. Use finger and thumb or a pair of scissors.
Pruning, Cutting back — more extensive cutting out of excessive growth. Use secateurs, scissors or a knife. Whenever possible cut just above a growth bud.
Trimming — removal of dead leaves, damaged parts and faded flowers.

The main purpose of stopping is to induce branching in many bushy and trailing plants, such as Coleus, Zebrina, Tradescantia and Pilea. The plants should be actively growing and the stem should have at least three leaves. The result is a plant crowded with stems, but with some climbing plants the opposite effect is desired. Here one or more strong main shoots are selected and trained as required, the weak side shoots being cut out cleanly at their junction with the main stems.

Many plants soon get out of hand and deteriorate if not regularly pruned and trimmed. Some climbing plants, such as Ivy and Philodendron scandens, regularly produce stems bearing abnormally small and pale leaves if kept too warm in winter. This growth should be cut back when spring arrives. Always cut out dead and diseased stems, crowded stems and all-green shoots on variegated plants. Cut back over-long branches and old leafless stems.

Prune flowering plants with care—there are no general rules. Some, such as (Fuchsia, Pelargonium, and Hydrangea), bear blooms on new growth. Others, such as Hoya, flower on previous growth. Only prune when the Secrets of Success tell you to do so.

Training — support of stems to ensure maximum display.
Training on supports is, of course, essential for climbing plants. It is also necessary for non-climbers with long, weak stems (e.g. Fatshedera), heavy flower heads (e.g. Hydrangea) and brittle stems (e.g. Impatiens).

Avoid the single cane wherever possible; use a framework of three or four canes. The canes should reach the bottom of the pot. Many other types of support are available — trellises, moss sticks (page 43) and wire hoops for inserting within the pot and climbing frames of wire and wood outside the pot.

Do not tie stems too tightly to the support. Train new growth before it has become long enough to be untidy and difficult to bend. Vines must be trained frequently or the tendrils will tie the stems together. A few untrained shoots hanging down from a climber can sometimes improve its appearance.

CHAPTER 7

POTS AND POTTING

Most of this book is devoted to descriptions of hundreds of different varieties of indoor plants, but not one of them can be grown if it is not planted in a suitable growing medium inside a suitable container. When you buy a plant the nurseryman will have already made a satisfactory choice, but in a year or two it will become pot-bound. The time has come for repotting – you will have to choose a satisfactory pot and the correct compost to house the roots, and you will have to ensure that the plant will settle down successfully in its new home. This chapter will show you how.

GROWING MEDIA

Soil taken straight from the garden is totally unsuitable for filling pots for the cultivation of indoor plants. It may well contain pests and disease organisms which would flourish under the warmer conditions indoors, and its restriction within a pot which is then regularly watered is almost bound to lead to a complete loss of structure. For these reasons indoor plants are grown in special mixtures known as *composts*. In nearly every case multipurpose composts are used, but you can buy special mixes for Orchids, Cacti and lime-hating plants such as Azalea and Cyclamen.

Soil Composts

The basis of soil composts is loam, made from turves stacked grass-downwards until well-rotted. Shortage of supply has meant that good-quality topsoil has been substituted in most cases; poor-quality soil will always produce an unsatisfactory compost. Other organic ingredients are added, and all are either steam- or chemically-sterilised before blending with fertilizer, lime and sand. The introduction of the John Innes Composts has removed the need for a wide array of bewildering mixtures.

Soilless Composts

Because loam is difficult to obtain and its quality is variable, modern composts are based on peat, or peat and sand. These soilless composts have many advantages over soil-based composts. Their quality does not vary and they are lighter and cleaner to handle. Perhaps the most important advantage of all is that the plant to be repotted was almost certainly raised in a peat-based compost, and plants do not like a change in growing medium at repotting time. Most manufacturers of soilless composts produce a single grade which provides an average plant with enough food for a few months. This fertilizer content makes potting compost too rich for sowing seeds or taking cuttings.

Soilless composts can have one or two drawbacks. All-peat composts tend to be difficult to water once they have been allowed to dry out but some (such as the Baby Bio Composts) contain an additive which makes the peat easy to wet. Lightness can be a disadvantage when a large top-heavy plant is to be potted — use a clay pot and add some sharp sand to the compost.

Do not compress these composts too firmly. They are based on peat, so excessive compaction impairs proper aeration which is vital for plant roots.

Aggregates

In hydroculture, porous clay aggregates replace compost as anchorage for the roots, and both roots and aggregates are bathed in a dilute fertilizer solution. The system is housed in a special container — the hydropot. These hydropots first appeared in 1976 and can be seen in many public buildings where regular maintenance is difficult. They are expensive, but have the advantage of requiring water only once every few weeks. Fertilizer is added through a special filler tube.

The plants grown in hydroculture develop thick, fleshy roots in place of the thin fibrous ones which grow in soil. Some plants succeed better than others. Cacti do surprisingly well, so do Aglaonema, Philodendron, Scindapsus and Spathiphyllum. Repotting can be a problem, and compost-raised plants cannot simply be transferred to a hydropot.

HOW TO RECOGNISE A POT-BOUND PLANT

Most house plants thrive best in pots which appear to the beginner to be too small for the amount of leaf and stem present. It is a mistake to repot into a larger container unless the plant is definitely pot-bound. Check in the A-Z guide — some plants will only flower when in this condition and there are others, such as Bromeliads, which should never need repotting.

Stem and leaf growth very slow even when the plant is fed regularly in spring and summer

Soil dries out quickly, so frequent watering is required

Roots growing through drainage hole

Final check:
Remove the pot in the way described on page 112. If the plant is pot-bound there will be a matted mass of roots on the outside, and not much soil will be visible.

If it is not pot-bound, simply replace the soil ball back into the original pot; no harm will have been done.

REPOTTING

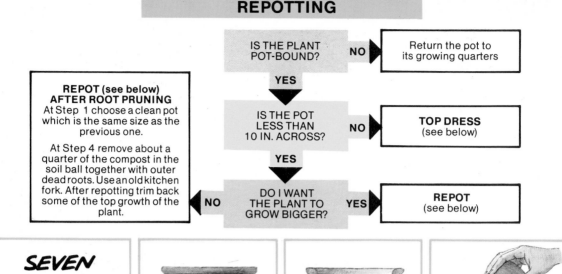

| IS THE PLANT POT-BOUND? | **NO** → | Return the pot to its growing quarters |

YES ↓

| IS THE POT LESS THAN 10 IN. ACROSS? | **NO** → | **TOP DRESS** (see below) |

YES ↓

| DO I WANT THE PLANT TO GROW BIGGER? | **YES** → | **REPOT** (see below) |

NO ←

REPOT (see below) AFTER ROOT PRUNING
At Step 1 choose a clean pot which is the same size as the previous one.

At Step 4 remove about a quarter of the compost in the soil ball together with outer dead roots. Use an old kitchen fork. After repotting trim back some of the top growth of the plant.

SEVEN STEPS TO SUCCESSFUL REPOTTING

The best time is in spring, so that the roots will have plenty of time to become established before the onset of the resting season. Choose a pot which is only slightly larger than the previous one; too large a difference will result in a severe check to growth (see page 113).

① If the pot has been used before, it must be thoroughly scrubbed out. A new clay pot should be soaked in water overnight before use.

② If a clay pot is used, cover the drainage hole with 'crocks' (broken pieces of pot or brick). Place a shallow layer of potting compost over the crock layer.

③ Water the plant. One hour later remove it from the pot by spreading the fingers of the left hand over the soil surface. Invert, and gently knock the rim on the edge of a table. Run a knife around the edge if necessary. Remove the pot with the right hand.

④ Take away the old crocks. Carefully tease out some of the matted outside roots. Remove any rotten roots but avoid at all costs causing extensive root damage.

⑤ Place the plant on top of the compost layer in the new pot and gradually fill around the soil ball with potting compost, which should be slightly damp.

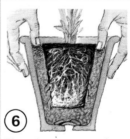

⑥ Firm the compost down with the thumbs, adding more until level of the base of the stem is reached. Finally, tap the pot on the table several times to settle the compost.

⑦ Water carefully and place in the shade for about a week, misting the leaves daily to avoid wilting. Then place the plant in its growing quarters and treat normally.

TOP DRESSING

For a variety of reasons, especially with large pots and trained specimens, you may not wish or be able to disturb by repotting. In this case the pot should be top dressed every spring by carefully removing the top inch of compost (2 inches for large pots). The removed material is then replaced by fresh potting compost.

CONTAINERS

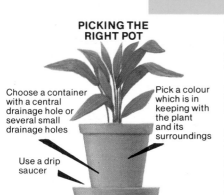

Choose a container with a central drainage hole or several small drainage holes

Pick a colour which is in keeping with the plant and its surroundings

Use a drip saucer

The basic container is the clay or plastic pot. Each type has its own group of devotees, but both sorts will support perfectly good plants. Their watering requirements are rather different, so try to keep a plant in one type or the other — repotting from a plastic pot into a clay one will mean that you will have to change your watering routine.

All clay pots have the same earthy terracotta appearance, but plastic pots come in a wide variety of shapes and surfaces. If your room is unheated in winter the insulating properties of foam plastic pots can be a distinct advantage.

Clay and plastic are not the only materials — wood, fibreglass and glazed earthenware containers are all available. The choice is up to you, but do remember the basic requirement for good drainage. If holes are not present at the bottom of the pot then bore suitable water outlets. It may be impractical to have drainage holes in a large tub for an indoor tree, but a small undrained pot is extremely difficult to care for — life for the plant inside it will be a constant struggle against waterlogging.

Clay Pots v Plastic Pots

Advantages:
- Heavy; much less liable to topple over.
- Waterlogging is less likely because of porous nature.
- Traditional 'natural' appearance — no chance of colour clashes.
- Damaging salts are leached away from the compost.

Advantages:
- Lightweight; much less liable to break if dropped.
- Watering is needed less often.
- Decorative and colourful forms available.
- No crocking needed; easy to clean.

Standard Pots

Half Pots — use for Bulbs, Azalea, Bromeliads, Begonia semperflorens and Saintpaulia

Seed Pans

The Standard Pot

Watering Space
This is the recommended distance from the compost level to the top of the pot.

Pot Size	Watering Space
2½ — 5 in.	½ in.
5½ — 7½ in.	¾ in.
8 — 9 in.	1 in.
10 — 12 in.	1½ in.
15 in.	2 in.

Diameter inside rim
This is the size of the pot — a 5 in. pot has a 5 in. diameter inside rim.

Height
The height of the pot is approximately the same as the diameter.

Pot Size
A wide range is available between 1½ and 15 inches. Ideally you should move up only 1 in. every time you repot, but this would call for a large store of pots. You can manage by taking the following steps when repotting, provided you use a good peat-based compost and follow the instructions on page 112. If you wish to stop before the 10 in. stage, root prune before repotting.

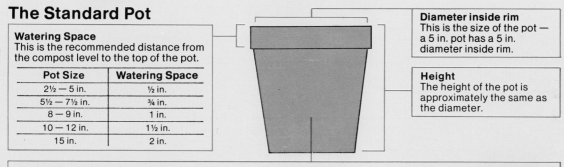

2½ in. 3½ in. 5 in. 7 in. 10 in.

The Self-Watering Pot

The range of self-watering pots continues to increase, and you can now buy any size from a small plastic container for the windowsill to a floor-standing tub which will house a large indoor garden. They all work on the same two-pot principle — the main container, which houses the compost and plant, draws its water by capillary action from the lower container, or reservoir, which is kept topped up through a filler tube. Liquid feed as well as water is added through this tube.

The self-watering pot can be a boon for areas where watering cannot take place at frequent intervals — weekend cottages, offices, etc. Plants which like to be kept moist at all times grow successfully during the active growing season, but the compost tends to be too wet in winter. For plants which require a period of dryness between waterings, the reservoir should dry out completely for a few days before refilling. Unfortunately, this removes the "automatic" virtue of these containers.

CHAPTER 8

INCREASING YOUR STOCK

Some indoor plants cannot be raised at home without special equipment — you either have to invest in a thermostatically-controlled propagator or leave it to the nurseryman. But a vast number of different varieties can be propagated quite simply in the kitchen or spare room, and it is strange that there are so many people who grow their own vegetables and paint their own homes and yet are daunted by the idea of raising their own house plants. We now have so many aids which were unknown in grandmother's day — rooting hormone, transparent polythene bags, special composts, rooting bags and so on, yet the Victorians propagated a higher proportion of their own plants than we do.

There are four basic reasons for raising plants at home — to have more plants without having the expense of buying them every time, to replace ageing specimens with vigorous new ones, to have plants which would otherwise be unobtainable and to provide welcome gifts for friends. This final reason is responsible for the term 'friendship plants' given to varieties such as Busy Lizzie and Wandering Jew which are more usually raised at home than bought in a garden shop.

PLANTLETS

A few species produce miniature plants at the end of flowering stems (e.g. Chlorophytum, Saxifraga sarmentosa and Tolmiea) or on mature leaves (e.g. Bryophyllum daigremontianum and Asplenium bulbiferum).

Propagation is easy. If no roots are present on the plantlet, peg it down in moist Seed and Cutting Compost — see 'Layering' below for details. Sever the plantlet from the parent plant when rooting has taken place. If the plantlet bears roots, it can be propagated by removing it from the parent plant and potting up as a rooted cutting.

OFFSETS

Some species produce miniature plants as side shoots from the main stem (e.g. Bromeliads, Cacti and Succulents) or as tiny bulbils or bulblets next to the parent bulb (e.g. Hippeastrum and Oxalis).

Stem offsets should be cut off as near the main stem as possible — preserve any roots which may be attached. A Bromeliad offset is ready for propagating when it is about a quarter of the size of the parent plant. Pot up each offset in Seed and Cutting Compost and treat as an ordinary cutting — see page 116. Bulb offsets should be separated from the parent bulb and potted up; it will take one or two years before flowering occurs.

DIVISION

A number of house plants form several clumps or daughter rosettes as they develop, and these plants can be easily propagated by division. Examples are Chlorophytum, Cyperus, Maranta, Saintpaulia, Sansevieria and many Ferns.

Knock the plant out of its pot in spring or early summer and carefully pull off one or more segments. Do this by gently removing some compost so as to expose the connection between the clump and the rest of the plant. Break this join by hand or with a sharp knife. Never divide a plant by simply cutting it in two.

Transplant the segments into pots using Seed and Cutting Compost. Trickle compost between the roots and gently firm to prevent air pockets. Water sparingly until new growth appears.

LAYERING

Most climbers and trailers with long, flexible stems can be propagated by layering —the disadvantage of this method is that rooting takes a long time.

Pick a vigorous stem and in spring or early summer pin it down into Seed and Cutting Compost in a small pot, using a hairpin or U-shaped piece of wire. A small nick cut into the underside of the stem will speed up rooting. Several stems arising from the parent plant can be layered at the same time. Once rooting has taken place, fresh growth will appear and the stem can then be cut, thus freeing the new plant.

AIR LAYERING

Polythene film

Healthy leaf 4 in. or less above cut section

½ in. section from which bark has been stripped and then painted with Bio Roota

Wire tie

Damp sphagnum moss

When thick-stemmed plants such as Dieffenbachia, Dracaena, Ficus elastica decora or Monstera become leggy due to the loss of their lower leaves, new compact plants can be produced by air layering.

Make the air layer as shown in the illustration; the cut should not be more than 2 ft from the tip of the plant. After a couple of months roots will be seen inside the plastic bag. Sever the stem just below the bottom wire tie, remove the polythene and pot up carefully in Potting Compost. The old plant need not be thrown away; it will produce new shoots on the shortened stem if the compost is kept just moist.

CUTTINGS

Cuttings are by far the most usual way to raise indoor plants at home. The chance of success depends on the variety—some woody plants are difficult or impossible to propagate without special equipment, whereas several popular plants, such as Tradescantia, Impatiens and Ivy, will root quite readily in a glass of water. Even with easy-to-root cuttings there can be inexplicable failures so always take several cuttings and do not be disappointed if a few of them fail.

STEM CUTTINGS

Most house plants can be propagated from stem cuttings. Choose a sturdy and healthy non-flowering shoot. Some non-woody plants will root at any time of the year but woody varieties are generally more reliant on active growing conditions so in this latter case always follow the timing specified in the A-Z guide and always use a rooting hormone. As a general rule spring or early summer is the best time for all plants, but late summer is a popular time for striking Fuchsia and Geranium cuttings.

Stem cuttings should be inserted in the compost as soon as they have been prepared, but a Cactus or Succulent cutting should be left to dry for several days before insertion.

With shrubby plants it is preferable to take heel cuttings rather than the stem-tip cuttings illustrated on the right. Pull off a side shoot with a 'heel' (strip of bark from the main stem) attached. Trim any ragged edges and dip the bottom inch in Bio Roota.

Cutting should be 3-6 in. long, depending on the size of the parent plant

Cut off leaves from lower half of cutting

Cut straight across with a razor blade or sharp knife below a leaf joint

Dip bottom ½ in. in Bio Roota

Insert cutting; firm around the base with the pencil

Make a hole with a pencil

LEAF CUTTINGS

Some plants do not have stems; the leaves arise directly from the crown of the plant. Obviously stem cuttings are impossible, but leaf cuttings provide an easy way to propagate many of these varieties.

Whole Leaf plus Stalk

Standard method for Saintpaulia, Gloxinia, small-leaved Peperomias and some Begonias.

Mature leaf taken from the base of the plant

Leaf stalk 2 in. long

Dip end into Bio Roota

Cut straight across with a razor blade or sharp knife

Insert cutting with the back of leaf towards the back of the pot. Leaf base should be just above the compost. Firm around the base with the pencil

Make a hole at 45° with a pencil

Whole Leaf

Standard method for Succulents such as Sedum, Echeveria and Crassula.

Mature fleshy leaf. Large leaves should be allowed to dry for a couple of days before planting

Cover surface with sharp sand

Lay small leaves on the surface; press lightly into the compost

Push the ends of large leaves into the compost

Part Leaf

Standard method for Begonia rex, Begonia masoniana, Streptocarpus and Sansevieria.

Begonia 1-1½ in. triangle cut from a mature, healthy leaf

Sansevieria 2-3 in. section cut from a mature, healthy leaf. Note: the plant produced will not be variegated

Streptocarpus Section of a leaf—an adult leaf will produce 3 or 4 cuttings

Insert cutting and wooden labels for support at 45°. Bury a quarter of the cutting

Insert cutting vertically. Bury half the cutting

CANE CUTTINGS

A number of important house plants which produce thick and erect stems are propagated by means of cane cuttings. The best time to do this is when one or more stems have lost their lower leaves and are no longer attractive. The bare trunk is cut into several pieces, and each piece is inserted into Seed & Cutting Compost. The cane cuttings can be placed horizontally, as illustrated, or planted upright. If planted upright, make sure you bury the end which was the lower part on the stem. Cane cuttings can be used for Cordyline, Dracaena and Dieffenbachia; ready-to-plant canes ('Ti-Plants') can be bought in gift shops.

Cutting should be 2-3 in. long, bearing at least 1 node. Leaf buds must point upward. Bury lower half in compost

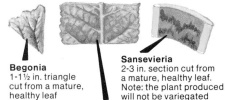

HOW TO ROOT CUTTINGS
The Pot Method

A 5 in. clay or plastic pot will take three to six average-sized cuttings. The rooting medium must be sterile, free-draining, firm enough to hold the cuttings and contain not too much fertilizer. A specially formulated Seed & Cutting Compost is ideal.

Fill the pot with compost and lightly firm to leave a ½ in. watering space at the top. The cuttings should be inserted close to the side of the pot; make sure that they are properly firmed in as an air space around the cut surface is fatal. Some cuttings are inserted vertically and others at 45°; the instructions on the previous page will tell you when the cutting should be put in at an angle. Water in very gently.

Nearly all cuttings will need a humid atmosphere—in dry air large leaves soon shrivel and die, as there is no root system to replace the rapid loss of moisture. Place four canes in the pot and drape a polythene bag over them; secure with a rubber band. There are three important exceptions to this polythene bag technique—do not cover Cactus, Succulent or Geranium cuttings.

Place the pot in light shade or in a bright spot out of direct sunlight. The temperature should be 65°F or more. Pick off any leaves that turn yellow or start to rot.

The great enemy now is impatience—do not keep lifting the cuttings to see if roots are appearing. In a few weeks the tell-tale signs of success should appear—new growth at the tips of stem cuttings, and tiny plantlets at the base of leaf cuttings.

Potting-on time has arrived. Water the compost and then lift out each rooted stem cutting, taking care not to disturb the compost around the roots. Transfer each cutting to a 2½ or 3½ in. pot—fill with Potting Compost. Firm gently and water to settle the compost around the roots. Put the pots back in the same spot for a week or two; then transfer to their permanent quarters.

The technique with leaf cuttings which produce several plantlets is different. When the new plants are large enough to handle, cut away the parent leaf, gently separate and pot on. Make sure that each plantlet has some roots.

The Rooting Bag Method

A recent innovation is the rooting bag, in which Seed & Cutting Compost is tightly packed and sealed in a stout polythene bag. There are two basic advantages compared to the pot method—the covered compost stays moist much longer and weak cuttings are supported by the polythene. The method consists of cutting fourteen slits in the upper surface and inserting a cutting through each slit. If the cuttings wilt after a few hours, the rooting bag is slipped into a large plastic bag which is blown up and the top tied with a wire tie or self-adhesive tape.

The Propagator Method

A propagator is a useful piece of equipment if you intend to raise a large number of house plants. Basically it consists of a firm tray to hold the compost and a transparent cover which bears air vents. A simple unheated model will meet the needs of the average indoor gardener, but if you plan to raise delicate plants which need a propagating temperature of 70°F or more then you will need a heated propagator. This contains a heating element to raise the temperature of the compost and a thermostat to ensure that the temperature stays constant.

SEED SOWING

Unlike raising plants for the garden, seed sowing is not a popular method of propagating house plants. Nearly all of them require time, skill and heated conditions, but there are special cases where seed sowing is the method to use. Some plants, such as Thunbergia, Exacum and the Garden Annuals have to be raised in this way, and seed sowing allows large numbers of plants such as Coleus to be grown for indoor bedding at very little cost. Lastly, the young (and not-so-young) delight in sowing pips, fruit stones, beans, etc., to produce short-lived foliage plants.

Fill a pot or seed pan with Seed & Cutting Compost; firm lightly with the fingertips or a board and water lightly. Sow seeds thinly—space out each seed if they are large enough to handle. Cover large seeds with a layer of compost; small seeds not at all. Place a polythene bag over the container and secure with a rubber band.

Stand the pot in a shady place at a temperature of 60°-70°F. As soon as the seeds have germinated move the pot to a bright spot, away from direct sunlight. Remove the plastic cover, keep the compost surface moist and turn the pot regularly to avoid lop-sided growth.

As soon as the seedlings are large enough to handle they should be pricked out into small pots filled with Potting Compost.

SPORE SOWING

Ferns produce dust-like spores, not seeds, and it is always a challenge to try to raise fern plants from these spores at home. Collect them in a paper bag from ripe spore-cases which are found on the underside of the fronds. Leave them to dry for a couple of weeks and then spread them very thinly on the surface of moist Seed & Cutting Compost. The compost should be in a plastic pot which has been sterilised by immersion in boiling water. Cover the pot with a sheet of glass after sowing the spores and place it in a shady spot. When the plants are large enough to handle transplant them into small pots.

CHAPTER 9

PLANT TROUBLES

It is always disappointing when a cherished specimen suddenly looks sickly, and it is so often the more expensive types which succumb first.

There is not going to be much pleasure in growing indoor plants unless you learn how to avoid plant troubles. Specific pests and diseases are not usually to blame; in most cases the cause of ill-health or death is either too much or too little of one or more of the essential growth factors—light, water, warmth, humidity and food.

To keep your plants in perfect condition, your first task is to choose only those types which can be expected to flourish in the conditions you can provide. Then choose carefully and buy healthy specimens, protect them on their way home and finally provide them with the right conditions. Even so, leaf, stem and flower problems can still occur and you should learn to recognise the cause of problems so that you can take immediate action—pages 118-121 will help you. Many troubles can be stopped or cured if tackled quickly enough—delay or the wrong treatment can lead to the death of the plant.

Finally, a word for the beginner. As you will have seen on pages 79-95, not all flowering plants can survive indoors. So there is no need to feel you have failed when Cineraria, Chrysanthemum, Gloxinia, Cyclamen and so on die down once their flowering display is over.

Plant collapse

There are scores of possible reasons which can account for the death of an indoor plant. The seven most common fatal factors are:

- **SOIL DRYNESS** No life can survive without water. Many plants can cope with infrequent watering in winter but failure to provide sufficient water during the growing season soon leads to wilting of the leaves and finally to the death of the plant.

- **OVERWATERING** The most usual cause of plant death in winter is overwatering. The leaves of affected plants droop, and the owner thinks that they are short of water. So the plants are thoroughly watered and collapse soon follows.

  It is obviously vital not to confuse the symptoms of drought with those of over-watering. Both cause leaves to wilt and sometimes to drop, but too much water results in yellowing of the foliage, whereas dryness is much more likely to cause shrivelling and browning of the leaves. Also waterlogged clay pots are covered with green slime.

- **COLD NIGHTS** The harmful effects of cold nights are heightened if the plants are kept under warm or hot conditions during the day, as it is the sudden fluctuation in temperature rather than cold air which usually causes the damage.

  Frost is generally fatal, and plants standing on windowsills are the ones most likely to suffer. Never leave pots between the windows and drawn curtains on a cold night; if frost is expected and the room is unheated then move the plants away from the window.

- **STRONG SUNSHINE** Some plants will quickly succumb if exposed to direct sunlight even if the air temperature is not unusually high. Some flowering plants, such as Pelargonium, thrive in a sunny window but even these, in common with all other plants, should have the pot and soil surface shaded in the hot summer months. If this is not done, the soil may be baked and the roots killed.

- **HOT DRY AIR** With central heating, and with most forms of artificial heat, the air lacks moisture and conditions are not favourable for most indoor plants. Delicate plants may die under such winter conditions, and it is necessary to increase the Relative Humidity of the surrounding air by one of the techniques on page 107.

- **DRAUGHTS** When a door *and* window are opened in a room, and when the temperature outside the room is lower than within, then a cross-current of air occurs and these draughts are an important cause of plant failure. For this reason, avoid standing plants in a direct line between door and windows.

  Another spot which is subject to draughts is the windowsill where there are cracks in the window frame. If delicate plants are to be grown on a windowsill, it is essential to block up all cracks.

- **NO LIGHT** Poor light conditions in an average room do not usually kill; the result is generally pale, weak growth and no flowers. There is a level, however, at which the amount of light is not sufficent to support house plant life and this can occur in dark passages, corners of large rooms, hallways, etc. If you wish to keep plants in such areas, return them at regular intervals to a moderately well-lit spot for a fortnight's holiday.

Cultural faults

UPPER LEAVES FIRM BUT YELLOW
This is generally due to the use of CALCIUM in the compost of lime-hating plants or the use of HARD WATER for watering such plants.

LEAVES DULL AND LIFELESS
TOO MUCH LIGHT is the probable culprit; another possibility is RED SPIDER MITE (see page 120). Even healthy green leaves can be rendered dull and lifeless by dust and grime — follow the cleaning instructions on page 110.

SPOTS OR PATCHES ON LEAVES
If spots or patches are crisp and brown, UNDERWATERING is the most likely cause. If the areas are soft and dark brown, OVERWATERING is the probable reason. If spots or patches are white or straw-coloured, the trouble is due to WATERING WITH COLD WATER, WATER SPLASHES ON LEAVES, AEROSOL DAMAGE, TOO MUCH SUN or PEST/DISEASE DAMAGE (see pages 120-121).If spots are moist and blister-like or dry and sunken, the cause is DISEASE (see page 121). Several PESTS can cause speckling of the leaf surface (see page 120).

BROWN TIPS OR EDGES ON LEAVES
If edges remain green, the most likely cause is DRY AIR. Another possible reason is BRUISING — people or pets touching the tips can be the culprit, so can leaf tips pressing against a wall or window. If edges are yellow or brown, the possible causes are many and varied — OVERWATERING, UNDERWATERING, TOO LITTLE LIGHT, TOO MUCH SUN, TOO LITTLE HEAT, TOO MUCH HEAT, OVERFEEDING, DRY AIR or DRAUGHTS. To pinpoint the cause, look for other symptoms.

LEAVES CURL AND FALL
Curling followed by leaf fall is a sign of TOO LITTLE HEAT, OVERWATERING or COLD DRAUGHTS.

WILTING LEAVES
The most usual cause is either SOIL DRYNESS (caused by underwatering) or WATERLOGGING (caused by impeded drainage or watering too frequently). Other possible causes are TOO MUCH LIGHT (especially if wilting takes place regularly at midday), DRY AIR, TOO MUCH HEAT, POT-BOUND ROOTS or PEST DAMAGE (see page 120).

SUDDEN LEAF FALL
Rapid defoliation without a prolonged preliminary period of wilting or discolouration is generally due to a SHOCK to the plant's system. There may have been a large drop or rise in temperature, a sudden increase in daytime light intensity or an intense cold draught. DRYNESS at the roots below the critical level can result in this sudden loss of leaves, especially with woody specimens.

LEAF FALL ON NEW PLANTS
It is quite normal for a newly repotted plant, a new purchase or a plant moved from one room to another, to lose one or two lower leaves. Keep MOVEMENT SHOCK to a minimum by repotting into a pot which is only slightly larger than the previous one, by protecting new plants on the way home from the shop and by never moving a plant from a shady spot to a very bright one without a few days in medium light.

LEAVES TURN YELLOW AND FALL
It is quite normal for an occasional lower leaf on a mature plant to turn yellow and eventually fall. When several leaves turn yellow at the same time and then fall, the most likely cause is OVERWATERING or COLD DRAUGHTS.

LOWER LEAVES DRY UP AND FALL
There are three common causes — TOO LITTLE LIGHT, TOO MUCH HEAT or UNDERWATERING.

PLANT GROWING SLOWLY OR NOT AT ALL

In winter this is normal for nearly all plants, so do not force it to grow. In summer the most likely cause is UNDERFEEDING, OVER-WATERING or TOO LITTLE LIGHT. If these factors are not responsible, and the temperature is in the recommended range, then the plant is probably POT-BOUND (see page 111).

SMALL, PALE LEAVES; SPINDLY GROWTH

This occurs in winter and early spring when the plant has been kept too warm and the compost too wet for the limited amount of light available. Where practical, prune off this poor quality growth. If these symptoms appear in the growing season, the most likely cause is either UNDER-FEEDING or TOO LITTLE LIGHT.

FLOWER BUDS FALL

The conditions which cause leaf drop can also lead to loss of buds and flowers. The commonest causes are DRY AIR, UNDER-WATERING, TOO LITTLE LIGHT, MOVING THE POT and INSECT DAMAGE (see page 120).

NO FLOWERS

If the plant has reached flowering size and blooms do not appear at the due time of year, several factors can be responsible. The most likely causes are lighting problems — TOO LITTLE LIGHT or WRONG DAYLENGTH. Other possibilities are OVERFEEDING, DRY AIR, THRIPS (see page 120) or REPOTTING (some flowering plants need to be pot-bound before they will flower).

VARIEGATED LEAVES TURN ALL-GREEN

The simple explanation here is that the foliage is not receiving sufficient light. Remove the all-green branch (if practical) and move the pot closer to the window.

FLOWERS QUICKLY FADE

The commonest culprits are UNDERWATERING, DRY AIR, TOO LITTLE LIGHT and TOO MUCH HEAT.

ROTTING LEAVES AND STEMS

This is due to disease attack where growing conditions are poor. The fault often lies with OVERWATERING in winter or LEAVING WATER ON LEAVES at night.

HOLES AND TEARS IN LEAVES

There are two basic causes — PHYSICAL DAMAGE by pets or people (merely brushing against an opening leaf bud can occasionally be responsible) or INSECT DAMAGE (see page 120).

GREEN SLIME ON CLAY POT

A sure sign of watering problems — OVERWATERING or BLOCKED DRAINAGE is the cause.

WHITE CRUST ON CLAY POT

There are two possible causes — use of excessively HARD WATER or OVERFEEDING.

Pests

Pest attacks are less common indoors than in the garden, but if they do occur and are allowed to get out of hand then serious damage can result. Apply the appropriate remedy as soon as the first signs are seen.

APHID (Greenfly)

Small, sap-sucking insects, usually green but may be black, grey or orange. All plants with soft tissues can be attacked; shoot tips and flower buds are the preferred site. Flowering pot plants are especially susceptible. The plant is weakened and sticky honeydew is deposited. Spray with Bio Sprayday — alternatively use malathion or derris. Repeat as necessary.

CATERPILLAR

Caterpillars of many types can infest the plants in a conservatory but these pests are rarely found on specimens in the living room. The tell-tale sign is the presence of holes in the leaves; some species of caterpillar spin leaves together with silken threads. Pick off and destroy individual caterpillars — spraying with fenitrothion or derris is usually not necessary.

CYCLAMEN MITE

Minute mites, looking like a film of dust on the underside of leaves. Cyclamen, Impatiens, Pelargonium and Saintpaulia are susceptible. The infested plant is stunted; leaf edges are curled, stems are twisted, flower buds wither. Unlike red spider mite, this pest will flourish in humid conditions. Spraying with standard insecticides is not effective — destroy infested leaves.

EARWIG

A familiar garden and household pest with a dark brown body and pincer-like tail. It is rarely if ever seen on house plants as it hides during the day, feeding at night on leaves and flower petals. Ragged holes are produced and leaves may be skeletonised. Pick off the insects — look under the leaves and shake the flowers. Spraying with malathion is rarely necessary.

EELWORM

Fortunately these miscroscopic, soil-living worms are not common house plant pests. If a plant collapses for no apparent reason remove it from its pot — large, corky swellings on the roots are a sure sign of root knot eelworm attack. Destroy the plant immediately — do not put it on the compost heap. In future use sterilised compost and buy plants from a reputable supplier.

FUNGUS GNAT

The small, black, adult insects which fly around the plant are harmless, but they lay eggs on the compost and the tiny, black-headed maggots they produce can be harmful. The maggots normally feed on organic matter in the compost but they will occasionally devour young roots. Fungus gnats can be troublesome in over-damp conditions — water with malathion solution.

MEALY BUG

Small pests covered with white, cottony fluff. Large clusters can occur on the stems and under the leaves of a wide variety of plants. A serious attack leads to wilting, yellowing and leaf fall. A light infestation is easily dealt with — wipe off with a damp cloth or a babycare cotton bud. A severe infestation is difficult to control — spray weekly with malathion or systemic insecticide.

RED SPIDER MITE

Minute, sap-sucking pests which can infest the underside of leaves of nearly all house plants growing in hot and dry conditions. The upper surface becomes speckled with yellow blotches and the leaves fall prematurely; white webbing is sometimes produced between the leaves and stems. Daily misting will help to prevent attacks; spray with derris, malathion or systemic insecticide as soon as the first signs are seen. Repeat as necessary.

SCALE

Small, brown discs attached to the underside of leaves, especially along the veins. These immobile adults are protected from sprays by the outer waxy shells, but they can be wiped off with a damp cloth or a babycare cotton bud. After removal spray the whole plant with malathion. If a plant is allowed to become badly infested the leaves turn yellow and sticky with honeydew; eradication is difficult or impossible at this stage.

THRIPS

These tiny, black insects are a minor pest of house plants, but Begonia, Codiaeum and Fuchsia are sometimes disfigured. They fly or jump from leaf to leaf, causing tell-tale silvery streaks, but the worst damage is to flowers which are spotted and distorted. Growth is stunted. Control is not difficult — spray with Bio Sprayday, malathion or derris at the first sign of attack and repeat as necessary.

VINE WEEVIL

The adult beetles attack leaves, but it is the 1 in. creamy grubs which do the real damage. They live in the compost and rapidly devour roots, bulbs and tubers. Control is difficult or impossible — the root system will have been seriously damaged by the time the plant has started to wilt. Water immediately with spray-strength Hexyl. Use as a precautionary measure if beetles are noticed on Cyclamen or Primula leaves.

WHITEFLY

Tiny, white moth-like insects which can be troublesome, especially to Begonia, Fuchsia, Impatiens and Pelargonium. The adult flies are unsightly; the greenish larvae on the underside of the leaves suck sap and deposit sticky honeydew. Badly infested leaves turn yellow and drop. Whitefly can occur in great numbers and rapidly spread from plant to plant. Eradication is difficult — spray with Bio Sprayday and repeat at 3-day intervals.

Diseases

The appearance of disease is usually a sign of poor growing conditions. Speedy action is essential — cut out the affected area as soon as it is seen, use a fungicide if one is recommended and correct the cultural fault.

ANTHRACNOSE

Sunken black spots appear on the foliage of Palms, Ficus and other susceptible plants. Dark brown streaks may occur at the leaf tips. This disease is associated with warm and very moist conditions, and it is therefore much more likely in the greenhouse than in the living room. Remove and burn infected leaves, spray the plant with Benlate and keep it on the dry side without misting for several weeks.

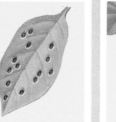

BLACK LEG

A disease of stem cuttings, especially Pelargonium. The base of the cutting turns black, due to the invasion of the Botrytis fungus. Remove the infected cutting as soon as possible. The cause is over-watering or overcompaction of the compost which has prevented proper drainage. Make sure that the Seed and Cutting Compost is kept drier next time you take Pelargonium cuttings; do not cover with glass or polythene.

BOTRYTIS (Grey Mould)

Familiar grey, fluffy mould which can cover all parts of the plant — leaves, stems, buds and flowers if the growing conditions are cool, humid and still. All soft-leaved plants can be affected — Begonia, Cyclamen, Gloxinia and Saintpaulia are particularly susceptible. Cut away and destroy all affected parts. Remove mouldy compost. Spray with Benlate. Reduce watering and misting; improve ventilation.

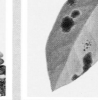

CROWN & STEM ROT

Part of the stem or crown has turned soft and rotten. When the diseased area is at the base of the plant it is known as basal rot. The fungus usually spreads rapidly and kills the plant — the usual course is to throw the pot, compost and plant away. If you have caught the trouble early you can try to save it by cutting away all diseased tissue. In future avoid overwatering, under-ventilating and keeping the plant too cool.

DAMPING OFF

The damping off fungi attack the root and stem bases of seedlings. Shrinkage and rot occur at ground level and the plants topple over. The golden rules are to use sterilised compost, sow thinly and never overwater. At the first sign of attack remove collapsed seedlings, improve the ventilation and move the seedlings to a cooler spot. Water the remainder with Cheshunt Compound.

LEAF SPOT

Brown, moist spots appear on the foliage of Citrus, Dracaena, Dieffenbachia and other susceptible plants. In a bad attack the small spots enlarge and merge, killing the whole leaf. Both bacteria and fungi can cause this effect — the best general treatment is to remove and burn infected leaves, spray the plant with Benlate and keep it on the dry side without misting for several weeks.

OEDEMA (Corky Scab)

Hard corky growths sometimes appear on the underside of leaves. This disease is not caused by either a fungus or bacterium; it is the plant's response to waterlogged compost coupled with low light intensity. Badly affected leaves will not recover so they should be removed. Transferring the plant to a better lit spot and reducing the frequency of watering will result in healthy new foliage.

POWDERY MILDEW

A fungus disease which grows on the surface of leaves, spotting or coating them with a white powdery deposit. Unlike Botrytis this complaint is neither common nor fatal, but it is disfiguring and can spread to stems and flowers. Remove badly mildewed leaves and spray the plants with Benlate or dinocap. Alternatively lightly dust the leaves with sulphur. Improve ventilation around the plants.

ROOT ROT (Tuber Rot)

A killer disease to which Cacti, Succulents, Begonia, Palms and Saintpaulia are particularly prone. The first sign is usually the yellowing and wilting of the leaves which is rapidly followed by browning and collapse. The cause is fungal decay of the roots due to waterlogging and you can only save the plant if the trouble is spotted in time and you follow the Root Rot Surgery technique on page 122.

RUST

An uncommon disease which need not concern the ordinary house plant owner. The only plant you are likely to see infected with rust is the Pelargonium — brown concentric rings of spores on the underside of the leaves. It is difficult to control — remove and burn infected leaves, improve the ventilation around the plants and spray with Dithane. Do not propagate cuttings infected with this disease.

SOOTY MOULD

A black fungus which grows on the sticky honeydew which is deposited by aphid, scale, whitefly and mealy bug. The unsightly mould does not directly harm the plant, but it does reduce growth and vigour by blocking the pores and shading the surface from sunlight. Remove sooty mould by wiping with a damp cloth; rinse with clean warm water. Control future attacks by spraying promptly against the pests which produce honeydew.

VIRUS

There is no single symptom of virus infection. The growth may be severely stunted and stems are often distorted. The usual effect on leaves is the appearance of pale green or yellow spots or small patches. Coloured flowers may bear large white streaks. The infection was brought in by insects or was already present in the plant at the time of purchase. There is no cure — throw away the plant if you are sure of your diagnosis.

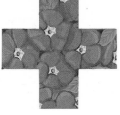

First aid for house plants

House plant varieties have changed over the years, but one would expect their problems to be quite unchanging. This surprisingly is not so — the menace of coal gas fumes has disappeared in recent years but it has been replaced by an equally serious but completely different menace — the hot, desert-dry air of the centrally heated room. Even pests and diseases change — Pelargonium rust was virtually unknown until a few years ago.

The problems that can occur are many and varied. Inspect the plants regularly, especially under the leaves. You may detect the first signs of rot because you forgot to reduce watering as winter approached, or you may notice symptoms of light deficiency if you have redecorated using much darker wallpaper. Use pages 118-121 to put a name to the problems you see, then take prompt action. The secret of green fingers is to look for and act on the first signs of trouble.

PREVENTION IS BETTER THAN CURE

Don't bring trouble in with the compost
Never use unsterilised soil. Buy a specially-prepared compost, which you can be sure will be pest- and disease-free. Alternatively sterilise soil if you wish to prepare a home-made compost.

Don't bring trouble in with the plants
Inspect new plants carefully and take any remedial action which may be necessary before putting them with the other plants.

Don't put plants in the danger spots:
- Between an open window and a door
- Near an air-conditioning heating duct
- On the TV or radiator unless extra humidity is provided
- On a windowsill with poor-fitting frames
- In an unlit corner or a dark passageway
- Between closed curtains and the window during frosty weather

Remove dead flowers and dying leaves
Hygiene is important. Fallen leaves can become covered in grey mould, and this will spread rapidly to healthy leaves if conditions are cool and humid.

Prevent trouble by following the rules
Look up the plant in the A-Z guide — nearly all problems arise from inadequate care.

Act promptly when there is trouble
Don't wait. Move the plant to a better location or spray the leaves if such treatment is recommended.

GOOD SPRAYING PRACTICE

Use the right product
Make sure that it is recommended for the pest or disease to be controlled, and make sure that there is no warning against spraying the plant to be treated.

Buy a brand recommended for house plants
Where possible obtain a product which is specially recommended for use indoors—Bio Sprayday will not harm surrounding furnishings or fabrics.

Spray the right way
Before spraying read the instructions — avoid using too little or too much. Cover fish bowls and aquaria before you start. Spray thoroughly both above and below the leaves. Wash out the sprayer after use.

Spray the right plants
With the quick-moving invaders, such as aphid and whitefly, spray all the neighbouring plants. With slow-moving pests, such as scale and mealy bug, only plants which are infested need be sprayed.

ROOT ROT SURGERY

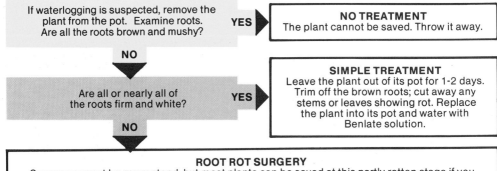

If waterlogging is suspected, remove the plant from the pot. Examine roots. Are all the roots brown and mushy?

YES →

NO TREATMENT
The plant cannot be saved. Throw it away.

NO ↓

Are all or nearly all of the roots firm and white?

YES →

SIMPLE TREATMENT
Leave the plant out of its pot for 1-2 days. Trim off the brown roots; cut away any stems or leaves showing rot. Replace the plant into its pot and water with Benlate solution.

NO ↓

ROOT ROT SURGERY
Success cannot be guaranteed, but most plants can be saved at this partly rotten stage if you follow the steps listed below.
Remove all the compost from around the roots by holding the soil ball under the tap. Lay the plant on a table and cut off all the brown, mushy roots with a sharp knife. Cut away any stems or leaves showing rot, and remove some healthy top growth to balance the loss of roots.
Repot carefully using a new pot and fresh Potting Compost. Water with Benlate solution. Keep the pot in a reasonably well-lit spot away from direct sunlight. Do not water again until fresh growth appears and then be careful to avoid overwatering.

CHAPTER 10

HOUSE PLANT GROWER'S DICTIONARY

ACID MEDIUM A compost which contains little or no lime and has a pH of less than 6.5.

AERIAL ROOT A root which grows out from the stem above ground level. Aerial roots are commonly seen on mature specimens of Monstera deliciosa.

AIR LAYERING A method of propagating single-stem plants, such as Ficus elastica decora, which have lost their lower leaves. See page 114 for details.

ALTERNATE Leaf form, where the leaves are arranged singly at different heights on the stem. Compare *opposite* and *whorled*.

ANNUAL A plant which completes its life cycle within one year of germination. Compare *biennial* and *perennial*.

ANTHER The part of the flower which produces pollen. It is the upper section of the *stamen*.

AQUATIC A plant which grows partly or wholly in water. Compare *terrestrial* and *epiphyte*.

AREOLE A small well-defined area, usually hairy and cushion-like, found on the stem of cacti. From them arise spines or *glochids*.

AROID A plant belonging to the Araceae or Arum-lily family. Popular aroids include Aglaonema, Anthurium, Dieffenbachia, Monstera and Philodendron.

AXIL The angle between the upper surface of a leaf or leaf stalk and the stem that carries it. A growth or flower bud ("axillary bud") often appears in the axil.

BICOLOUR A flower with petals which bear two distinctly different colours.

BIENNIAL A plant which completes its life cycle in two seasons. Compare *annual* and *perennial.*

BLADE The expanded part of a leaf or petal.

BLEEDING The loss of sap from plant tissues which have been cut.

BLIND The loss of the growing point, resulting in stoppage of growth. Also, failure to produce flowers or fruit.

BLOOM A natural mealy or waxy coating covering the leaves of some house plants.

BONSAI The art of dwarfing trees by careful root and stem pruning coupled with root restriction.

BRACT A modified leaf, often highly coloured and sometimes mistaken for a petal. Examples of house plants with showy bracts are Poinsettia, Aphelandra and Bougainvillea.

BREAK Production of a side shoot after removal of the growing point.

BULB A storage organ, usually formed below ground level, used for propagation. A true bulb consists of fleshy scales surrounding the central bud, but the term is often loosely applied to *corms, rhizomes* and *tubers.*

BULBIL An immature small bulb formed on the stem of a plant; e.g Lily.

BULBLET An immature small bulb formed at the base of a mature bulb; e.g Hyacinth.

CALYX The outer ring of flower parts, usually green but sometimes coloured.

CAPILLARY ACTION The natural upward movement of water in confined areas, such as the spaces between soil particles.

CARBOY A large and heavy glass vessel, originally designed for the storage of chemicals but now commonly used as a container for bottle gardens.

CHLOROSIS An abnormal yellowing or blanching of the leaves due to lack of chlorophyll. See Chapter 9 for possible causes.

CLADODE A modified stem which has taken on the form of a leaf; e.g the needle-like "leaves" of Asparagus Fern.

COLOURED LEAF A leaf with one or more distinct colours apart from green, white or cream. Compare *variegated leaf.*

COMPOST Usual meaning for the house plant grower is a potting or seed/cutting mixture made from peat ("soilless compost") or sterilised soil ("loam compost") plus other materials such as sand, lime and fertilizer. Compost is also a term for decomposed vegetable matter.

COMPOUND FLOWER A flower made up of many *florets*; e.g Chrysanthemum.

COMPOUND LEAF A leaf made up of two or more *leaflets* attached to the leaf stalk; e.g Schefflera.

CORM A swollen, underground stem base used for propagation; e.g Crocus.

COROLLA The ring of separate or fused petals which is nearly always responsible for the main floral display.

CRISTATE Cockscomb-like growth of leaves (e.g Pteris cretica cristata), stems (Cereus peruvianus monstrosus) or flowers (Celosia cristata).

CROCK A piece of broken pot used to help drainage. See Chapter 7.

CROWN The region where shoot and root join, usually at or very near ground level.

CULTIVAR See *Naming House Plants*, page 125.

CUTTING A piece of a plant (leaf, stem or root) which can be used to produce a new plant.

DAMPING OFF Decay of young seedlings at ground level following fungal attack. See Chapter 9.

DEAD-HEADING The removal of faded heads of flowers.

DECIDUOUS A plant which loses its leaves annually at the end of the growing season. Compare *evergreen.*

DISTILLED WATER Pure water free from dissolved salts. Formerly made by distillation, now produced chemically by demineralisation.

DIVISION A method of propagating plants by separating each one into two or more sections and then repotting.

DORMANT PERIOD The time when a plant has naturally stopped growing and the leaves have fallen or the top growth has died down. The dormant period is usually, but not always, in winter. Compare *resting period.*

DOUBLE FLOWER A flower with many more petals than are present in the single form.

DOUBLE POTTING An American term for placing a potted plant in a larger pot with damp peat in between. See page 107.

DRAWN Excessively tall and weak growth, caused by plants being grown in too little light or too closely together.

EPIDERMIS The transparent protective skin which covers non-woody plants.

EPIPHYTE A non-parasitic plant which grows above ground attached to other plants or on mossy rocks; e.g Orchids and Bromeliads. Compare *aquatic* and *terrestrial.*

EVERGREEN A plant which retains its leaves throughout the year. Compare *deciduous.*

EXOTIC Strictly speaking, a plant which is not native to the area, but popularly any unusual or striking house plant.

EYE Two unrelated meanings – an undeveloped growth bud or the centre of a flower.

F₁ HYBRID A first generation offspring of two pure-bred strains. An F₁ hybrid is generally more vigorous than an ordinary hybrid.

FAMILY See *Naming House Plants*, page 125.

FLORET A small flower which is part of a much larger compound flower head; e.g Cineraria.

FLOWER SPIKE A flower head made up of a central stem with the flowers growing directly on it.

FORCING The process of making a plant grow or flower before its natural season.

FROND A leaf of a fern or palm.

FUNGICIDE A chemical used to control diseases caused by fungi.

FUNGUS A primitive form of plant life which is known to the house plant grower as the most common cause of infectious disease – powdery mildew, sooty mould and grey mould are examples.

GENUS See *Naming House Plants*, page 125.

GERMINATION The first stage in the development of a plant from seed.

GESNERIAD A plant belonging to the Gesneriaceae or African Violet family. Popular gesneriads include Saintpaulia, Gloxinia, Streptocarpus and Columnea.

GLABROUS Plant surface which is smooth and hairless.

GLAUCOUS Plant surface which is covered with a bluish-grey bloom.

GLOCHID A small hooked hair borne on some cacti.

GRAFTING The process of joining a stem or bud of one plant on to the stem of another.

GROWING POINT The tip of a stem, which is responsible for extension growth.

HALF HARDY An indoor plant which requires a minimum temperature of 50°–55°F for healthy growth. Compare *hardy* and *tender.*

HARDENING OFF Gradual acclimatisation to colder conditions.

HARDY An indoor plant which can withstand prolonged exposure to temperatures at or below 45°F. Compare *half hardy* and *tender.*

HEEL A strip of bark and wood remaining at the base of a side shoot cutting pulled off a main shoot. Some cuttings root more readily if a heel is attached.

HERB A plant grown for flavouring or medicinal purposes.

HERBACEOUS A plant with a non-woody stem.

HONEYDEW Sticky, sugary secretion deposited on plants by insects such as aphid and whitefly.

HUMIDIFIER A piece of equipment used to raise the humidity of the air in a room.

HYBRID A plant with parents which are genetically distinct. The parent plants may be different *cultivars, varieties, species* or *genera* but not different *families.*

HYDROPONICS A method of growing a plant in water containing dissolved nutrients.

HYGROMETER An instrument used to measure the Relative Humidity of the air.

INFLORESCENCE The arrangement of flowers on the stem.

INORGANIC A chemical or fertilizer which is not obtained from a source which is or has been alive.

INSECTICIDE A chemical used to control insect pests.

INTERNODE The part of the stem between one node and another.

KNOCKING OUT The temporary removal of a plant from its pot in order to check the condition of the root ball.

LATERAL SHOOT A side branch growing from the main stem.

LATEX Milky sap which exudes from cut surfaces of a few house plants, such as Ficus elastica decora and Euphorbia.

LEAF MOULD Partially decayed leaves used in some potting mixtures. It must be sieved and sterilised before use.

LEAFLET A leaf-like section of a compound leaf.

LEGGY Abnormally tall and spindly growth.

LOAM Good quality soil used in preparing compost. Adequate supplies of clay, sand and fibre must be present.

LONG DAY PLANT A plant which requires light for a longer period than it would normally receive from daylight in order to induce flowering. E.g Saintpaulia.

MACRAMÉ Decoratively knotted rope or cord forming a harness-like structure for hanging pots.

MICROCLIMATE The warmth and humidity of the air in close proximity to a plant. It may differ significantly from the general climate of the room.

MIST PROPAGATION The ideal method of propagation under glass, using automatic mist generators and soil heaters.

MOUTH The open end of a bell-shaped or tubular flower.

MULTICOLOUR A flower with petals which bear at least three distinctly different colours.

MUTATION A sudden change in the genetic make-up of a plant, leading to a new feature. This new feature can be inherited.

NEUTRAL Neither acid nor alkaline; pH 6.5–7.5.

NODE The point on a stem where a leaf or bud is attached.

OFFSET A young plantlet which appears on a mature plant. An offset can generally be detached and used for propagation.

OPPOSITE Leaf form, where the leaves are arranged in opposite pairs along the stem. Compare *alternate* and *whorled.*

ORGANIC A chemical or fertilizer which is obtained from a source which is or has been alive.

OSMUNDA FIBRE The roots of the fern Osmunda regalis, used for making Orchid Compost.

OVER-POTTING Repotting a plant into a pot which is too large to allow successful establishment.

PEAT (Peat moss in the U.S) Partially decomposed sphagnum moss or sedge used in making composts. Valuable for its pronounced air- and water-holding capacity and its freedom from weeds and disease organisms.

PERENNIAL A plant which will live for three years or more under normal conditions.

PETIOLE A leaf stalk.

pH A measure of acidity and alkalinity. Below pH 6.5 is acid, above pH 7.5 is alkaline.

PHOTOSYNTHESIS The food-making process which occurs in the leaf. This process requires water, air and adequate light.

PINCHING OUT The removal of the growing point of a stem to induce bushiness or to encourage flowering. Also known as *stopping*.

PIP Two distinct meanings – the seed of some fruits (e.g Orange) and the rootstock of some flowering plants (e.g Convallaria).

PISTIL The female reproductive parts of the flower.

PLUNGING The placing of a pot up to its rim outdoors in soil, peat or ashes.

POT-BOUND A plant growing in a pot which is too small to allow proper leaf and stem growth.

POTTING ON The repotting of a plant into a proper-sized larger container which will allow continued root development.

PRICKING OUT The moving of seedlings from the tray or pot in which they were sown to other receptacles where they can be spaced out individually.

RESTING PERIOD The time when a plant has naturally stopped growing but when there is little or no leaf fall. Compare *dormant period*.

RHIZOME A thickened stem which grows horizontally below or on the soil surface.

ROOT BALL Matted roots plus enclosed compost within the pot.

RUNNER A creeping stem (scientific name: *stolon*) which roots and produces a plantlet when it comes in contact with moist soil.

SELF-COLOUR A flower with single-coloured petals.

SESSILE A stalkless leaf or flower which is borne directly on the stem.

SHARP SAND Coarse, lime-free sand.

SHORT DAY PLANT A plant which requires light for a shorter period than it would normally receive from daylight in order to induce flowering. E.g Chrysanthemum and Poinsettia.

SHRUB A woody plant with a framework of branches and little or no central stem. Compare *tree*.

SINGLE FLOWER A flower with the normal number of petals arranged in a single layer.

SPADIX A fleshy flower spike in which tiny *florets* are embedded.

SPATHE A large bract, sometimes highly coloured, surrounding or enclosing a *spadix*. The spathe flower is characteristic of the *aroids*, such as Anthurium and Spathiphyllum.

SPECIES See *Naming House Plants*, on this page.

SPORE A reproductive cell of non-flowering plants, such as ferns.

SPORT A plant which shows a marked and inheritable change from its parent; a *mutation*.

STAMEN The male reproductive parts of a flower.

STANDARD A plant which does not normally grow as a tree but is trained into a tree-like form.

STERILISED SOIL A rather misleading term, as steam- or chemically-sterilised soil is only partially sterilised. Harmful organisms have been killed but helpful bacteria have been spared.

STOLON See *runner*.

STOPPING See *pinching out*.

STOVE PLANT A plant which requires warm greenhouse conditions in winter.

SUB-SHRUB A plant which at the adult stage has woody stems near the base and a framework of soft green growth.

SUCCULENT A plant with swollen leaves and/or stems which store water.

SUCKER A shoot which arises from an underground shoot or root of a plant.

SYSTEMIC A pesticide which goes inside the plant and travels in the sap stream.

TENDER An indoor plant which requires a minimum temperature of 60°F. Occasional short exposure to temperatures below this level may be tolerated. Compare *hardy* and *half hardy*.

TENDRIL A thread-like stem or leaf which clings to any nearby support.

TERMINAL The uppermost bud or flower on a stem.

TERRESTRIAL A plant which grows in soil in its natural habitat. Compare *aquatic* and *epiphyte*.

TOPIARY The art of clipping and training woody plants to form geometric shapes or intricate patterns. Box and Myrtle are suitable types.

TRANSPIRATION The loss of water through the pores of the leaf.

TREE A woody plant with a distinct central trunk. Compare *shrub*.

TUBER A storage organ used for propagation. It may be a fleshy root (e.g Dahlia) or a swollen underground stem.

VARIEGATED LEAF A green leaf which is blotched, edged or spotted with yellow, white or cream. Compare *coloured leaf*.

VARIETY See *Naming House Plants*, below.

WHORLED Leaf form, where three or more leaves radiate from a single node.

XEROPHYTE A plant which is able to live under very dry conditions.

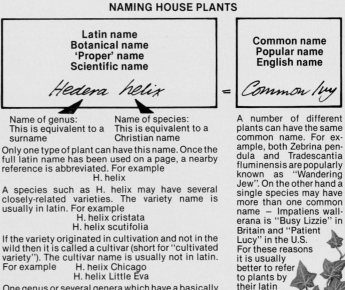

NAMING HOUSE PLANTS

Latin name Botanical name 'Proper' name Scientific name		Common name Popular name English name
Hedera helix	=	*Common Ivy*

Name of genus:
This is equivalent to a surname

Name of species:
This is equivalent to a Christian name

Only one type of plant can have this name. Once the full latin name has been used on a page, a nearby reference is abbreviated. For example
H. helix

A species such as H. helix may have several closely-related varieties. The variety name is usually in latin. For example
H. helix cristata
H. helix scutifolia

If the variety originated in cultivation and not in the wild then it is called a cultivar (short for "cultivated variety"). The cultivar name is usually not in latin. For example   H. helix Chicago
H. helix Little Eva

One genus or several genera which have a basically similar floral pattern make up a family. Hedera, Fatsia, Dizygotheca and Schefflera all belong to the Araliaceae or Ivy family.

A number of different plants can have the same common name. For example, both Zebrina pendula and Tradescantia fluminensis are popularly known as "Wandering Jew". On the other hand a single species may have more than one common name – Impatiens wallerana is "Busy Lizzie" in Britain and "Patient Lucy" in the U.S. For these reasons it is usually better to refer to plants by their latin names.

CHAPTER 11

PLANT INDEX

A

	page
ABUTILON MEGAPOTAMICUM	21
ABUTILON STRIATUM THOMPSONII	21
ACACIA ARMATA	60
ACALYPHA HISPIDA	60
ACALYPHA WILKESIANA	21
ACHIMENES HYBRIDA	80
ACORUS GRAMINEUS VARIEGATUS	22
ADIANTUM CUNEATUM	35
ADIANTUM HISPIDULUM	35
ADIANTUM RADDIANUM	35
AECHMEA CHANTINII	25, 63
AECHMEA FASCIATA	25, 63
AECHMEA FULGENS DISCOLOR	25, 63
AECHMEA MACRACANTHA	25
AECHMEA RHODOCYANEA	25, 63
AEONIUM ARBOREUM ATROPURPUREUM	55
AEONIUM TABULAEFORME	55
AESCHYNANTHUS LOBBIANUS	60
AFRICAN MARIGOLD	87
AFRICAN VIOLET	76
AGAPANTHUS AFRICANUS	60
AGAVE AMERICANA	55
AGAVE AMERICANA MEDIOPICTA	55
AGAVE FILIFERA	55
AGAVE VICTORIAE-REGINAE	55
AGERATUM	87
AGERATUM HOUSTONIANUM	87
AGLAONEMA CRISPUM SILVER QUEEN	21
AGLAONEMA MODESTUM	21
AGLAONEMA PICTUM	21
AGLAONEMA PSEUDOBRACTEATUM	21
AGLAONEMA TREUBII SILVER SPEAR	21
ALOE ARBORESCENS	55
ALOE ARISTATA	55
ALOE HUMILIS	55
ALOE VARIEGATA	55
ALUMINIUM PLANT	49
AMARYLLIS	90
AMAZONIAN ZEBRA PLANT	63
ANANAS BRACTEATUS STRIATUS	25
ANANAS COMOSUS	25
ANANAS COMOSUS VARIEGATUS	25
ANANAS SATIVUS	25
ANGEL WING BEGONIA	62
ANGEL'S WINGS	27
ANNUALS	87
ANTHURIUM ANDREANUM	61
ANTHURIUM CRYSTALLINUM	23
ANTHURIUM SCHERZERIANUM	61
ANTIRRHINUM MAJUS	87
APHELANDRA SQUARROSA BROCKFELD	61
APHELANDRA SQUARROSA DANIA	61
APHELANDRA SQUARROSA LOUISAE	61
APOROCACTUS FLAGELLIFORMIS	100
APPLE-SCENTED GERANIUM	47
ARALIA	33
ARALIA ELEGANTISSIMA	29
ARALIA SIEBOLDII	33
ARAUCARIA EXCELSA	22
ARAUCARIA HETEROPHYLLA	22
ARDISIA CRISPA	61
ARROWHEAD VINE	53
ARTILLERY PLANT	49
ARUM LILY	95
ASPARAGUS ASPARAGOIDES	23
ASPARAGUS FALCATUS	23
ASPARAGUS FERN	23
ASPARAGUS MEYERI	23
ASPARAGUS PLUMOSUS	23
ASPARAGUS SETACEUS	23
ASPARAGUS SPRENGERI	23
ASPIDISTRA ELATIOR	22
ASPLENIUM BULBIFERUM	35
ASPLENIUM NIDUS	35
ASTILBE JAPONICA	80
ASTROPHYTUM CAPRICORNE	98
ASTROPHYTUM MYRIOSTIGMA	98
AUCUBA JAPONICA VARIEGATA	22
AZALEA	80
AZALEA INDICA HYBRID	80

B

	page
BABY RUBBER PLANT	46
BABY'S TEARS	40
BASKET BEGONIA	81
BASKET GRASS	44
BAY TREE	41
BEAD PLANT	91
BEAUCARNEA RECURVATA	23
BEEFSTEAK PLANT	41
BEGONIA ARGENTEO-GUTTATA	62
BEGONIA BOWERI	26
BEGONIA CLEOPATRA	26
BEGONIA COCCINEA	62
BEGONIA FIREGLOW	81
BEGONIA FUCHSIOIDES	62
BEGONIA GLAUCOPHYLLA	62
BEGONIA GLOIRE DE LORRAINE	81
BEGONIA HAAGEANA	62
BEGONIA LUCERNA	62
BEGONIA MASONIANA	26
BEGONIA METALLICA	62
BEGONIA MULTIFLORA	81
BEGONIA PENDULA	81
BEGONIA REX	26
BEGONIA REX HER MAJESTY	26
BEGONIA REX MERRY CHRISTMAS	26
BEGONIA REX SILVER QUEEN	26
BEGONIA REX YULETIDE	26
BEGONIA SEMPERFLORENS	62
BEGONIA SERRATIPETALA	62
BEGONIA TUBERHYBRIDA	81
BEGONIA VINE	58
BELOPERONE GUTTATA	63
BENGAL FIG	37
BILLBERGIA NUTANS	63
BILLBERGIA WINDII	63
BIRD OF PARADISE	78
BIRD'S NEST BROMELIAD	25
BIRD'S NEST FERN	35
BIRD'S NEST PHILODENDRON	48
BIRD'S NEST SANSEVIERIA	51
BISHOP'S CAP	98
BLACK-EYED SUSAN	95
BLACK GOLD	48
BLACK LEAF PANAMIGA	49
BLECHNUM GIBBUM	35
BLEEDING HEART VINE	65
BLOOD LEAF	41
BLUE AFRICAN LILY	60
BLUE ECHEVERIA	55
BLUE FLOWERED TORCH	63
BLUE GUM	32
BLUSHING BROMELIAD	25
BOAT LILY	50
BOSTON FERN	35
BOTTLEBRUSH PLANT	64
BOUGAINVILLEA GLABRA	63
BOUVARDIA DOMESTICA	64
BOX	26
BRAIN CACTUS	98
BRASSAIA ACTINOPHYLLA	51
BROMELIADS	24, 63
BRONZE INCH PLANT	57
BROWALLIA SPECIOSA	82
BROWN SPIDERWORT	57
BRUNFELSIA CALYCINA	62
BRYOPHYLLUM DAIGREMONTIANUM	55
BRYOPHYLLUM TUBIFLORUM	55
BUDDHIST PINE	50
BULBS	88
BUNNY EARS	99
BURRO'S TAIL	55
BUSH VIOLET	82
BUSY LIZZIE	70
BUTTERFLY FLOWER	94
BUTTERFLY ORCHID	73
BUTTON FERN	35
BUXUS MICROPHYLLA	26
BUXUS SEMPERVIRENS	26

C

	page
CABBAGE TREE	31
CACTI	96
CALADIUM HORTULANUM CANDIDUM	27
CALADIUM HORTULANUM FRIEDA HEMPLE	27
CALADIUM HORTULANUM LORD DERBY	27
CALADIUM HORTULANUM MRS. HALDERMAN	27
CALADIUM HORTULANUM ROSEBUD	27
CALAMONDIN ORANGE	65
CALATHEA INSIGNIS	42
CALATHEA LANCIFOLIA	42
CALATHEA MAKOYANA	42
CALATHEA ORNATA	42
CALATHEA ZEBRINA	42
CALCEOLARIA HERBEOHYBRIDA	82
CALENDULA OFFICINALIS	87
CALLA LILY	95
CALLISIA ELEGANS	57
CALLISTEMON CITRINUS	64
CAMELLIA	64
CAMELLIA JAPONICA	64
CAMPANULA ISOPHYLLA	64
CANARY DATE PALM	45
CANARY ISLAND IVY	39
CANDLE PLANT	56
CAPE COWSLIP	91
CAPE GRAPE	58
CAPE HART'S TONGUE	56
CAPE HEATH	85
CAPE IVY	52
CAPE JASMINE	68
CAPE LEADWORT	74
CAPE PRIMROSE	78
CAPSICUM ANNUM	82
CARDINAL FLOWER	93
CAREX MORROWII VARIEGATA	26
CARISSA GRANDIFLORA	65
CARRION FLOWER	77
CASCADE CHRYSANTHEMUM	83
CAST IRON PLANT	22
CASTOR OIL PLANT	33
CATTLEYA	73
CEDAR GUM	32
CELOSIA CRISTATA	82
CELOSIA PLUMOSA	82
CENTURY PLANT	55
CEPHALOCEREUS SENILIS	98
CEREUS PERUVIANUS	98
CEREUS PERUVIANUS MONSTROSUS	98
CEROPEGIA WOODII	55
CESTRUM AURANTIACUM	65
CESTRUM ELEGANS	65
CESTRUM NOCTURNUM	65
CESTRUM PARQUI	65
CHAIN CACTUS	100
CHAMAECEREUS SILVESTRII	98
CHAMAEDOREA ELEGANS	45
CHAMAEDOREA SEIFRIZII	45
CHAMAEROPS HUMILIS	45
CHEIMANTHA BEGONIA	81
CHENILLE PLANT	60
CHESTNUT VINE	58
CHICKEN GIZZARD	41
CHINESE EVERGREEN	21
CHINESE FAN PALM	45
CHINESE PRIMROSE	93
CHIONODOXA	88
CHLOROPHYTUM COMOSUM VARIEGATUM	27
CHRISTMAS CACTUS	100
CHRISTMAS FERN	36
CHRISTMAS HEATHER	85
CHRISTMAS PEPPER	82
CHRYSANTHEMUM FRUTESCENS	83
CHRYSANTHEMUM MORIFOLIUM	83
CIGAR PLANT	67
CINERARIA	84
CINNAMON CACTUS	99
CISSUS ANTARCTICA	58
CISSUS DISCOLOR	58
CISSUS RHOMBIFOLIA	58
CISSUS STRIATA	58
CITRUS LIMON PONDEROSA	65
CITRUS MITIS	65
CITRUS RETICULATA	65
CITRUS SINENSIS	65
CLEISTOCACTUS STRAUSSII	98
CLERODENDRUM THOMSONAE	65
CLEYERA JAPONICA TRICOLOR	28
CLIANTHUS FORMOSUS	66
CLIANTHUS PUNICEUS	66
CLIVIA MINIATA	66
CLOAK FERN	35
CLOG PLANT	69
COBAEA SCANDENS	87
COBWEB HOUSELEEK	56
COCKSCOMB	82
COCONUT PALM	45
COCOS WEDDELIANA	45
CODIAEUM AUCUBIFOLIUM	28
CODIAEUM BRAVO	28
CODIAEUM CRAIGII	28
CODIAEUM GOLDEN RING	28
CODIAEUM MRS ICETON	28
CODIAEUM REIDII	28
CODIAEUM VARIEGATUM PICTUM	28
COELOGYNE	73
COELOGYNE CRISTATA	73
COFFEA ARABICA	28
COFFEE PLANT	28
COLEUS	29
COLEUS BLUMEI	29
COLEUS BLUMEI CANDIDUM	29
COLEUS BLUMEI FIREBIRD	29
COLEUS BLUMEI KLONDYKE	29
COLEUS BLUMEI SALMON LACE	29
COLEUS BLUMEI VOLCANO	29
COLEUS PUMILUS TRAILING QUEEN	29
COLUMN CACTUS	98
COLUMNEA BANKSII	66
COLUMNEA GLORIOSA	66
COMMON BOX	26
COMMON IVY	39
COMMON PINEAPPLE	25
CONVALLARIA MAJALIS	85
COPPER LEAF	21
CORAL BERRY	61, 63
CORDATUM	48
CORDYLINE AUSTRALIS	31
CORDYLINE STRICTA	31
CORDYLINE TERMINALIS	31
CORDYLINE TERMINALIS REDEDGE	31
CORDYLINE TERMINALIS TRICOLOR	31
CORN PALM	31
CORSAGE ORCHID	73
COTYLEDON UNDULATA	56
CRASSULA	74
CRASSULA ARGENTEA	55
CRASSULA FALCATA	55
CRASSULA LYCOPODIOIDES	55
CRASSULA PERFORATA	55
CREEPING CHARLIE	49
CREEPING FIG	37
CREEPING JENNY	49
CREEPING MOSS	52
CREEPING PEPEROMIA	46
CRISTATE TABLE FERN	36
CROCUS	88
CROSSANDRA UNDULIFOLIA	66
CROTON	28
CROWN OF THORNS	68
CRYPTANTHUS ACAULIS	25
CRYPTANTHUS BIVITTATUS	25
CRYPTANTHUS BROMELIOIDES TRICOLOR	25
CRYPTANTHUS FOSTERIANUS	25
CRYPTANTHUS ZONATUS	25
CRYSTAL ANTHURIUM	23
CTENANTHE OPPENHEIMIANA TRICOLOR	42
CUP & SAUCER VINE	87
CUPHEA IGNEA	67
CUPID PEPEROMIA	46
CUPID'S BOWER	80
CYANOTIS KEWENSIS	57
CYCAS REVOLUTA	45
CYCLAMEN	84
CYCLAMEN PERSICUM	84
CYPERUS ALTERNIFOLIUS	29
CYPERUS DIFFUSUS	29
CYPRIPEDIUM	73
CYPRIPEDIUM INSIGNIS	73
CYRTOMIUM FALCATUM	35
CYTISUS CANARIENSIS	85
CYTISUS RACEMOSUS	85

D

	page
DAFFODIL	88
DARWIN TULIPS	88
DAVALLIA CANARIENSIS	35
DELTA MAIDENHAIR	35
DESERT CACTI	97
DESERT PRIVET	46
DEVIL'S IVY	52
DIDYMOCHLAENA TRUNCATULA	35
DIEFFENBACHIA	32
DIEFFENBACHIA AMOENA	32
DIEFFENBACHIA OERSTEDII	32
DIEFFENBACHIA PICTA EXOTICA	32
DIEFFENBACHIA PICTA RUDOLPH ROEHRS	32
DIEFFENBACHIA PICTA SUPERBA	32
DINNER PLATE ARALIA	50
DIPLADENIA SANDERI	67
DIZYGOTHECA ELEGANTISSIMA	29
DRACAENA	30
DRACAENA DEREMENSIS	31
DRACAENA DEREMENSIS BAUSEI	31
DRACAENA DEREMENSIS JANET CRAIG	31
DRACAENA DEREMENSIS RHOERSII	31
DRACAENA DEREMENSIS WARNECKII	31
DRACAENA DRACO	31
DRACAENA FRAGRANS	31
DRACAENA FRAGRANS LINDENII	31
DRACAENA FRAGRANS MASSANGEANA	31
DRACAENA GODSEFFIANA	31
DRACAENA INDIVISA	31
DRACAENA MARGINATA	31
DRACAENA MARGINATA TRICOLOR	31
DRACAENA SANDERIANA	31
DRACAENA TERMINALIS	31
DRAGON TREE	31

	page
DUCHESNEA INDICA	67
DUMB CANE	32
DUTCH HYACINTH	88
DWARF POMEGRANATE	93

E

	page
EARLY DOUBLE TULIP	88
EARLY NARCISSUS	88
EARLY SINGLE TULIP	88
EARTH STAR	25
EASTER CACTUS	100
EASTER LILY	91
ECHEVERIA AGAVOIDES	55
ECHEVERIA DERENBERGII	55
ECHEVERIA GIBBIFLORA METALLICA	55
ECHEVERIA GLAUCA	55
ECHEVERIA HARMSII	55
ECHEVERIA SETOSA	55
ECHINOCACTUS GRUSONII	98
ECHINOCEREUS KNIPPELIANUS	98
ECHINOCEREUS PECTINATUS	98
ECHINOFOSSULOCACTUS ZACATECASENSIS	98
ECHINOPSIS EYRIESII	98
ECHINOPSIS RHODOTRICHA	98
EGYPTIAN STAR CLUSTER	74
ELATIOR RIEGER BEGONIA	81
ELEPHANT'S EAR	48
ELEPHANT'S EAR BEGONIA	62
EMERALD RIPPLE	46
ENGLISH IVY	39
EPIPHYLLUM HYBRID	100
EPISCIA CUPREATA	67
EPISCIA DIANTHIFLORA	67
ERICA GRACILIS	85
ERICA HYEMALIS	85
ESPOSTOA LANATA	98
EUCALYPTUS CITRIODORA	32
EUCALYPTUS GLOBULUS	32
EUCALYPTUS GUNNII	32
EUONYMUS JAPONICUS MEDIO-PICTUS	33
EUONYMUS JAPONICUS MICROPHYLLUS	33
EUPHORBIA FULGENS	68
EUPHORBIA MILII SPLENDENS	68
EUPHORBIA OBESA	56
EUPHORBIA PULCHERRIMA	92
EUPHORBIA TIRUCALLI	56
EUROPEAN FAN PALM	45
EURYA JAPONICA	28
EXACUM AFFINE	85
EYELASH BEGONIA	26

F

	page
FAIRY PRIMROSE	93
FAT-HEADED LIZZIE	33
FATSHEDERA LIZEI	33
FATSHEDERA LIZEI VARIEGATA	33
FATSIA JAPONICA	33
FATSIA JAPONICA VARIEGATA	33
FAUCARIA TIGRINA	56
FEATHER FERN	35
FERNS	34
FEROCACTUS LATISPINUS	98
FICUS BENGHALENSIS	37
FICUS BENJAMINA	37
FICUS DELTOIDEA	37
FICUS DIVERSIFOLIA	37
FICUS ELASTICA	37
FICUS ELASTICA BLACK PRINCE	37
FICUS ELASTICA DECORA	37
FICUS ELASTICA DOESCHERI	37
FICUS ELASTICA ROBUSTA	37
FICUS ELASTICA TRICOLOR	37
FICUS LYRATA	37
FICUS PANDURATA	37
FICUS PUMILA	37
FICUS RADICANS VARIEGATA	37
FICUS REPENS	48
FIDDLE LEAF	37
FIDDLE LEAF FIG	37
FIG	37
FINGER ARALIA	29
FINGERNAIL PLANT	25
FIRECRACKER FLOWER	66
FIRECRACKER PLANT	72
FISH HOOK CACTUS	98
FISHTAIL FERN	35
FITTONIA ARGYRONEURA	38
FITTONIA ARGYRONEURA NANA	38
FITTONIA VERSCHAFFELTII	38
FLAME NETTLE	29
FLAME OF THE WOODS	71
FLAME VIOLET	67
FLAMING DRAGON TREE	31
FLAMING KATY	71
FLAMING SWORD	25, 63
FLAMINGO FLOWER	61
FLOWERING MAPLE	21
FOREST CACTI	100
FOREST LILY	95

	page
FRAGARIA INDICA	67
FRECKLE FACE	40
FRENCH MARIGOLD	87
FRIENDSHIP PLANT	49
FROSTED SONERILA	53
FUCHSIA BEGONIA	62
FUCHSIA HYBRIDA	86
FUCHSIA TRIPHYLLA	86

G

	page
GARDENIA JASMINOIDES	68
GASTERIA VERRUCOSA	56
GENISTA	85
GERANIUM	75
GERMAN IVY	52
GHOST PLANT	56
GLORIOSA ROTHSCHILDIANA	87
GLORY BOWER	65
GLORY LILY	87
GLORY PEA	66
GLOXINIA	90
GOAT'S HORN CACTUS	98
GOLD DUST DRACAENA	31
GOLD DUST PLANT	22
GOLDEN BARREL	98
GOLDEN BIRD'S NEST	51
GOLDEN EVERGREEN	21
GOLDEN LILY CACTUS	98
GOLDEN POTHOS	52
GOLDENHEART IVY	39
GOLDFINGER CACTUS	99
GOLDFISH PLANT	55
GOOD LUCK PLANT	55
GOOSE FOOT PLANT	53
GRAPE HYACINTH	88
GRAPE IVY	58
GRAPTOPETALUM PARAGUAYENSE	56
GRASS PALM	31
GREEN BRAKE FERN	35
GREVILLEA ROBUSTA	38
GUM	32
GUZMANIA LINGULATA	25
GYMNOCALYCIUM MIHANOVICHII HIBOTAN	98
GYNURA AURANTIACA	38
GYNURA SARMENTOSA	38

H

	page
HAAGEOCEREUS CHOSICENSIS	98
HAMATOCACTUS SETISPINUS	98
HARE'S FOOT FERN	36
HART'S TONGUE FERN	35
HAWORTHIA FASCIATA	56
HAWORTHIA MARGARITIFERA	56
HAWORTHIA REINWARDTII	56
HAWORTHIA TESSELLATA	56
HEDERA CANARIENSIS GLOIRE DE MARENGO	39
HEDERA HELIX	39
HEDERA HELIX CHICAGO	39
HEDERA HELIX CRISTATA	39
HEDERA HELIX GLACIER	39
HEDERA HELIX IVALACE	39
HEDERA HELIX JUBILEE	39
HEDERA HELIX LITTLE EVA	39
HEDERA HELIX LUTZII	39
HEDERA HELIX MARMORATA	39
HEDERA HELIX SAGITTAEFOLIA	39
HEDERA HELIX SCUTIFOLIA	39
HEDGEHOG ALOE	55
HELIOTROPE	68
HELIOTROPIUM HYBRIDA	68
HELXINE SOLEIROLII	40
HEMIGRAPHIS COLORATA	40
HEMIGRAPHIS EXOTICA	40
HENS & CHICKENS	55
HEPTAPLEURUM ARBORICOLA	40
HERRINGBONE PLANT	42
HIBISCUS ROSA-SINENSIS	69
HIBISCUS ROSA-SINENSIS COOPERI	69
HIEMALIS BEGONIA	81
HIPPEASTRUM HYBRIDA	90
HOLLY FERN	35
HORTENSIA	90
HOUSE LIME	77
HOWEA BELMOREANA	45
HOWEA FORSTERIANA	45
HOYA BELLA	69
HOYA CARNOSA	69
HYACINTH	88
HYDRANGEA	90
HYDRANGEA MACROPHYLLA	90
HYPOCYRTA GLABRA	69
HYPOESTES SANGUINOLENTA	40
HYPOESTES TAENIATA	68

I

	page
IMPATIENS HAWKERI HYBRIDA	70
IMPATIENS LINEARIFOLIA HYBRIDA	70
IMPATIENS WALLERANA	70
IMPATIENS WALLERANA HOLSTII	70

	page
IMPATIENS WALLERANA PETERSIANA	70
IMPATIENS WALLERANA SULTANII	70
IMPATIENS WALLERANA SULTANII VARIEGATA	70
INCH PLANT	57
INDIAN AZALEA	80
INDIAN STRAWBERRY	67
INDOOR OAK	44
IPOMOEA TRICOLOR	87
IRESINE HERBSTII	41
IRESINE HERBSTII AUREORETICULATA	41
IRIS RETICULATA	88
IRON CROSS BEGONIA	26
ITALIAN BELLFLOWER	64
IVORY PINEAPPLE	25
IVY	39
IVY-LEAVED GERANIUM	75
IVY PEPEROMIA	46
IVY TREE	33
IXORA COCCINEA	71

J

	page
JACARANDA	41
JACARANDA MIMOSIFOLIA	41
JACOBINIA CARNEA	71
JADE PLANT	55
JAPANESE AZALEA	80
JAPANESE SEDGE	26
JASMINE	71
JASMINE PLANT	64
JASMINUM POLYANTHUM	71
JASMINUM PRIMULINUM	71
JELLY BEAN PLANT	56
JERUSALEM CHERRY	95
JESSAMINE	65
JONQUIL NARCISSUS	88
JOSEPH'S COAT	28

K

	page
KAFFIR LILY	66
KALANCHOE BEHARENSIS	56
KALANCHOE BLOSSFELDIANA	71
KALANCHOE TOMENTOSA	56
KANGAROO THORN	60
KANGAROO VINE	58
KENTIA BELMOREANA	45
KENTIA FORSTERIANA	45
KENTIA PALM	45
KING OF THE BROMELIADS	25
KING'S CROWN	71
KLEINIA ARTICULATA	56
KURUME AZALEA	80

L

	page
LACE FERN	35
LACE FLOWER	67
LACHENALIA ALOIDES	91
LACY LEAF IVY	39
LACY TREE PHILODENDRON	48
LADY PALM	45
LADY'S EARDROPS	86
LANTANA CAMARA	72
LAUREL	41
LAURUS NOBILIS	41
LEAF CACTUS	99
LEMAIREOCEREUS MARGINATUS	99
LEMON-SCENTED GERANIUM	47
LEMON-SCENTED GUM	32
LEOPARD LILY	32
LILIUM LONGIFLORUM	91
LILY-FLOWERED TULIP	88
LILY OF THE VALLEY	85
LILY TURF	44
LIPSTICK VINE	60
LITHOPS FULLERI	56
LITHOPS PSEUDO-TRUNCATELLA	56
LITHOPS SALICOLA	56
LIVING STONES	56
LIVISTONA CHINENSIS	45
LOBELIA	87
LOBELIA ERINUS	87
LOBIVIA AUREA	98
LOBIVIA FAMATIMENSIS	98
LOLLIPOP PLANT	73
LORRAINE BEGONIA	81
LUCKY CLOVER	92

M

	page
MADAGASCAR DRAGON TREE	31
MADAGASCAR JASMINE	78
MAIDENHAIR FERN	35
MAMMILLARIA BOCASANA	99
MAMMILLARIA BOMBYCINA	99
MAMMILLARIA WILDII	99
MANDEVILLA SPLENDENS	67
MANETTIA INFLATA	72
MARANTA LEUCONEURA ERYTHROPHYLLA	42
MARANTA LEUCONEURA KERCHOVEANA	42
MARANTA LEUCONEURA MASSANGEANA	42

	page
MARANTA MAKOYANA	42
MARANTA TRICOLOR	42
MARGUERITE CHRYSANTHEMUM	83
MERMAID VINE	58
METAL LEAF BEGONIA	62
MEXICAN SNOWBALL	55
MEXICAN SUNBALL	99
MILK BUSH	56
MILTONIA	73
MIMOSA PUDICA	41
MIND YOUR OWN BUSINESS	40
MING ARALIA	50
MINIATURE GRAPE IVY	58
MINIATURE ROSE	94
MINIATURE WAX PLANT	69
MISTLETOE CACTUS	100
MISTLETOE FIG	37
MONDO GRASS	44
MONSTERA DELICIOSA	43
MONSTERA DELICIOSA BORSIGIANA	43
MORNING GLORY	87
MOSAIC PLANT	38
MOSES IN THE CRADLE	50
MOTHER-IN-LAW'S TONGUE	51
MOTHER OF THOUSANDS	50
MOTHER SPLEENWORT	35
MYRTILLOCACTUS GEOMETRIZANS	99
MYRTLE	72
MYRTUS COMMUNIS	72

N

	page
NARCISSUS	88
NASTURTIUM	87
NATAL PLUM	65
NEANTHE BELLA	45
NEEDLEPOINT IVY	39
NEOREGELIA CAROLINAE MARECHALII	25
NEOREGELIA CAROLINAE TRICOLOR	25
NEOREGELIA SPECTABILIS	25
NEPHROLEPIS EXALTATA	35
NEPHROLEPIS EXALTATA BOSTONIENSIS	35
NEPHROLEPIS EXALTATA FLUFFY RUFFLES	35
NEPHROLEPIS EXALTATA WHITMANNII	35
NEPHTHYTIS	53
NERINE FLEXUOSA	91
NERIUM OLEANDER	72
NERTERA DEPRESSA	91
NERVE PLANT	38
NEVER NEVER PLANT	42
NICODEMIA DIVERSIFOLIA	44
NICOTIANA AFFINIS	87
NIDULARIUM INNOCENTII	25
NIGHT JESSAMINE	65
NORFOLK ISLAND PINE	22
NOTOCACTUS LENINGHAUSII	99
NOTOCACTUS OTTONIS	99

O

	page
ODONTOGLOSSUM	73
ODONTOGLOSSUM GRANDE	73
OLD MAN CACTUS	98
OLD MAN OF THE ANDES	99
OLEANDER	72
ONCIDIUM	73
OPHIOPOGON JAPONICUS	44
OPLISMENUS HIRTELLUS VARIEGATUS	44
OPUNTIA BERGERIANA	99
OPUNTIA BRASILIENSIS	99
OPUNTIA CYLINDRICA	99
OPUNTIA MICRODASYS	99
OPUNTIA RUFIDA	99
ORCHID CACTUS	100
ORCHIDS	73
OREOCEREUS CELSIANUS	99
ORNAMENTAL PEPPER	47
OXALIS DEPPEI	92

P

	page
PACHYPHYTUM OVIFERUM	56
PACHYSTACHYS LUTEA	73
PAINTED LADY	55
PAINTED NET LEAF	38
PAINTED TONGUE	94
PAINTER'S PALETTE	61
PALMS	45
PANAMIGA	49
PANDA PLANT	56
PANDANUS VEITCHII	44
PANICUM	44
PANSY ORCHID	73
PAPER FLOWER	63
PARASOL PLANT	40
PARLOUR PALM	45
PARODIA CHRYSACANTHION	99
PARODIA SANGUINIFLORA	99
PARROT BILL	66
PARTRIDGE BREAST	55

	page
PASSIFLORA CAERULEA	74
PASSION FLOWER	74
PATIENT LUCY	70
PEACE LILY	77
PEACOCK FERN	52
PEACOCK PLANT	42
PEANUT CACTUS	98
PEARL PLANT	56
PELARGONIUM CAPITATUM	47
PELARGONIUM CRISPUM	47
PELARGONIUM DOMESTICUM ELSIE HICKMAN	75
PELARGONIUM DOMESTICUM HYBRID	75
PELARGONIUM GRAVEOLENS	47
PELARGONIUM HORTORUM BLACK COX	75
PELARGONIUM HORTORUM CAROLINE SCHMIDT	75
PELARGONIUM HORTORUM DISTINCTION	75
PELARGONIUM HORTORUM HAPPY THOUGHT	75
PELARGONIUM HORTORUM HYBRID	75
PELARGONIUM HORTORUM MARECHAL MACMAHON	75
PELARGONIUM HORTORUM MRS HENRY COX	75
PELARGONIUM HORTORUM MRS POLLOCK	75
PELARGONIUM HORTORUM VERONA	75
PELARGONIUM ODORATISSIMUM	47
PELARGONIUM PELTATUM	75
PELARGONIUM PELTATUM L'ELEGANTE	75
PELARGONIUM TOMENTOSUM	47
PELLAEA ROTUNDIFOLIA	35
PELLAEA VIRIDIS	35
PELLIONIA DAVEAUANA	47
PELLIONIA PULCHRA	47
PELLIONIA REPENS	47
PENTAS LANCEOLATA	74
PEPEROMIA ARGYREIA	46
PEPEROMIA CAPERATA	46
PEPEROMIA CAPERATA VARIEGATA	46
PEPEROMIA GRISEO-ARGENTEA	46
PEPEROMIA HEDERAEFOLIA	46
PEPEROMIA MAGNOLIAEFOLIA	46
PEPEROMIA OBTUSIFOLIA	46
PEPEROMIA PROSTRATA	46
PEPEROMIA ROTUNDIFOLIA	46
PEPEROMIA SANDERSII	46
PEPEROMIA SCANDENS VARIEGATA	46
PEPEROMIA VERTICILLATA	46
PEPPER FACE	46
PEPPERMINT GERANIUM	47
PERESKIA ACULEATA	99
PERESKIA GODSEFFIANA	99
PERSIAN VIOLET	85
PERUVIAN OLD MAN	98
PETUNIA	87
PETUNIA HYBRIDA	87
PHEASANT LEAF	25
PHILODENDRON ANDREANUM	48
PHILODENDRON BIPINNATIFIDUM	48
PHILODENDRON BURGUNDY	48
PHILODENDRON DOMESTICUM	48
PHILODENDRON ELEGANS	48
PHILODENDRON HASTATUM	48
PHILODENDRON MELANOCHRYSON	48
PHILODENDRON OXYCARDIUM	48
PHILODENDRON PANDURAEFORME	48
PHILODENDRON PERTUSUM	43
PHILODENDRON RED EMERALD	48
PHILODENDRON SCANDENS	48
PHILODENDRON SELLOUM	48
PHILODENDRON TUXLA	48
PHILODENDRON WENDLANDII	48
PHLEBODIUM AUREUM	36
PHLOX	87
PHLOX DRUMMONDII	87
PHOENIX CANARIENSIS	45
PHOENIX ROEBELINII	45
PHYLLITIS SCOLOPENDRIUM	35
PIGGYBACK PLANT	53
PILEA BRONZE	49
PILEA CADIEREI	49
PILEA DEPRESSA	49
PILEA INVOLUCRATA	49
PILEA MICROPHYLLA	49
PILEA MOON VALLEY	49
PILEA MUSCOSA	49
PILEA NUMMULARIFOLIA	49
PILEA REPENS	49
PILEA SPRUCEANA	49
PINCUSHION CACTUS	99
PINEAPPLE	25
PINK ALLAMANDA	67
PINK JASMINE	71
PINK SPOT BEGONIA	62
PIPER CROCATUM	47
PLATYCERIUM ALCICORNE	36
PLATYCERIUM BIFURCATUM	36

	page
PLECTRANTHUS AUSTRALIS	49
PLECTRANTHUS COLEOIDES MARGINATUS	49
PLECTRANTHUS OERTENDAHLII	49
PLEOMELE ANGUSTIFOLIA HONORARIAE	31
PLEOMELE REFLEXA VARIEGATA	31
PLEOMELE THALIOIDES	31
PLUMBAGO CAPENSIS	74
PLUME ASPARAGUS	23
PLUME FLOWER	82
PODOCARPUS MACROPHYLLUS	50
POINSETTIA	92
POISON PRIMROSE	93
POLKA DOT PLANT	40
POLYPODIUM AUREUM	36
POLYSCIAS BALFOURIANA	50
POLYSCIAS FRUTICOSA	50
POLYSTICHUM ACROSTICHOIDES	36
POLYSTICHUM TSUS-SIMENSE	36
POMEGRANATE	93
PONY TAIL	23
POOR MAN'S ORCHID	94
POT CHRYSANTHEMUM	83
POT MARIGOLD	87
PRAYER PLANT	42
PRIMROSE	93
PRIMROSE JASMINE	71
PRIMULA ACAULIS	93
PRIMULA KEWENSIS	93
PRIMULA MALACOIDES	93
PRIMULA OBCONICA	93
PRIMULA SINENSIS	93
PTERIS CRETICA	36
PTERIS CRETICA ALBOLINEATA	36
PTERIS CRETICA CRISTATA	36
PTERIS ENSIFORMIS VICTORIAE	36
PTERIS TREMULA	36
PUNICA GRANATUM NANA	93
PURPLE HEART	57
PURPLE PASSION VINE	38
PYGMY DATE PALM	45

Q

	page
QUEEN'S TEARS	63

R

	page
RABBIT TRACKS	42
RABBIT'S FOOT FERN	35
RAINBOW STAR	25
RAT TAIL PLANT	55
RAT'S TAIL CACTUS	100
RATTLESNAKE PLANT	42
REBUTIA MINISCULA	99
REBUTIA PYGMAEA	99
RECHSTEINERIA CARDINALIS	93
REED PALM	45
RED-HOT CATSTAIL	60
RED IVY	40
REGAL PELARGONIUM	75
REX BEGONIA	26
RHAPHIDOPHORA AUREA	52
RHAPIS EXCELSA	45
RHIPSALIDOPSIS GAERTNERI	100
RHIPSALIS CASSUTHA	100
RHIPSALIS PARADOXA	100
RHODODENDRON OBTUSUM HYBRID	80
RHODODENDRON SIMSII	80
RHOEO DISCOLOR	50
RHOICISSUS CAPENSIS	58
RHOICISSUS RHOMBIFOLIUS ELLEN DANICA	58
RHOICISSUS RHOMBOIDEA	58
RIBBON FERN	36
RIBBON PLANT	31
ROCHEA COCCINEA	74
ROCHEA FALCATA	55
ROMAN HYACINTH	88
ROSA CHINENSIS MINIMA HYBRID	94
ROSARY VINE	94
ROSE	94
ROSE MAIDENHAIR	35
ROSE OF CHINA	69
ROSE-SCENTED GERANIUM	47
RUBBER PLANT	37
RUGBY FOOTBALL PLANT	46

S

	page
SAGO PALM	45
ST. BERNARD'S LILY	27
SAINTPAULIA IONANTHA	76
SALPIGLOSSIS SINUATA	94
SALVIA	87
SALVIA SPLENDENS	87
SANCHEZIA NOBILIS	77
SANSEVIERIA HAHNII	51
SANSEVIERIA HAHNII VARIEGATA	51
SANSEVIERIA TRIFASCIATA	51

	page
SANSEVIERIA TRIFASCIATA LAURENTII	51
SANSEVIERIA ZEYLANICA	51
SAUCER PLANT	55
SAXIFRAGA SARMENTOSA	50
SAXIFRAGA SARMENTOSA TRICOLOR	50
SCARBOROUGH LILY	78
SCARLET PLUME	68
SCENTED-LEAVED GERANIUM	47
SCHEFFLERA ACTINOPHYLLA	51
SCHIZANTHUS HYBRIDA	94
SCHLUMBERGERA GAERTNERI	100
SCHLUMBERGERA TRUNCATA	100
SCILLA	88
SCINDAPSUS AUREUS	52
SCINDAPSUS AUREUS MARBLE QUEEN	52
SCINDAPSUS PICTUS	52
SCOLOPENDRIUM VULGARE	35
SCREW PINE	44
SEDGE	26
SEDUM ADOLPHII	56
SEDUM MORGANIANUM	56
SEDUM PACHYPHYLLUM	56
SEDUM RUBROTINCTUM	56
SEDUM SIEBOLDII MEDIOVARIEGATUM	56
SELAGINELLA MARTENSII	52
SELAGINELLA UNCINATA	52
SEMPERVIVUM ARACHNOIDEUM	56
SEMPERVIVUM TECTORUM	56
SENECIO CRUENTUS	84
SENECIO CRUENTUS GRANDIFLORA	84
SENECIO CRUENTUS NANA	84
SENECIO CRUENTUS STELLATA	84
SENECIO MACROGLOSSUS VARIEGATUS	52
SENECIO MIKANIOIDES	52
SENECIO ROWLEYANUS	56
SENSITIVE PLANT	41
SENTRY PALM	45
SETCREASEA PURPUREA	57
SHRIMP PLANT	63
SHRUB VERBENA	72
SIDERASIS FUSCATA	57
SILK OAK	38
SILVER LACE FERN	36
SILVER NET LEAF	38
SILVER RIPPLE	46
SILVER RUFFLES	56
SILVER TORCH CACTUS	98
SILVER VINE	52
SILVERY INCH PLANT	57
SINNINGIA SPECIOSA	90
SLIPPER FLOWER	82
SLIPPER ORCHID	73
SMALL-LEAVED BOX	26
SMILAX	23
SMITHIANTHA HYBRIDA	94
SNAKE PLANT	51
SNAKESKIN PLANT	38
SNAPDRAGON	87
SNOWDROP	88
SOLANUM CAPSICASTRUM	95
SOLANUM PSEUDOCAPSICUM	95
SONERILA MARGARITACEA	53
SONG OF INDIA	31
SPANISH BAYONET	58
SPANISH MOSS	24
SPARMANNIA AFRICANA	77
SPATHIPHYLLUM MAUNA LOA	77
SPATHIPHYLLUM WALLISII	77
SPIDER PLANT	27
SPINELESS YUCCA	58
SPIRAEA	80
SPLIT LEAF PHILODENDRON	43
SPOTTED ANGEL WING BEGONIA	62
SPOTTED FLOWERING MAPLE	21
SPOTTED LAUREL	22
STAG'S HORN FERN	36
STAPELIA GIGANTEA	77
STAPELIA VARIEGATA	77
STAR OF BETHLEHEM	64
STAR WINDOW PLANT	56
STARFISH PLANT	25
STEPHANOTIS FLORIBUNDA	78
STRAWBERRY GERANIUM	50
STRELITZIA REGINAE	78
STREPTOCARPUS CONSTANT NYMPH	78
STREPTOCARPUS HYBRIDUS	78
STRING OF BEADS	56
STRING OF BUTTONS	55
STRIPED INCH PLANT	57
STROMANTHE AMABILIS	42
SUCCULENTS	54
SUGAR ALMOND PLANT	56
SUNSET CACTUS	98
SWEDISH IVY	49
SWEET FLAG	22
SWEETHEART IVY	39
SWEETHEART PLANT	48
SWISS CHEESE PLANT	43
SYNGONIUM PODOPHYLLUM	53

	page
SYNGONIUM PODOPHYLLUM EMERALD GEM	53
SYNGONIUM PODOPHYLLUM GREEN GOLD	53
SYNGONIUM PODOPHYLLUM IMPERIAL WHITE	53

T

	page
TABLE FERN	36
TAGETES ERECTA	87
TAGETES PATULA	87
TEDDY BEAR VINE	57
TEMPLE BELLS	94
TETRASTIGMA VOINIERIANUM	58
THREAD AGAVE	55
THUNBERGIA ALATA	95
TI PLANT	31
TIGER ORCHID	73
TIGER'S JAWS	56
TILLANDSIA IONANTHA	25
TILLANDSIA LINDENII	63
TILLANDSIA USNEOIDES	24
TOBACCO PLANT	87
TOLMIEA MENZIESII	53
TOM THUMB CACTUS	99
TOUCH-ME-NOT	41
TRADESCANTIA ALBOVITTATA	57
TRADESCANTIA BLOSSFELDIANA VARIEGATA	57
TRADESCANTIA FLUMINENSIS TRICOLOR	57
TRADESCANTIA FLUMINENSIS VARIEGATA	57
TRAILING FIG	37
TREE ALOE	55
TREE OPUNTIA	99
TREE PHILODENDRON	48
TREMBLING FERN	36
TRICHOCEREUS CANDICANS	99
TROPAEOLUM MAJUS	87
TROUT BEGONIA	62
TSUSINA HOLLY FERN	36
TULIP	88
TURKISH TEMPLE	56

U

	page
UMBRELLA PLANT	29
UMBRELLA TREE	51
URN PLANT	25, 63

V

	page
VALLOTA SPECIOSA	78
VARIEGATED IVY TREE	33
VARIEGATED ROSE OF CHINA	69
VARIEGATED TABLE FERN	36
VARIEGATED WAX PLANT	69
VASE PLANT	25
VELTHEIMIA CAPENSIS	95
VELVET LEAF	56
VELVET PLANT	38
VERBENA	87
VERBENA HYBRIDA	87
VINES	58
VRIESIA FENESTRALIS	25
VRIESIA HIEROGLYPHICA	25
VRIESIA SPECIOSA	63
VRIESIA SPLENDENS	25, 63

W

	page
WAFFLE PLANT	40
WANDERING JEW	57
WART PLANT	56
WATERMELON PEPEROMIA	46
WAX BEGONIA	62
WAX PLANT	69
WEEPING CHINESE LANTERN	21
WEEPING FIG	37
WHITE CALLA LILY	95
WHITE-EDGED SWEDISH IVY	49
WHORLED PEPEROMIA	46
WINTER CHERRY	95
WOOD SORREL	92

Y

	page
YESTERDAY, TODAY & TOMORROW	62
YUCCA ALOIFOLIA	58
YUCCA ELEPHANTIPES	58

Z

	page
ZANTEDESCHIA AETHIOPICA	95
ZEBRA HAWORTHIA	56
ZEBRA PLANT	42, 61
ZEBRINA PENDULA	57
ZEBRINA PURPUSII	57
ZONAL PELARGONIUM	75
ZYGOCACTUS TRUNCATUS	100